THE
ASHES
MATCH OF MY LIFE

THE
ASHES
MATCH OF MY LIFE
Fourteen Ashes Legends Relive Their Greatest Test

Sam Pilger and Rob Wightman

This edition first published by Pitch Publishing 2013

Pitch Publishing
A2 Yeoman Gate
Yeoman Way
Durrington
BN13 3QZ
www.pitchpublishing.co.uk

A CIP catalogue record is available for this book from the
British Library

ISBN 978-1-90917-897-7

Typesetting and origination by Pitch Publishing.

Printed in Great Britain by CPI Gruop (UK) Ltd, Croydon, CR0 4YY

Contents

Editors' Acknowledgements

From Sam

I WOULD LIKE to thank the eight cricketers I collaborated with: Glenn McGrath, Justin Langer, Mike Hussey, Mark Taylor, Ashley Giles, David Gower, Merv Hughes and Paul Collingwood. I am also grateful to Carmen Gunn and Warren Craig at Titan Management, Cheri Gardiner, Diana van Bunnens at SFX, Alison Prosser and Tracy Gaffey and Neil Fairbrother at ISM. Special thanks to Tony Harper and Adam Burnett for their help and advice. Thank you to Justyn, Geoff, Leo and Louis for the good times and trips to the bar each summer. I am very grateful to Paul Camillin and Jane Camillin at Pitch Publishing for their hard work, and to Duncan Olner for his brilliant cover. Thank you to my co-writer Rob for being a great ally on this project. Thank you to my Mum for those early trips to the MCG, and to my Dad for that first trip to the SCG in 1984, and to both for all their love and support. Most of all, thank you to my wife Esther, and my children Louis and Matilda, who are my best friends and the inspiration for everything I do. Their love makes it all worthwhile.

From Rob

I WOULD LIKE to thank all the cricketers for their enthusiasm and insight. Particular gratitude goes to those with whom I worked: Neil Harvey, Ray Illingworth, Jeff Thomson, Geoff Boycott, Bob Willis and John Emburey. Thank you to Paul Camillin and the team at Pitch Publishing for all their efforts in bringing out the book. Thanks also to Simon Mann, David Willis, Middlesex County Cricket Club, Eivion Bowen at Cricket Victoria, and Stephen Gray at Queensland Cricket. Thank you to my co-writer Sam for his humour, conscientiousness and determination to make this project a success. Special thanks to my family for their support and those trips to New Road, Worcester. Above all, thank you to Tamsin and Natasha for all the love, encouragement and understanding I value so much.

Sam Pilger and Rob Wightman
March 2013

Introduction

THERE WAS A sick feeling in the pit of my stomach as I sat on the top deck of the number three bus winding its way towards The Oval in September 2005.

I was headed to the final day of the fifth Ashes Test aware I could be about to encounter the sight I had gleefully avoided since I was at school: an England captain holding the Ashes.

For 16 years I had enjoyed a succession of Australian victories; I had been at Lord's in 1989 to watch Allan Border's side begin this era of dominance and then at the SCG in 2003 as Steve Waugh's team collected the Ashes after an eighth consecutive series win.

Every two years, five or six Tests were played, and then a group of men wearing baggy green caps got to have their picture taken with the urn.

But on that day eight years ago my fears were realised as I watched Michael Vaughan lift the Ashes and lead his side on a lap of honour. As I left The Oval an electronic sign above the Hobbs Gate flashed 'The Ashes are Home' in to the night sky, while England fans spilled out of the surrounding pubs.

Since then this scene of English joy has become quite common and been repeated twice more with Andrew Strauss holding aloft the Ashes at The Oval in 2009, and again at the Sydney Cricket Ground in 2011 to usher in a new era of England dominance.

I hope the following chapters have captured both the unique spirit and the enduring appeal of the Ashes. The long history of the battle for the urn has, for the most part, been about the pursuit of glory, and not about humiliating the other side. The concept of 'Mateship' extends to the opposition dressing room.

Each player in this book speaks about their all-consuming desire to triumph, but also to win the respect, and sometimes friendship, of the opposition players and fans. Without sacrificing any passion, and there remains plenty of rancour, the Ashes have managed to avoid much of the pettiness and ugliness of other sports.

As the former England captain Andrew Strauss has so neatly said, 'The Ashes represents all that is best about cricket.'

The Ashes have provided the stage for some of England and Australia's finest ever players to prove themselves, and here, those that I worked with give a fascinating insight in to the struggle behind their triumphs.

A year after being humbled by the West Indies, David Gower captained England to the Ashes in 1985; Mark Taylor was on the brink of becoming a surveyor before the tour of 1989 turned him in to one of the game's greats; Merv Hughes overcame a poor start to his Test career and a succession of injuries to bowl Australia to the Ashes in 1993.

Justin Langer recounts his decade-long journey from being what he calls 'the invisible man of Australian cricket' to scoring 250 at the MCG in 2002.

After being out of the game for a year with an ankle injury it was assumed Glenn McGrath was finished, but he returned to take his 500th wicket during a devastating spell at Lord's in 2005, while Ashley Giles was branded not good enough after defeat in that first Test, but seven weeks later was out in the middle guiding England to the Ashes at The Oval.

Mike Hussey had long given up on ever playing Test cricket for Australia, but found himself hitting the winning runs at the Adelaide Oval to complete Australia's greatest ever Ashes comeback at Adelaide in 2006.

Paul Collingwood endured the pain of being whitewashed 5-0 in that series in 2006/07, but four years later he returned triumphant, helping England to win the Ashes in Australia for the first time in 24 years in the final Test of his career.

Wickets and runs against every other Test nation have always been gratefully accepted, but each of these players has found that real greatness can only truly be grasped in the Ashes.

Sam Pilger
March 2013

Introduction

LIKE MANY ENGLISH and Australian cricket fans, I have a JFK moment. I remember exactly where I was when the Ashes first caught my imagination. It was a Monday afternoon in July 1981 and, by chance, I switched on my family's portable black-and-white television to see Ian Botham smashing the increasingly frustrated Australians to all parts of Headingley.

As a nine-year-old, I knew little about the intricacies of Test cricket but sensed from Botham's swagger and Dennis Lillee's scowl that I was witnessing something special. My eyes were then fully opened to the rich entertainment and raw emotion of the Ashes when Bob Willis's devastating spell of fast bowling completed England's sensational comeback.

During the rest of that memorable series I began to appreciate why the ebb and flow of England–Australia series has enthralled millions of cricket followers for over a century.

Despite being a team sport, cricket is based on individual showdowns, and Ashes matches consistently provide compelling sub-plots that are great events in their own right, like Lillee v Botham, Thomson v Boycott and McGrath v Pietersen.

But however intense the rivalry and clash of sporting cultures, there is generally a healthy dose of mutual respect between the two sides. England and Australia slug it out on the field, sometimes employing the most ruthless tactics to gain an advantage, and afterwards the teams have a laugh over a few beers.

By speaking to cricketers from a period that spans five decades, I quickly learned that from Bradman's 1948 Invincibles to Mike Gatting's 1986/87 winners, the Ashes inspired as much pride and passion in the players as the spectators.

This book provides evocative insider accounts of the agony, ecstasy, controversy and camaraderie of the most fiercely contested series from 1948 to the most recent battles. Each chapter reflects an individual character, voice and era of the game, while giving enormous insight into the thoughts of many of England and Australia's finest post-war players during the key matches of their careers.

There is Neil Harvey's fresh-faced ebullience on his first tour; Ray Illingworth's ingenuity in becoming the first England captain since the 1930s to reclaim the Ashes in Australia; Jeff Thomson's super-confidence in just his second Test; Geoff

Boycott's relentless desire to succeed on his return from three years in exile; Bob Willis's commitment to the cause and John Emburey's pure love of the game.

Although many of the contributors have long retired, their enthusiasm for the Ashes is undiminished. I hope you will now enjoy reliving many of the classic Ashes encounters through the eyes of the players who made them great.

Rob Wightman
March 2013

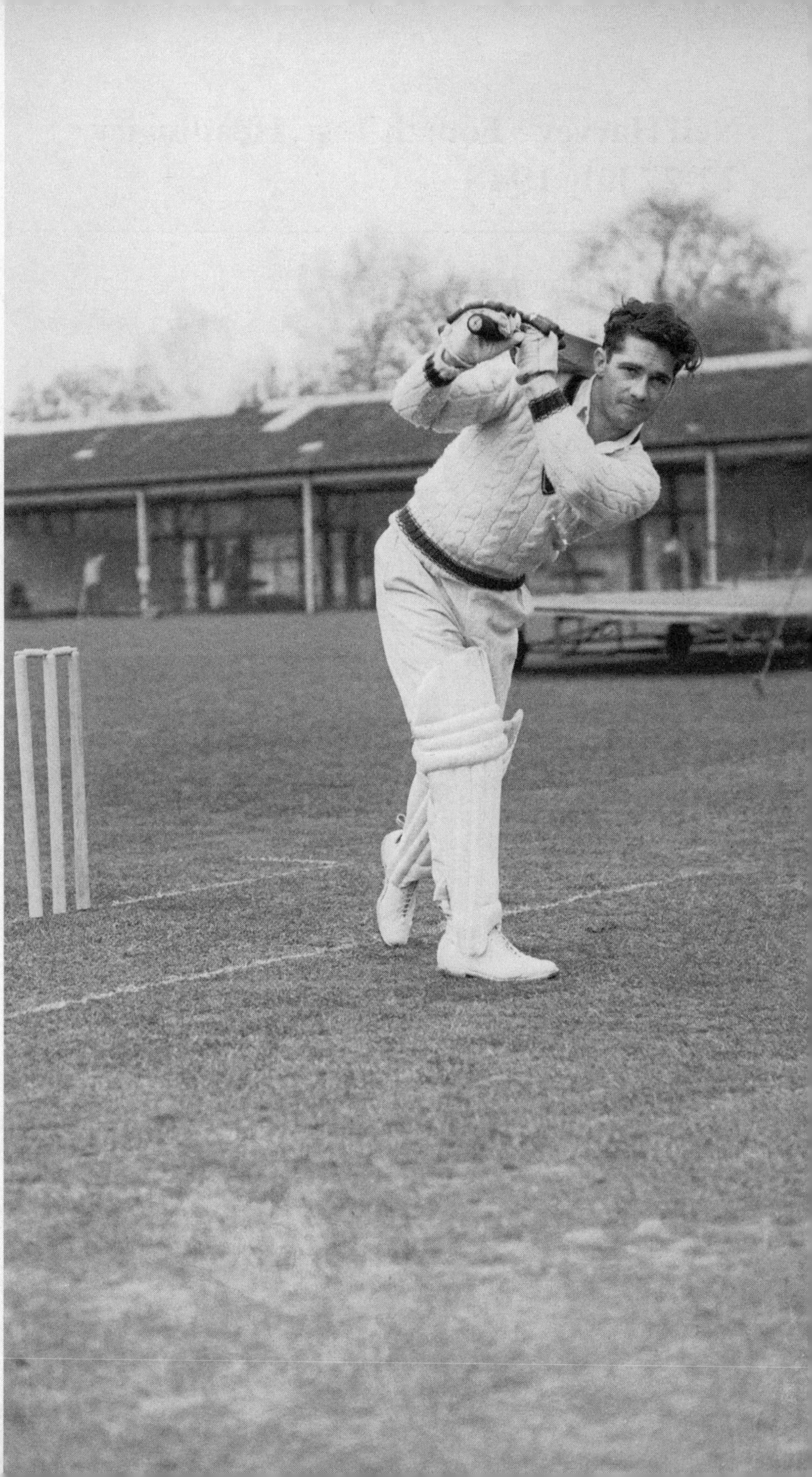

NEIL HARVEY

Neil Harvey – Fourth Test, Headingley, 22-27 July 1948

A dashing left-hander and exuberant fielder, Neil Harvey earned a reputation as one of Australia's finest batsmen in a Test career that spanned 15 years. Harvey played a prominent role in eight Ashes campaigns, finishing on the winning side in five series. His 2,416 Ashes runs included six hundreds and 12 half-centuries, though, surprisingly, his average of 38.34 against England was significantly lower than his overall Test average of 48.41.

Left-handed batsman
Born: 8 October 1928, Melbourne, Victoria
Test debut: January 1948 v India
Last Test: February 1963 v England
Test record: 79 matches, 6,149 runs at an average of 48.41

The state of play
Australia had already retained the Ashes with three Tests of the five-match series played having won the first two, followed by a draw in the third, then rubbed salt in England's wounds by snatching a seemingly impossible fifth-day victory in the fourth Test. They then won the fifth for a 4-0 series victory.

Scoreboard

England first innings

L. Hutton		b Lindwall	81
C. Washbrook	c Lindwall	b Johnston	143
W.J. Edrich	c Morris	b Johnson	111
A.V. Bedser		c & b Johnson	79
D.C.S. Compton	c Saggers	b Lindwall	23
J.F. Crapp		b Toshack	5
N.W.D. Yardley		b Miller	25
K. Cranston		b Loxton	10
T.G. Evans	c Hassett	b Loxton	3
J.C. Laker	c Saggers	b Loxton	4
R. Pollard		not out	0
Extras	(b 2, lb 8, w 1, nb 1)		12
Total	(all out, 192.1 overs)		496

Bowling	O	M	R	W
Lindwall	38	10	79	2
Miller	17.1	2	43	1
Johnston	38	12	86	1
Toshack	35	6	112	1
Loxton	26	4	55	3
Johnson	33	9	89	2
Morris	5	0	20	0

Australia first innings

A.R. Morris	c Cranston	b Bedser	6
A.L. Hassett	c Crapp	b Pollard	13
D.G. Bradman		b Pollard	33
K.R. Miller	c Edrich	b Yardley	58
R.N. Harvey		b Laker	112
S.J.E. Loxton		b Yardley	93
I.W.G. Johnson	c Cranston	b Laker	10
R.R. Lindwall	c Crapp	b Bedser	77
R.A. Saggers	st Evans	b Laker	5
W.A. Johnston	c Edrich	b Bedser	13
E.R.H. Toshack		not out	12
Extras	(b 9, lb 14, nb 3)		26
Total	(all out, 136.2 overs)		458

Bowling	O	M	R	W
Bedser	31.2	4	92	3
Pollard	38	6	104	2
Cranston	14	1	51	0
Edrich	3	0	19	0
Laker	30	8	113	3
Yardley	17	6	38	2
Compton	3	0	15	0

England second innings

L. Hutton	c Bradman	b Johnson	57
C. Washbrook	c Harvey	b Johnston	65
W.J. Edrich	lbw	b Lindwall	54
D.C.S. Compton	c Miller	b Johnston	66
J.F. Crapp		b Lindwall	18
N.W.D. Yardley	c Harvey	b Johnston	7
K. Cranston	c Saggers	b Johnston	0
T.G. Evans		not out	47
A.V. Bedser	c Hassett	b Miller	17
J.C. Laker		not out	15
Extras	(b 4, lb 12, nb 3)		19
Total	(8 wickets dec, 107 overs)		365

Bowling	O	M	R	W
Lindwall	26	6	84	2
Miller	21	5	53	1
Johnston	29	5	95	4
Loxton	10	2	29	0
Johnson	21	2	85	1

Australia second innings (target: 404 runs)

A.R. Morris	c Pollard	b Yardley	182
A.L. Hassett		c & b Compton	17
D.G. Bradman		not out	173
K.R. Miller	lbw	b Cranston	12
R.N. Harvey		not out	4
Extras	(b 6, lb 9, nb 1)		16
Total	(3 wickets, 114.1 overs)		404

Bowling	O	M	R	W
Bedser	21	2	56	0
Pollard	22	6	55	0
Cranston	7.1	0	28	1
Laker	32	11	93	0
Yardley	13	1	44	1
Compton	15	3	82	1
Hutton	4	1	30	0

Neil Harvey

ON THE FIRST morning of the Headingley Test, I was about to attack a kipper for breakfast when Don Bradman came up to me and said, 'You're playing today.' Of course the kipper got thrust to one side and the butterflies took over in my stomach.

There I was at the age of 19, about to play my very first Test against England. It was a complete and utter shock.

I was very fortunate because I was the first youngster to play for Australia after the Second World War. We had England out in Australia in 1946/47 for an Ashes series that the home side won 3-0. Aged 18, I broke into the Victoria team for the last three games of that season, which included one against England.

I made 69 and I was batting against Doug Wright, who was a pretty good leg-spinner. Anyway, he bowled me this wrong'un, which I didn't pick, and I was caught behind. As I started to walk from the crease, a voice behind me said, 'Well played, son, I'll see you in England next year.' That was Godfrey Evans, the wicketkeeper. I have never, ever forgotten that. It was one of those nice things that used to happen on the cricket field when blokes of my vintage played.

The next summer I made my Test debut against India at Adelaide. I only made 13 and thought my career was finished already. But they gave me another game because we had already won the series, and I made 153.

I guess that got me into the great team of 1948, which was captained by Don Bradman.

It was one of the highlights of my cricketing life just to get selected for the 1948 tour of England, especially since I was seven years younger than anybody else in the party. We had a tremendous side, which I believe is still the yardstick for all teams to try and better because it was so beautifully balanced, with great batsmen, bowlers, all-rounders, and wicketkeepers, the lot.

The tour was the first time I had left Australia. The furthest I had been was from Melbourne to Brisbane and Sydney, playing for Victoria, so to go on a month-long voyage from Fremantle to London was incredible.

I hardly knew the other blokes because I hadn't played with most of them. But because we were on the boat for a month, we got to know each other as people, as friends. By the time we got to England, we were a pretty close-knit bunch.

Fortunately, I had a very good room-mate in Sammy Loxton, the Victoria all-rounder. When I first played for Victoria, I went to meet the team at Spencer Street Station in Melbourne and all I had was a plastic bag with my cricket whites and no other kit.

Lindsay Hassett, the captain, welcomed me and looked around and said, 'Sam, you're closest, you look after him.' And that's how Sam and I became very good friends and room-mates on the boat, throughout the tour and in later series. I was only 19 so I wasn't really in with a lot of the other guys. They had all been in the services and gone through the war together, so I was left out of that sort of thing.

We got a bit of practice on board, using rope balls and half-sized bats. And the other players welcomed me into that, so it wasn't long before I became one of the boys. During the day we played a little bit of deck tennis because you can keep quite fit with that if you ignore the rules, and the older fellows like Bradman played deck quoits, which was more sedate.

Every night there was a cocktail party before dinner, which went down well. There were quite a few wealthy people on the boat and they liked to entertain. Basically, it was 28 days of getting to know each other and getting off at the other end as a good and happy team.

When the *Strathaird* docked at Tilbury, Essex, on Friday 16 April 1948, it didn't take me long to realise that England had really been knocked around by the war. After disembarking, we travelled to our hotel in Piccadilly and saw a lot of the damage on the way. We asked ourselves how Londoners had ever coped with this.

But this Ashes tour did so much for English morale. It was the first since 1938, when a drawn series had seen Australia retain the Ashes. The people needed a boost and this Australian side provided it. The grounds were full for both the Tests and the games against the counties for every day of every match.

Only four of our party had been to England before, so most of the guys took quite some time to get used to warm English beer. Bill Brown, Keith Miller and Sid Barnes had been to England previously and had already sampled a few! And, of course, it didn't bother Bradman, who wasn't a beer drinker but liked his wine and sherry. It didn't affect me either because I didn't drink at all in those days. I never touched a drop until I was 29. That was the way I was brought up and it just stuck with me until I moved from Melbourne to Sydney and got a job with a hotel supplier and my habits changed a bit.

I struggled for form early in the tour and was very worried because after four county games I was averaging about seven. I started saying to myself, 'Jeez, I can't handle this.' The ball was moving around a lot and I felt I was doing something wrong. I was finding it hard to adapt to the green English pitches and damp conditions, which were totally different to what we had in Australia.

Because Bradman was 20 years older than me, I didn't feel I could go and talk to him about it. But Loxton was a good friend of Bradman's, so I asked Sam to do me a favour and ask the boss what I was doing wrong. He went to Bradman and said, 'My little mate's got a problem. He's not making any runs. Can you tell him what he's doing wrong?'

Well, Bradman never told me anything in his life, so he said to Sam, 'You go back and tell your little mate that if he keeps the ball on the ground, he can't get out.' I ended up making four first-class centuries on the tour, so it must have been good advice.

As well as Bradman, Australia had many other fine players. One of them was Arthur Morris, who had a tremendous tour, scoring more runs than anybody else. He made 696 runs at an average of 87, including three centuries and three fifties. Although Bradman didn't do quite as well, he still managed to average 72. And you can't forget old Sid Barnes, whom Morris said was one of the best players he had ever seen. Sid averaged 82.

Another key factor was Bill Johnston, who was one of the most underrated bowlers ever. He was a great new-ball bowler and when the shine came off Bradman could call on him to bowl finger-spinners, which not everybody can do. Bill took 27 wickets in the series – which was equalled by Ray Lindwall – at an average of 23.

Lindwall was our main strike bowler and still the best and most skilful fast bowler I have ever come across. He got his 27 wickets at 19 apiece. He was quicker than Glenn McGrath and maybe fractionally quicker than Steve Harmison, but much more skilful. He wasn't as quick, maybe, as Frank Tyson, Jeff Thomson or Wes Hall, but skill-wise, he was the best. If Ray wanted to bowl a yorker he bowled a yorker. He had the most lethal bouncer because he didn't have to pitch as short as most people do; it was a sort of skidding bouncer. He used to unsettle a lot of batsmen.

Then there was Keith Miller, the greatest all-rounder Australia has ever produced. Keith took 13 wickets at 23 and scored 184 runs at 26. Len Hutton always said Keith was the most dangerous bowler he ever faced. And coming from him, the best English batsman I've ever seen, that's a great compliment. After all, Len scored almost 7,000 Test runs at an average of 56. By his standards, he didn't have a great series in 1948, but still averaged 42, scoring 342 runs over four matches.

Other than Hutton, we saw Denis Compton as England's most dangerous batsman. We were right because Compton was tremendous, scoring 562 runs at an average of 62. England also had the best bowler I have ever played against, Alec Bedser. He was their top wicket-taker, with 18 at an average of 38. He made you play six balls out of six. He would take the new ball and bowl these great big in-swingers, which were lethal, as away-swingers, to left-handers like myself. He got Bradman out in the first couple of Tests, caught by Hutton at short leg, with deliveries that swung in to him.

The other thing about Alec was that when the shine went he used to bowl great big leg-cutters. He would bowl top batsmen with these deliveries that pitched on leg stump and knocked out off stump. Bedser could bowl beautifully anywhere in the world; England, Australia, the West Indies, anywhere.

I didn't expect to be in the team for the first Test at Trent Bridge. I hadn't made a lot of runs against the counties and when you've got a batting line-up of Morris, Barnes, Bradman, Hassett, and Miller, how do you expect to get a game?

But I thoroughly enjoyed watching from the dressing room and was fortunate enough to field a bit as a substitute for injured bowlers. Getting on in an Ashes match was the greatest thing that had ever happened to me at that point, even if it was as 12th man.

It was vital to get off to a good start in the first Test. We had rolled over a few of the counties without too much trouble and we were looking forward to the Ashes. The first match is the most important because if you get one up, you're on your way.

That was what happened as we won fairly comfortably by eight wickets. England captain Norman Yardley won the toss and decided to bat on a damp day, but England slumped to 165 all out. Our bowling hero was Bill Johnston, who took 5-36.

Our openers then made a good start to the Australian reply, putting on 73 before Morris was bowled by Laker for 31. That brought Bradman to the crease. Bedser worried him a little bit because there was still a bit of shine on the ball, but Don tried so hard because it was his first Test back in England for ten years and he wanted to do well.

He was such a dedicated batsman that you could see him trying his brains out to make a score. Being the great player he was, even at 39, he was able to go on scoring runs. Bradman got his usual hundred (138) and Hassett got 137 as we piled on 509 all out.

So England needed a good score in their second innings. Cyril Washbrook went early, followed by Bill Edrich, but Hutton (71) and Compton then shared a century stand. Compton played beautifully for his 184. I fielded for Lindwall for a while and I reckoned Compton's bat that day was twice as wide as it should have been. Our bowlers just couldn't get the ball past him. It was one of the best innings I've ever seen an Englishman play.

Despite Compton's efforts, England's 441 all out meant we only needed 98 to win on the last day. The game ended rather farcically because we needed only a few more runs when Barnes and Hassett were batting together after Morris and Bradman had gone.

Lindsay hit Bedser for what he thought was the winning run, so Sid pinched one of the stumps and disappeared off into the dressing room. But we still needed another run, so poor old Sid had to come back with the stump, which they placed back in the ground. Lindsay hit the next ball off Bedser for a single and we won the game, but by the time Sid had completed the run, all the stumps had gone. So Sid missed out. The players then had champagne in the dressing room as they do today.

All Australians love playing at Lord's. It is the home of cricket and every other ground is secondary. Our winning margin of 409 runs didn't really matter; it was just the victory that counted. We batted first and made 350 all out, with Morris contributing 105. Lindwall then took 5-70 as England were dismissed for just 215.

I have never seen a better opening partnership than Barnes and Morris, who put on 122 for the first wicket in the second innings. As a right-and left-hander respectively, they went well together. Barnes made 141, Morris 62, Bradman 89 and Miller 74 in a big second innings total of 460/7 declared. That left England almost 600 to win, but they managed a paltry 186, with left-arm seamer Ernie Toshack returning figures of 5-40.

We were 2-0 up, but if it hadn't rained so much at Old Trafford, we would have lost the third Test. Compton made 145 not out in England's first innings of 363, even though he had to retire hurt for some time after Lindwall hit him on the head with a bouncer early in his innings. Morris's 51 was the top score in our reply of 221 as Bedser and Dick Pollard shared seven wickets.

By the end of the third day, England had reached 174/3, with Washbrook 85 not out. But rain washed out the fourth day, so England declared on the fifth morning. That left us a target of 317 on the last day. But play didn't begin until 2.15pm, which meant England were the only team likely to win. We lost an early wicket but Morris and Bradman had seen us through to 92/1 when the game ended.

A drawn Test meant that we retained the Ashes because, with two games left to play, England could not overhaul our two-match lead. We didn't really celebrate, though, until after the Leeds Test.

After we got out of jail at Old Trafford, we began to believe we could go unbeaten on the tour. No Australian side had ever done that in England and they haven't since. It would be quite a feat to remain undefeated in 34 matches on uncovered wickets, but confidence was sky high.

I played at Leeds because Barnes got injured during the third Test. He was fielding at silly mid-on when Pollard was batting. Dick was a genuine number 11 and liked to hit the ball out of the park, so when Ian Johnson rolled him up this gentle off-spin delivery, Dick took his customary big whack at it. Sid turned his back and the ball hit him right in the kidneys. He went down like a stunned mullet.

Four Bobbies appeared and carried him off, so I went to field in his place. When we went back to the dressing room after taking the last wicket, Sid sat bolt upright on the treatment table and said, 'You know, fellas, that would have killed a normal human being.' He ended up spending 12 days in hospital.

Even so, I didn't expect to play because Sid was an opener and our backup was Bill Brown, who had played in the first two Tests. I can still remember going down to breakfast at Leeds, at the Queen's Hotel, and I ordered my 527th kipper because they were just about all you could get there in those days. That was when Don told me I was playing and I pushed away my breakfast untouched.

That match probably made my cricket career. We were confident because we had won the Ashes, but we lost the toss on a pretty good track and England got off to a great start. Hutton and Washbrook put on 168 for the first wicket, with Washbrook going on to make 143 in a total of 496, which also included a century from Bill Edrich.

England had amassed a formidable total and we were pretty down. We were playing on uncovered wickets, so we couldn't be sure the pitch would play the same for us. When our turn came to bat, Bradman and Hassett took us to 63/1 at stumps on the second day, with Morris the man out.

Then there was a bit of rain overnight and that made the wicket a bit greasy, and the ball was seaming around. Pollard did some damage, having Lindsay caught at second slip by Jack Crapp and then bowling Bradman for 33. That meant we were in trouble at 68/3 when I went out to bat in my first Ashes match. It was very daunting.

I had to really hurry to get my pads on because the wickets went down so quickly. I only had one pad on when I heard this great roar. I looked out of the dressing-room window and saw Bradman's off stump out of the ground. As I passed him on my way out to the middle, all he said was, 'Good luck, son.'

Miller was out there and he always maintained I said to him, 'What's going on out here, Nugget? Let's get stuck into them.' I don't know whether I said that, but I had so much to thank Keith for with this innings because he said, 'You get up the other end and I'll take the bowling while you get yourself organised.' I replied, 'That'll do me, mate.' I couldn't get up the non-striker's end quick enough.

So I watched as Keith took the bowling for a few overs. Then Yardley brought on Jim Laker, the off-spinner, and Miller hit his third ball over my head and into the crowd for six. Three balls later, the same thing happened and I thought to myself, 'Jeez, this can't be such a tough game after all.'

To get off the mark, I pushed a very nervous single off Bedser. Alec was, for sure, the most difficult of the England bowlers, the ultimate opposition bowler as far as I was concerned. I suppose it was a hell of an advantage for me being left-handed. Bowlers were used to bowling to right-handers and when they were suddenly confronted with a left-hander, they had to change their line.

When I got to 50, I felt that was a landmark in itself, I was feeling fairly pleased with myself. I never thought I would get to a hundred. Keith and I put on a partnership of 121 before he got out, caught Edrich off the bowling of Yardley, for 58.

That brought my old mate Sam Loxton to the crease at 189/4. He said, 'You've got to continue with this.' He got on my back a little bit and made me carry on. Sam was a great help to me and he played the innings of his life. He made 93, including five sixes, all off Laker.

I was on 70 at the end of the morning session, but I couldn't eat any lunch. I was still nervous and if I wasn't out at lunch, I wouldn't eat, no matter what sort of game it was. I used to get keyed up during the break and even more so on this occasion because it was my first Ashes Test.

I started thinking about the possibility of getting a century, although I felt I had already done alright to get 70. As usual, Bradman didn't say anything to me. He just left me to my own devices. Even after I got the hundred, he only said, 'Well played.' But that was about it.

When I was on 99, Laker bowled me one on off stump. I just pushed forward gently and the ball went between mid-off and extra cover, and I took off like a rabbit. The ball was shied in at the bowler's end and I put one hand over my head and ducked for cover as I finished the run. I turned around and Jim Laker came over and gave me a pat on the back. I will never forget that.

Scoring a century was out of this world. I was so happy with myself and Sam came down the wicket and shook my hand like nobody's business. He was even more delighted than I was.

English crowds have always been very good and I'll never forget the reception they gave me that day. Australian and English crowds are both very knowledgeable, but we get the more exuberant spectator who likes to abuse people if they don't get the entertainment they want. English people don't do that.

Loxton and I added 105 before I got out with the score on 294/5. It was a case of me thinking I had done enough, as you do at the age of 19. As my career progressed, I found out that was the wrong attitude to have.

Both the century stands took about an hour and a half, which was pretty good going. But that was our way of playing. All our batsmen were stroke players; I don't think we knew any other way. If the ball was there, we hit it. There was no inclination to get on the defensive, except when I was in the 90s and it took me ages to get from 93 to 100. I got very nervous in that situation. But up until that stage, I played as many shots as anybody.

Bradman later wrote a book called *Farewell to Cricket* and in it he mentioned my century at Headingley, which he praised a lot before adding, 'I only wish I'd been batting with him at the time. I might have been able to curb his natural, youthful exuberance.' Which is probably right.

I know I should have made more, but when you're 19 you do stupid things. When I had got to my hundred, I hit Laker for three fours in three balls. I tried to hit a fourth and was bowled by Laker for 112. Cover drives, square cuts and pulls were my most productive strokes during that innings. They were my trademark shots as I struck 17 boundaries.

I got a few pats on the back from my team-mates when I got back into the dressing room. That innings was a great experience and the only century we made in our first innings of 458. Ray Lindwall came in down the order and smashed 77, which helped us get to within 38 of England's total.

Then England batted again and piled on more runs to declare at 365/8, with Hutton, Washbrook, Edrich and Compton all passing 50. I can still see myself catching Washbrook down at long leg off the bowling of Johnston. It was a pretty good catch. I ran in about 30 metres from the boundary and caught it on my boot tops. I was an Aussie rules footballer, so I just drop-kicked it back to Ron Saggers, who was keeping wicket. It was one of those things you do on the spur of the moment.

Anyway, England's declaration left us 404 to get in 344 minutes on the last day, which was unheard of. But I witnessed one of the greatest partnerships ever: Morris at one end and Bradman at the other. I don't know whether Bradman went out there with the thought of winning the game when Hassett got out for 17. I think he intended to bat as long as he could to see out the day because the target was virtually impossible.

But they were both great stroke players and they played plenty of shots, including 62 fours between them. By mid-afternoon, our blokes started saying in the dressing room, 'Jeez, we could win this.' Don and Arthur were going so well that the atmosphere in the dressing room suddenly changed.

Admittedly, both Bradman and Morris gave stumping chances which were missed by Godfrey Evans. Anyway, they batted on and on until Arthur was caught by Pollard off the bowling of Yardley, for 182. That meant we were 358/2. Miller made 12 before getting out lbw to Ken Cranston with our score on 396, so we only needed eight more when I went in.

Then, with four needed, Cranston pitched one up to me on leg stump and I hit it through midwicket for the boundary that won the game 15 minutes before the close. I can still see Bradman running past me from the other end, at what seemed like 100 miles an hour, as the crowd started to invade the field, saying, 'Come on, son, let's get out of here.'

I didn't even think to grab a stump as a souvenir because I was so naive in those days. I have heard people say that Bradman allowed me the honour of hitting the winning runs, but I don't believe that. Don was 173 not out and I just happened to have the strike. I have been blamed ever since for the fact that Bradman didn't average 100 in Tests.

It was the only time I ever played with the bat I used in that match. Slazenger gave us two bats each when we arrived in England and I used one against the counties and kept the other one, saying that if I ever played a Test match against England, I would use it brand new. After the game, Stuart Surridge came up to me and said, 'I'd like you to use our gear from now on.' So I used their bats after that and never used the Slazenger again.

But years later when we were selectors together, Bradman wrote a message on the back of the Slazenger, which says, 'To my great friend Neil Harvey, this is a tribute to a great innings during Australia's greatest-ever Test victory at Leeds, 1948. Don Bradman.'

About an hour after the match finished, we travelled to Derby for our next county match. And it was there that we had a big dinner to celebrate the Ashes victory.

Bradman and I didn't bat together all that much, but it was always a great joy when we did. It was amazing to watch him, especially his footwork. They reckoned he was unorthodox and played with a cross bat, but if you look at old film and watch his footwork, you'll find his feet are always in the correct position, whether he's playing a square cut, a pull or a drive. His most magical shot was the glorious cover drive, where his front foot was about an inch from the ball when he hit it.

He was a dedicated run machine who didn't like getting out. He was a lesson to anybody else. I have never seen a batsman who could compare with him. There is nobody near him today. His record Test average of 99.94 will last forever, even though batting is so much easier these days. In fact, there should be many more people averaging 60-plus today, given the flatter pitches, shorter boundaries and jet-propelled bats.

Bradman was a tough captain. It wasn't on his agenda to give the opposition too much of a chance, he just wanted to win as easily as he could. He didn't even declare when we made 721 in a day against Essex at Southend. He was that sort of bloke. He played it hard, but he played it fair.

The Oval Test will always stick in my mind because when Bradman went out to bat, Yardley gathered all his boys together to give him three rousing cheers. I am still convinced that the reception Bradman got must have affected him. Don said it didn't, but I say it did. I think it would have brought a few tears to his eyes and that may have been a factor in him making that dreaded, infamous duck. He was bowled second ball by Eric Hollies, the leg-spinner.

We didn't know what to say to Don in the dressing room. We didn't even know he needed four runs to average 100 in Tests because nobody talked about stats in those days. But we knew it was going to be his last Test knock because we had bowled England out for 52 in the first innings and were on our way to a substantial lead.

We all felt so sorry for him, but we didn't feel we could go and commiserate with him. He came in, sat down on the bench in front of his locker and started to take his pads off. He just said, 'Fancy doing a thing like that!' Don took it all as the great man he was.

Lindwall and Morris were our main heroes in that match. Ray took 6-20 as England were skittled out in their first innings and he followed up with 3-50 in their second effort of 188. We only batted once, making 389, of which I made 17. That was enough for us to win by an innings and 149 runs as the series finished 4-0 in our favour.

Morris was the batsman of the series and he always remembers that the Bradman duck was the famous story of that match. People often ask Arthur if he played in that game and he says, 'Yeah, I did actually. I was up the other end, I was run out for 196!'

England took defeat pretty well. They were a good bunch of fellows and we used to get together after the game and have a few drinks. I didn't drink of course, but I was there.

I was delighted with my contributions. It took me a while to get going but I made up for it as I got used to English wickets. By the end, I had scored 1,129 first-class runs at an average of 53.76. We remained unbeaten throughout the tour but it wasn't until years later that people started to refer to the 1948 side as 'The Invincibles'.

There were plenty of funny moments on tour. A couple of the guys, Ron Hamence and Colin McCool, didn't play in a Test match so they composed a song called 'Groundstaff Bowlers'. That was because they used bowl to the other blokes all day in the nets. They were fine cricketers but couldn't find their way into the Test side, but they kept their sense of humour.

We had a few night owls, like Lindwall and Miller. Most of the blokes who had been in the services liked to have a good time. They had been through hard times during the war and a lot of them found the tour very relaxing. I can quite understand that because there were blokes who had been through the desert, been through New Guinea and the Philippines. Keith Miller flew Mosquitoes over Europe, so returning to England to play cricket was very relaxing in comparison.

But when the Test matches were on, they really applied themselves. We only had one team meeting on the entire tour and that was on the ship. Bradman said, 'We're going to play this game hard, we're going to play it fair, we're going to play it attractively. I don't care what you guys do so long as you are 100 per cent fit to play at 11 o'clock every morning.' The guys had a good time and there were some late nights, but they stuck to what Bradman wanted.

We went up to Scotland for a couple of games towards the end of the tour and had the marvellous experience of meeting King George and Queen Elizabeth at Balmoral Castle. We were invited there for an afternoon garden party and King George came out in his kilt. It was a tremendous afternoon and we thoroughly enjoyed it, although the English press got on Bradman's back because he walked on the lawns alongside the King with his hands in his pockets. But Bradman was in a friendly environment and I'm sure the King didn't mind.

Prince Philip was there with Princess Elizabeth, the current Queen. And Princess Margaret was there. I didn't find out until much later that Keith Miller and Princess Margaret had struck up a friendship while the team was playing in London. Apparently, Keith was invited out to some London clubs by Princess Margaret and her friends.

Keith liked to go to clubs and enjoy himself. I suppose you could call him the playboy of the Australian team. Because he had been in London during the war, he knew where to go, but it never affected his play on the field.

There is no series like Australia versus England. I would like to think that the blokes who play today think the same way and I hope they fraternise with the opposition like we used to. I still love going over to England.

I would like to thank the other 16 blokes I toured with and the rest of the party because they taught me a lot about cricket and about life, how to meet people and how to behave. Over half a century later I often think about what we achieved together on that extraordinary tour.

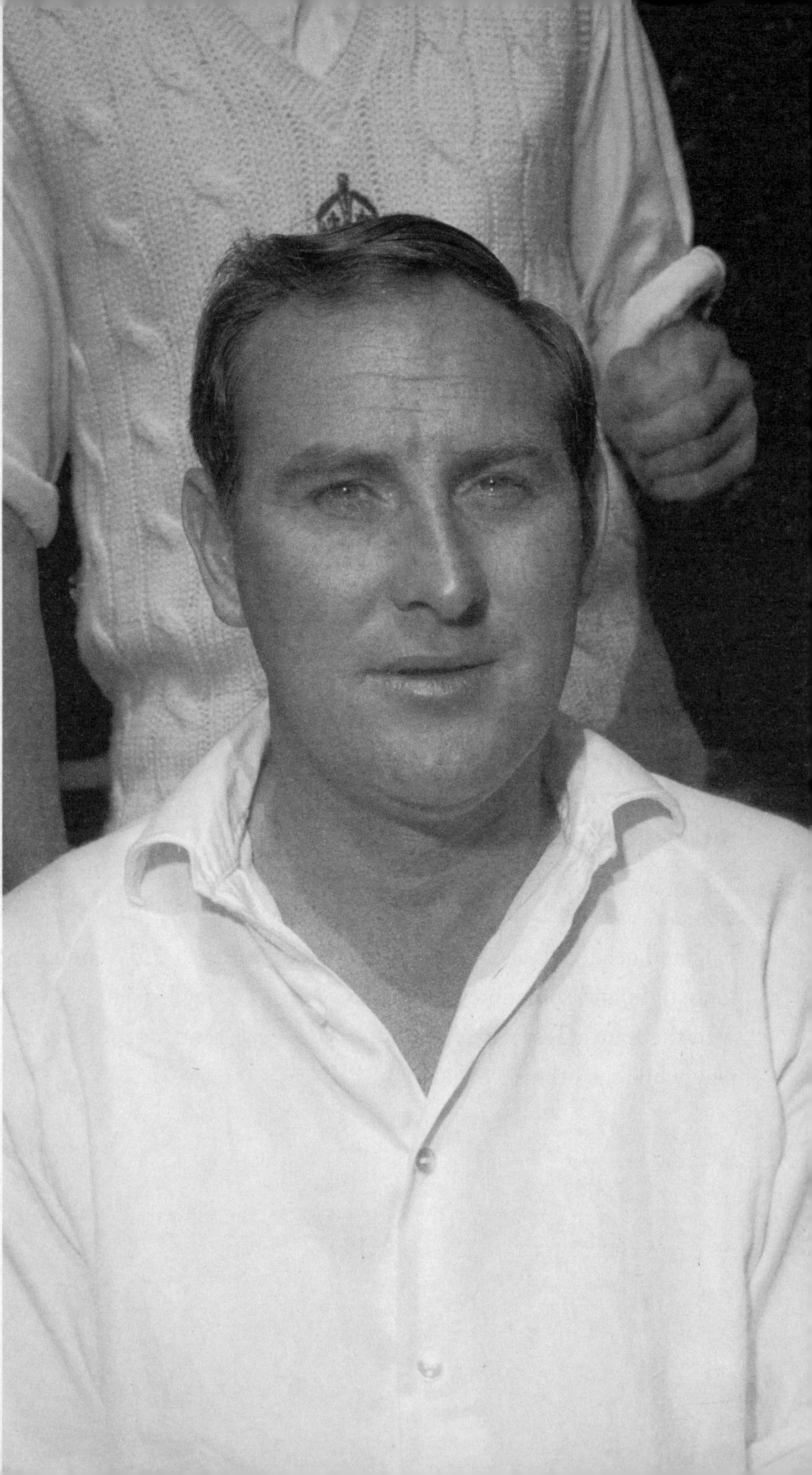

RAY ILLINGWORTH

Ray Illingworth – Seventh Test, Sydney Cricket Ground, 12-17 February 1971

Illingworth was a virtuoso captain capable of finding a strategy to deal with the most adverse situations. A determined batsman and canny bowler, he developed a happy habit of scoring vital runs and taking crucial wickets. The Yorkshireman scored two Test centuries and took five wickets in an innings on three occasions. Illingworth appeared in five Ashes series, but only finished on the winning side on two occasions, both when he was captain.

Right-arm off-break bowler, right-handed batsman
Born: 8 June 1932, Pudsey, Yorkshire
Test debut: July 1958 v New Zealand
Last Test: August 1973 v West Indies
Test record: 61 matches, 1,836 runs at an average of 23.24; 122 wickets at an average of 31.20

The state of play
England needed to avoid defeat to reclaim the Ashes at the end of a long, tight and sometimes controversial series. They led 1-0 having won the fourth Test with the third having been abandoned with no play, while the others were all draws.

Scoreboard

England first innings

J.H. Edrich	c G.S. Chappell	b Dell	30
B.W. Luckhurst	c Redpath	b Walters	0
K.W.R. Fletcher	c Stackpole	b O'Keeffe	33
J.H. Hampshire	c Marsh	b Lillee	10
B.L. D'Oliveira		b Dell	1
R. Illingworth		b Jenner	42
A.P.E. Knott	c Stackpole	b O'Keeffe	27
J.A. Snow		b Jenner	7
P. Lever	c Jenner	b O'Keeffe	4
D.L. Underwood		not out	8
R.G.D. Willis		b Jenner	11
Extras	(b 4, lb 4, w 1, nb 2)		11
Total	(all out, 76 overs)		184

Bowling	O	M	R	W
Lillee	13	5	32	1
Dell	16	8	32	2
Walters	4	0	10	1
G.S. Chappell	3	0	9	0
Jenner	16	3	42	3
O'Keeffe	24	8	48	3

Australia first innings

K.H. Eastwood	c Knott	b Lever	5
K.R. Stackpole		b Snow	6
R.W. Marsh	c Willis	b Lever	4
I.M. Chappell		b Willis	25
I.R. Redpath		c & b Underwood	59
K.D. Walters	st Knott	b Underwood	42
G.S. Chappell		b Willis	65
K.J. O'Keeffe	c Knott	b Illingworth	3
T.J. Jenner		b Lever	30
D.K. Lillee	c Knott	b Willis	6
A.R. Dell		not out	3
Extras	(lb 5, w 1, nb 10)		16
Total	(all out, 83.6 overs)		264

Bowling	O	M	R	W
Snow	18	2	68	1
Lever	14.6	3	43	3
D'Oliveira	12	2	24	0
Willis	12	1	58	3
Underwood	16	3	39	2
Illingworth	11	3	16	1

England second innings

J.H. Edrich	c I.M. Chappell	b O'Keeffe	57
B.W. Luckhurst	c Lillee	b O'Keeffe	59
K.W.R. Fletcher	c Stackpole	b Eastwood	20
J.H. Hampshire	c I.M. Chappell	b O'Keeffe	24
B.L. D'Oliveira	c I.M. Chappell	b Lillee	47
R. Illingworth	lbw	b Lillee	29
A.P.E. Knott		b Dell	15
J.A. Snow	c Stackpole	b Dell	20
P. Lever	c Redpath	b Jenner	17
D.L. Underwood	c Marsh	b Dell	0
R.G.D. Willis		not out	2
Extras	(b 3, lb 3, nb 6)		12
Total	(all out, 100.7 overs)		302

Bowling	O	M	R	W
Lillee	14	0	43	2
Dell	26.7	3	65	3
Walters	5	0	18	0
Jenner	21	5	39	1
O'Keeffe	26	8	96	3
Eastwood	5	0	21	1
Stackpole	3	1	8	0

Australia second innings (target: 223 runs)

K.H. Eastwood		b Snow	0
K.R. Stackpole		b Illingworth	67
I.M. Chappell	c Knott	b Lever	6
I.R. Redpath	c Hampshire	b Illingworth	14
K.D. Walters	c D'Oliveira	b Willis	1
G.S. Chappell	st Knott	b Illingworth	30
R.W. Marsh		b Underwood	16
K.J. O'Keeffe	c sub (Shuttleworth)	b D'Oliveira	12
T.J. Jenner	c Fletcher	b Underwood	4
D.K. Lillee	c Hampshire	b D'Oliveira	0
A.R. Dell		not out	3
Extras	(b 2, nb 5)		7
Total	(all out, 62.6 overs)		160

Bowling	O	M	R	W
Snow	2	1	7	1
Lever	12	2	23	1
D'Oliveira	5	1	15	2
Willis	9	1	32	1
Underwood	13.6	5	28	2
Illingworth	20	7	39	3
Fletcher	1	0	9	0

Ray Illingworth

MY TEAM-MATES PICKED me up and carried me off the field on their shoulders. Our celebrations usually consisted of a simple 'well done, kid', so this was really out of character, but it was touching. I had gone out to Australia with the intention of bringing back the Ashes and this moment was the reward for five months of very hard work. It was a marvellous feeling.

England were under pressure going into the 1970/71 series because the Australians had held the Ashes over the six previous series, since 1956. After all that time, we were in a similar position to the England side that reclaimed them in 2005.

But I didn't worry. We had a useful team and if we played to our potential, it would be a very good series, one we were capable of winning. I always believed I could win any game I played in.

Australia had a formidable batting line-up with Bill Lawry, Keith Stackpole, Ian Redpath, Ian and Greg Chappell, and Doug Walters. Lawry, Walters and Ian Chappell all made over 5,000 runs in their Test careers, which was a lot in those days, while Greg Chappell plundered over 7,000. Redpath scored over 4,500 and Stackpole almost 3,000, so I knew we would have to put on a tremendous bowling performance to overcome them.

At the start of the tour, my key players were John Snow and Alan Ward, who I thought would be a very fine fast-bowling pair. So it was a great disappointment when after a couple of State matches Wardy got shin splints and had to go home.

Fortunately we had good reserves in Ken Shuttleworth and Peter Lever, but we had to call up a replacement for Ward from England, and we decided on Bob Willis. I had never seen Willis play but John Edrich said the kid was young but quick. 'He'll do a job. He'll listen to you,' John told me.

So we had three quicks and Derek Underwood and myself to bowl spin, plus Basil D'Oliveira, who was a far better medium-pacer than people realised. That was a useful attack with a good balance between seam and spin.

I had gone for three opening batsmen, Geoff Boycott, Brian Luckhurst and John Edrich, because you often lose an opener early on the bouncy Australian wickets and I wanted our number three to be adept against the new ball. Boycs would always open and Lucky wanted to partner him. I knew John well because we were very close friends and I felt he had the temperament to wait, so it worked out well that he batted at three.

We were always a bit short in the number four position. Kipper [Colin Cowdrey] shouldn't have gone on the tour, to be quite honest. It took him three weeks to make his mind up to accept the vice-captaincy and I thought the selectors should have withdrawn the invitation. If a bloke takes that long to decide, he's not in the right frame of mind.

Cowdrey had already played over 100 Tests, scoring 22 centuries. But this was his fifth tour of Australia, so he tended to drift off and meet friends he had made on previous trips, turning up late for nets. I had a word with the tour manager, David Clark, who came from Kent as well, but David didn't want to do anything about it.

Kipper played early on but I told John Hampshire and Keith Fletcher, 'If this bloke doesn't do it, I don't care who he is, he won't be playing after a couple of Test matches. So I want you boys, while you can enjoy yourselves for a week or two, to keep fit and get plenty of practice, because you will come in.' In fact, Fletcher played throughout the tour and Hampshire came in later, so I kept my promise to them.

We then had D'Oliveira at number five, another who was good at waiting, which is so important in the middle order. I batted six and would sit and chat with Basil. We didn't get into panic stations, we were both calm before batting. Alan Knott was also relaxed before he went in. The three of us at five, six and seven all averaged 40 or above in Tests over a period of two years, which gave a lot of strength in the middle.

I insisted our bowlers had a good net before they came in to bat, and they made some useful runs. If a tail-ender can get 20 or 30 and they've still got a batsman with them it means the batsman can play with confidence and doesn't have to take silly risks.

It helped that I had played in Australia before under Ted Dexter in 1962/63, when a drawn series meant Richie Benaud's Australia retained the Ashes. I had played on all the grounds and knew which were good wickets, which might turn, which were more bouncy. I also knew what sort of barracking to expect from the crowds.

The team received some negative press coverage after we lost to Victoria a few weeks before the first Test, but we weren't too worried because the conditions were totally against us in that game. However, I was concerned about lack of practice. We had four first-class matches before the first Test in Brisbane and sides were batting for a long time against us, which meant our batsmen weren't getting much time in the middle.

For instance, Queensland's opener Sam Trimble was still batting on the third morning of a four-day match. They got 360 and we got 418/4 as the game ended in a draw. That was when I had a word with Boycs, saying, 'Somebody else needs to bat besides you, Geoffrey.' To be fair, he took it on board and at tea asked me what I wanted him to do. I said, 'You know my feelings, Geoff. I want another batsman to get a knock.' He replied, 'Well I won't get out, I'll retire hurt.' And he did so, on 124. That was fair enough.

Because of the way the State games had gone, I felt we were a bit under-cooked going into the first Test. We hadn't had a lot of batting practice, so we played the extra batsman, with Fletcher coming in at six and me at seven. Our bowlers were then Snowy, Shuttleworth, myself, Unders and Basil. Really, I wanted another quick but went without on this occasion.

We should have won the match. Australia got 433 in the first innings, but we were quite pleased with that after they were 308/2 at the end of the first day. Keith Stackpole made 207 but when he was on 18 we had him run out with a direct hit by Boycott, only for the umpire to rule against our appeal. A photo in the paper that night showed Keith was well short of safety. I got on to Stacky, who replied, 'Well, photographs can be misleading.' I said, 'Not when you're still two feet short and the stumps are flying through the air!'

It was the first of many things Stacky got away with over the six Tests. He must have been given not out six times when he was clearly out. That made a heck of a difference because he got over 600 runs in the series and we could have lost as a result. But we had a laugh over it in the end. Many years later I was working for the BBC and Stacky came to see me when he was over with a tour party. 'You know, all those decisions were out in Australia,' he said. 'Apart from the run out!'

In reply, we made 464, with half centuries from Luckhurst, Knott, Edrich and D'Oliveira. That gave us a lead of 31 and then we got Australia out cheaply in the second dig, for just 214. But our hopes of victory were dashed by wet weather, especially when the ground staff pulled the covers off and allowed water to spill all over the bowlers' run-ups, about a yard from the stumps, which meant we lost an hour and a half. Chasing 184, we finished on 39/1, but might have made the runs had we not lost so much time on the last day.

I had been working with Shuttleworth, getting him to get in closer to the stumps. He was bowling very well and got a five-for in Australia's second innings. But then he ruptured a groin muscle in a match upcountry and was out for most of the winter. After the early loss of Ward, this was a great disappointment and put us under more pressure.

Fortunately Lever improved by leaps and bounds. The next season, the Lancashire boys said they stood two or three yards deeper at slip to him than before. He worked with Snow quite a bit and put on that extra pace to add to his ability to swing the ball both ways. So with Lever, Snow and Willis, we still had a pretty useful pace attack.

Then we went to the WACA for the first ever Test at Perth. It was a very good wicket and a draw was always likely. We batted first and I went to see the groundsman to say I would like a light roller on the pitch. But before we went out, the umpires, Tom Brooks and Lou Rowan, came and told me I couldn't have a roller.

I said, 'I'm sorry, umpires, you are wrong. I can have a roller.' But, at lunchtime, they apologised to me and said we were entitled to a roller. I thought that was a good start for the umpires if they didn't know the bloody rules!

Roller or no roller, Boycott and Luckhurst put on 171 for the first wicket before Geoff was caught by McKenzie off Gleeson for 70. They worked well as a partnership. Lucky was a little bit more flamboyant than Boycs at the start, but Boycott soon hit superb form.

He said he would have batted against the devil in that series. While he wasn't going to hit sixes and fours all the time, he still scored at a good rate. I played with him for many years and never saw him bat better as he scored 669 Test runs at an average of 95.

Luckhurst went on to get 131 in our total of 397 before Australia put on 440, with centuries from Redpath and Greg Chappell, making his Test debut. Greg was a very upright batsman, stylish to watch and was clearly going to be a top-class Test player. On the last day, I declared at 287/6, with Edrich unbeaten on 115. That set Australia a target of 245, but the match was drawn with them finishing on 100/3. So the series was still locked at 0-0 after two Tests.

Afterwards, David Clark told the press he would rather Australia won the series than every game end in a draw. I was incensed. 'Hang on,' I said, 'these lads are playing their hearts out in a foreign country, it's hard going against a good side, and to come out with a statement like that is absolutely ridiculous.'

We wanted to win, but you don't throw a Test match away early on in the series. If you lose one, it's damned hard to win two back. I had a real go at David about his comments, as I did over many things. We felt we would probably be better off if he went home.

At least the tour manager had no say on selections. We had a selection committee, but I had overall control and wouldn't have taken the job any other way. Cowdrey was supposed to be on the committee but he didn't show much interest, so I just used to talk with Boycs and Edrich.

The third Test at Melbourne was completely washed out so MCC and the Australian Cricket Board agreed there would be a seventh match in Sydney later in the tour to replace it. The players were not consulted, which was completely wrong. So I said to David, 'That's seven Test matches and we're going to play five in six weeks after Christmas. If we get one injury, we're stuffed.' Anyone crocked would have no time to recover between matches, while Australia could call someone up from their domestic scene.

Snowy got a lot off his chest in the team meeting about that matter. We were only contracted for a certain number of matches, so that caused a row because we weren't getting paid for the extra one.

Eventually, David rang MCC, who said we must be paid for the seventh Test, so they offered us £25 apiece!

Every day at Melbourne we turned up thinking we were going to start, but it would just rain again. At one point, Ian Johnson, the former Australia captain and then secretary of Melbourne, said it was fit to play and walked on to the pitch in his best suit, only to slip over on his arse. He was covered in mud and there was an almighty roar from the dressing room. The rain cleared away on what would have been the last day, so we played the first-ever one-day international, which Australia won in front of a crowd of over 45,000.

We took on Tasmania over Christmas, a three-day game, with Christmas Day as a rest day. The team had Christmas dinner together but we didn't go mad, just had a few drinks. We were playing the next day so the boys looked after themselves and we beat Tasmania comfortably.

I trusted the players. At the start of the tour, I told them, 'You're out here to play cricket. You're grown men and I trust you. But if you turn up and you're not bloody fit because of having too much to drink, your feet won't touch the floor.' They responded positively to that rule and we had no problems.

Sydney is always a great place to play cricket. Providing there are no problems with the weather, you can nearly always get a result and I always preferred pitches like that. Boycs made 77 in our first-innings total of 332 before Australia were bowled out for 236 as Underwood took 4-66.

In the second innings, Boycott made a splendid 142 not out. He and I shared a partnership of 95 for the fifth wicket, and I hit 53 as we pushed towards a declaration that left Australia a massive 416 to win in about nine hours. They were 64/4 at stumps on the fourth day and had no chance of surviving the last day.

Before we went out to field on the last morning, I said to the players, 'I want you to go out there and imagine we're playing the last over of a Gillette one-day final at Lord's and the opposition need eight to win. How would you be fielding? Now, that's the fielding I want. If we do that, we can have this match sewn up.' Everyone responded and we won the match in no time as the Aussies collapsed to 116 all out. We were 1-0 up in the series.

Snowy bowled magnificently to take a memorable 7-40, making the ball bounce awkwardly and move off the seam. He performed as well as any quick bowler I've ever seen, including the likes of Fred Trueman, Brian Statham and Frank Tyson. Snowy's victims included the Chappells, Redpath, Stackpole and Marsh, so it was a heck of a display.

Before the Melbourne game, Willis, Lever and Snowy bowled at me in some good nets at the grammar school. The other two were doing nothing at all off the seam, while Snowy was nipping the ball about all the time. So I said to him, 'Let's have a look at that ball of yours.'

I thought he must have been fiddling with it but it was perfectly normal. He had the ability to hit the seam so often that he could easily make it go either way. He also got bounce from just short of a length, so didn't need to bowl bouncers, and frequently got batsmen turned around and caught in the slip and gully area.

I had to be pretty hard with Snowy early in the tour. He could be a lazy bugger in the field, just lolloping about. So I gave him a rollicking and explained that because of his fielding other bowlers were getting hit for three when it should have been two and things like that. I wouldn't accept it. The next day he went out and tried very hard in the field.

Snowy and I had a few words but he responded well and we became very good friends. He even wrote about me in his book, 'Bless his little cotton socks, he did understand fast bowlers.' Which was a nice thing to say.

We always had a few beers with the Aussies after play. People like Rodney Marsh, Ian Chappell and Doug Walters would be there, and sometimes the dressing room attendant would come and say, 'Are you buggers going home tonight?'

When we won the fourth Test the England boys celebrated with a few glasses of champagne. Some of our friends from the entertainment business were over, people like Leslie Crowther and Tony Mercer, and we had a drink or two with them at the hotel.

Confidence was high. We felt we were getting the upper hand while Australia were beginning to worry where they were going next. But the fifth Test at Melbourne was another draw. Australia batted first on what looked like a typical English green top. We spilled two or three chances early on and that swung the match because they went on to make 493/9 declared.

We dropped Ian Chappell on nought and he got a hundred. If we had have caught that, I doubt Chappelli, as he was known to the boys, would have captained Australia because he was struggling and in danger of being dropped. It just shows a dropped catch can change history.

Luckhurst and D'Oliveira then completed centuries in our total of 392. Basil was a good competitor, always wanted to win. He had come up the hard way in South Africa, where because he wasn't white, he could never play Test cricket under the apartheid regime, so representing England was a big thing in his career. Off the field he was a good character, you just had to watch he didn't get too much ale down him. Two pints could be enough, three was his absolute limit!

Australia declared their second innings on 169/4, leaving us about four hours to score 271 for victory. Unfortunately we couldn't have a go at the target because Luckhurst was off with a broken thumb and Dolly had injured a hamstring. Some people thought we should have gone for the runs, but if two of the top five can't bat, you are effectively starting at 0/2. So I told the boys to play normal cricket and Boycott and Edrich took us to 161 without loss by the end.

There were some strange umpiring decisions throughout the series, none more so than when Stackpole was given not out at the end of the first over of the fifth Test. The ball must have gone three feet in the air off his gloves as it lobbed through to

Knotty. But umpire Max O'Connell was already striding off to square leg and when we appealed he said it wasn't out.

Because of that incident I told the boys that even if it was an obvious catch, we still had to shout like we were appealing for a thin nick. If you don't shout, umpires don't think it's out. I didn't say we should appeal when we knew it wasn't out, as one national newspaper suggested. That was ridiculous.

We had a little chat with Stacky at the time, but didn't expect him to walk. Bill Lawry was at the other end and if he had middle stump knocked out, he would put it back in, you weren't going to get him to walk. After that, I told our players, 'It's up to you what you do, but I don't think we should walk.' We were losing out on two major decisions a match, and that's a lot if it's two of the main batsmen. But it wasn't easy not walking having spent the rest of your career doing so. You would take one step towards the pavilion and then go back again, which looked a bit guilty anyway.

For the sixth Test at Adelaide we had the best batting pitch I've ever seen. England made 470, with Edrich contributing 130, but Boycott was unhappy to be adjudged run out for 58. I saw it from the dressing room, which is dead square-on at the Adelaide Oval, and he was out. I think his bat may have bounced up when he went to run it in.

Nevertheless, Boycs threw his bat down and Greg Chappell picked it up, handed it to him and told him to get back to his mother in the stand. Of course the woman in the stand was Anne, Boycott's girlfriend at the time, who was 14 years older than him, so that didn't go down too well.

I had known Boycs a long time, having played at Yorkshire with him from 1962 to 1968. He was a complex character, whose number one priority always seemed to be his own runs, but he batted brilliantly on that tour and we got on very well. We both thought the other one was a good professional.

I had no trouble batting with Boycs because in the early days when he ran a few people out, I said to him, 'You won't run me out because if you do I'll sit you on your arse in the middle of the wicket.' From that day on, we had no problem running together.

I honestly don't know how we managed to bowl Australia out for 235 given how good the pitch was. But because we had to take the second new ball to dismiss them, Lever, who took four wickets, and Snowy were knackered. If both my main quick bowlers had problems it wasn't the wisest decision to make them bowl again on a really flat surface, so we didn't enforce the follow-on.

Our second innings of 233/4 declared included a fine century from Boycott and left Australia a day and a session to make 469. They reached 328/3 as Stackpole and Ian Chappell both made centuries, so the match finished in another draw, leaving us 1-0 up in the series with one Test to play.

Dennis Lillee made his debut for Australia at Adelaide and took 5-84 in our first innings. When we had encountered him playing for Western Australia, Dennis came steaming in to bowl his first ball at Boycs and it hit the peak of his cap and spun it around on his head. That was our introduction to him. Dennis was aggressive but I got on well with him.

He had a go at me once because he thought I had nicked one, but it had hit my elbow. He went on about how I should have walked and I called him a kangaroo or something.

Stacky told him at the end of the over that I hadn't hit it, so Dennis came into our dressing room later and said, 'Sorry about that, captain.' I responded, 'No trouble. See you tonight for a pint.'

We were 1-0 up going into the seventh Test, so to regain the Ashes, we just had to avoid defeat at Sydney. But everything seemed to be going wrong when we played at Western Australia in a one-day match four days before the decider. The pitch was wet and Boycott had his arm broken by a rising delivery from Garth McKenzie. That was the last thing we wanted with Boycott playing so well.

Australia's preparations were also less than perfect. They sacked Lawry as skipper and dropped him from the team. His replacement, Ian Chappell, was a better captain, more attacking and adventurous. It rained for two days prior to the Test, and they never got the covers off. So Chappelli had no hesitation putting us in when he won the toss. I top-scored with 42 in our innings of just 184, which was a hell of a struggle because the pitch was damp and the outfield hadn't been cut for two days, so you couldn't hit a four.

When it was obvious we were heading for a low score, I contemplated declaring because I thought Snowy and Lever could bowl out Australia for under 100 while the pitch was so lively and the outfield so slow. But we lost our last two wickets in no time and the decision was taken out of my hands. Fortunately that helped us win the match because we got them two down for 13 overnight, with openers Ken Eastwood and Stackpole both out.

During that little time we had at them on the first evening, they couldn't lay a bat on Snowy. It was going both ways off the seam and if we had have had another hour, we might have got five out by stumps. But Australia were in the box seat on the second morning because the wicket had changed so dramatically. The covers had been off since five o'clock in the morning with the sun beating down and the outfield was cut so that it was like a billiard table, meaning it was a lot easier to score runs. Still, our bowlers plugged away and Australia weren't able to build a massive lead despite half-centuries from Redpath and Greg Chappell.

When Australia were 195/7, a delivery from Snowy struck Terry Jenner, their leg-spinner, on the head and he was forced to retire hurt for a while. It was never a bouncer. I was at short bat and pad, and Snowy appealed for lbw. It might have gone six inches over the top, but not much more than that. Jenner himself realised he had made a mistake ducking into the ball. If he had stood up, he would have played it at waist height.

But umpire Lou Rowan started warning Snowy for intimidatory bowling. I got accused of wagging my finger at the official, but what I said was, 'He's bowled one bouncer. Under which law are you warning him?' He replied, 'Persistent intimidating bowling.'

He went over to Tom Brooks, his fellow official, but Brooks wouldn't support him. It got Snowy so riled, I was afraid what he might do. It was no surprise when his next ball whistled over the batsman's head and Snowy said, 'That's a bloody bouncer!' I was worried I might be forced to take him off.

By warning Snowy for no reason, the umpire whipped up the crowd, who became very hostile. When John went down to field on the boundary, some of the crowd threw cans and bottles in his direction. So I called the players into the middle and we sat down while the missiles were cleared off the outfield. But when Snowy returned to the boundary more cans and bottles were hurled, some of them full, and a spectator leaned over the fence and grabbed Snowy, who would have got in real trouble if he had bobbed him one back.

One of the bottles hit the sightscreen attendant, and he was carted off to hospital. That could easily have been a player, so I said to the umpires, 'If you're not going to do anything to stop this, I'm not prepared to have my players on the field.'

I couldn't understand the umpires' inaction because Rowan was the bloke who in the first Test stopped the game and walked all the way to the boundary just to tell a kid who was sat on the fence with his legs dangling to get them to the other side.

We went off to the pavilion and told the Sydney secretary to announce that we would go back on when the field was cleared, but if anything else happened we would go off again. We would not play in those conditions. Then the umpires started saying we could forfeit the Test. 'We can lose the match, but I won't get a player bloody killed for it,' I told them.

'You must get back on the field, Raymond,' David Clark said to me. Snowy let him have a few home truths then, while I told him to get out of the way, we would go back on when the field was fit for play, when the 30 or so cans and bottles had been cleared. Eventually they were removed and we went back out.

What pleased me more than anything was that all the Australian writers like Richie Benaud supported me. The ones who didn't were in the English press. E.W. Swanton said I should have put Snowy at cover-point. Well, I wasn't going to put my fast bowler at cover-point, doing all the running around when he had to bowl the next over. I wasn't going to let the crowd dictate where I put my fielders.

By and large, we had no trouble with Australian spectators. There was a pub in Adelaide, the Green Dragon, where we used to go for a drink, and we received quite a few telegrams from them saying well done in the series.

If you had a bit of fun with the crowds, they were okay. My arm had gone a bit by this time so you can imagine trying to throw the ball in from the boundary at Melbourne. The old wags were shouting out, 'Get a bloody catapult!' I would turn around and say, 'Have you got one?' Little things like that get you in with them. While they would have a go at you, they did it in good humour.

By the end of the second day Australia were 51 ahead with three wickets remaining. The next morning we did well to mop up the tail and restrict them to a lead of 80. I bowled 11 eight-ball overs for just 16 runs and picked up the wicket of Kerry O'Keeffe, the New South Wales leg-spinner.

Edrich and Luckhurst got our second innings off to a good start by both scoring half-centuries. The rest of the top nine batsmen all got into double figures, so it was a real team effort. We knuckled down and everybody tried their hardest. There was a little bit in the pitch all the time so it was hard work.

I got a whack on the knee during my knock of 29 and was struggling. My wife Shirley was out with us then and I had to send her down for bags of ice for my knee overnight. I kept the ice on throughout the rest day, so I was fit for day four.

Our second innings total of 302 was just about par for the course and set Australia a last-innings target of 223, but I felt we could have done with another 50 runs. Our prospects of victory were not improved when shortly after Snowy had dismissed Eastwood in Australia's second innings, we lost him with a dislocated finger after he had trapped it in the fence trying to take a catch.

That was a massive blow and I had to find other weapons to explode Australia's chances. Happily, I bowled really well and had Redpath caught by John Hampshire before bowling Stackpole to reduce Australia to 96/5. Stacky had scored 67 of their runs at that point, so his was a crucial wicket.

Going into the last day, Australia needed 100 more to win with five wickets in hand. I felt it would be very tight. We had lost Snowy and only had Plank [Peter Lever] and Willis to come charging in. It is always difficult to make decisions about your own bowling when you are captain, but I realised batsmen often don't start well against spin, so I opted to bowl myself and Underwood from the start.

My plan worked. Derek bowled Marshy to make it 131/6. Marsh was a very dangerous player chasing a small total because he could swat 40 or 50 in no time, so it was an important wicket. But the pivotal moment came when I got Greg Chappell out stumped for 30. I bowled him an arm ball that drifted out a little bit. He came down the pitch and it beat the outside edge, and Knotty whipped the bails off. It was a classic spinner's dismissal, good to watch on telly!

Knotty was the best keeper I've ever seen. His fingers were like a pianist's, not a mark on them. He caught bottom edges when stood up, things that other people wouldn't have even seen. Everybody who played with him will tell you he was brilliant, but earlier he had dropped Marshy off a little outside edge. So when we passed in the middle, I said, 'You've proved one thing.' He asked, 'What's that?' I replied, 'You're human. I didn't think you could miss them.'

He said that relaxed him so much, that I had shown such confidence in him, and of course he kept his cool to dismiss Chappell. If we hadn't got Greg, Australia would have won the match and retained the Ashes because he was in really good form. His departure left them 142/7, with another 81 required and we felt we would win then.

D'Oliveira picked up O'Keeffe and Lillee, both caught, with the score on 154. Then Derek had Jenner caught by Fletcher and Australia were all out for 160, which meant we had won by 62 runs and reclaimed the Ashes with a 2-0 series victory. I was delighted with my second-innings performance of 3-39 from 20 overs as I picked up the vital wickets of Stackpole, Redpath and Chappell.

My team-mates carried me from the field on their shoulders, which I really appreciated. Mind you, I was a bit worried because Shuttleworth, on as a substitute for Snow, and Edrich weren't the same height. There was about a foot's difference between them, so I was concerned they might drop me!

The Australians all came into our dressing room and said 'well played', and we had a few beers before leaving the ground. Chappelli, in particular, was a very good loser. That night, some of the entertainers from the *Black and White Minstrel Show*, whom we knew from seeing them in Scarborough and London, joined our celebrations.

We had played five Tests in six weeks and were bloody tired after the tension of that last match, so by the time we'd had two or three beers and something to eat, we were all a bit sleepy. Basil might have gone a bit off the straight and narrow that night, but nobody else really did. He had a lot of friends over and they all finished up partying in his room.

I had a steady series, scoring 333 runs at 37 and taking 11 wickets. A couple of times I threw my wicket away just going for quick runs for a declaration and I could have averaged over 40 if that hadn't happened.

I didn't bowl a lot but worked on making the ball leave the bat because of the lbw law at the time, which said that if the ball pitched outside off stump and the batsman was playing a shot, he couldn't be out leg before. That meant it was very difficult to get lbws and we only got one on the entire tour, and none in the Tests. So I had to get people to bowl out-swingers or the left-armers to turn the ball away. The fact that we bowled them out six times for under 300 shows my theory worked pretty well.

On the batting side, one of our strengths was we very rarely lost two wickets quickly. We always seemed to get off to a reasonable start and the opening pair put on over 100 four times during the series. We kept on hearing about how much interest we were creating back home, that people were staying up through the night to listen on the radio. But when we got back, there was very little excitement. That was disappointing compared with what goes on now.

Still, I was the first captain since Douglas Jardine, on the Bodyline tour 38 years earlier, to recapture the Ashes on Australian soil, which made me very proud. My emphasis as captain was always on the team. You can have stars within a team, but you've got to have unity.

Unless people have been to Australia, they don't realise how difficult it is to win a series down there. There is the climate for one thing – it can be 100 degrees or more. The crowds are massive and hostile, with 90 per cent of them against you, and the pitches are different. So winning back the Ashes in Australia was the absolute highlight of my cricket career.

JEFF THOMSON

Jeff Thomson – First Test, Brisbane, 29 November to 4 December 1974

Few bowlers in Test history can claim to have matched Jeff Thomson's lightning pace. He formed a fearsome partnership with Dennis Lillee, but while Lillee was noted for his classical action, Thomson's shuffling approach to the wicket and slinging delivery were utterly unorthodox. Thomson's speed was not measured as regularly or as accurately as that of modern-day bowlers, but one delivery against the West Indies at Perth in 1975 was timed at 99.70 mph. Thomson himself maintains he often bowled faster.

Right arm fast bowler
Born: 16 August 1950, Greenacre, Sydney
Test debut: December 1973/January 1974 v Pakistan
Last Test: August 1985 v England
Test record: 51 matches, 200 wickets at an average of 28.00

The state of play
In the opening Test of the 1974/75 Ashes, England got a rude awakening from Australia's fast-bowling duo, who would go on to wreak havoc throughout the rest of the series which the hosts won 4-1.

Scoreboard

Australia first innings

I.R. Redpath		b Willis	5
W.J. Edwards	c Amiss	b Hendrick	4
I.M. Chappell	c Greig	b Willis	90
G.S. Chappell	c Fletcher	b Underwood	58
R. Edwards	c Knott	b Underwood	32
K.D. Walters	c Lever	b Willis	3
R.W. Marsh	c Denness	b Hendrick	14
T.J. Jenner	c Lever	b Willis	12
D.K. Lillee	c Knott	b Greig	15
M.H.N. Walker		not out	41
J.R. Thomson		run out	23
Extras	(lb 4, nb 8)		12
Total	(all out, 92.5 overs)		309

Bowling	O	M	R	W
Willis	21.5	3	56	4
Lever	16	1	53	0
Hendrick	19	3	64	2
Greig	16	2	70	1
Underwood	20	6	54	2

England first innings

D.L. Amiss	c Jenner	b Thomson	7
B.W. Luckhurst	c Marsh	b Thomson	1
J.H. Edrich	c I.M. Chappell	b Thomson	48
M.H. Denness	lbw	b Walker	6
K.W.R. Fletcher		b Lillee	17
A.W. Greig	c Marsh	b Lillee	110
A.P.E. Knott	c Jenner	b Walker	12
P. Lever	c I.M. Chappell	b Walker	4
D.L. Underwood	c Redpath	b Walters	25
R.G.D. Willis		not out	13
M. Hendrick	c Redpath	b Walker	4
Extras	(b 5, lb 2, w 3, nb 8)		18
Total	(all out, 80.5 overs)		265

Bowling	O	M	R	W
Lillee	23	6	73	2
Thomson	21	5	59	3
Walker	24.5	2	73	4
Walters	6	1	18	1
Jenner	6	1	24	0

Australia second innings

I.R. Redpath		b Willis	25
W.J. Edwards	c Knott	b Willis	5
I.M. Chappell	c Fletcher	b Underwood	11
G.S. Chappell		b Underwood	71
R. Edwards	c Knott	b Willis	53
K.D. Walters		not out	62
R.W. Marsh		not out	46
Extras	(b 1, lb 7, w 1, nb 6)		15
Total	(5 wickets dec, 85 overs)		288

Bowling	O	M	R	W
Willis	15	3	45	3
Lever	18	4	58	0
Hendrick	13	2	47	0
Greig	13	2	60	0
Underwood	26	6	63	2

England second innings (target: 333 runs)

D.L. Amiss	c Walters	b Thomson	25
B.W. Luckhurst	c I.M. Chappell	b Lillee	3
J.H. Edrich		b Thomson	6
M.H. Denness	c Walters	b Thomson	27
K.W.R. Fletcher	c G.S. Chappell	b Jenner	19
A.W. Greig		b Thomson	2
A.P.E. Knott		b Thomson	19
P. Lever	c Redpath	b Lillee	14
D.L. Underwood	c Walker	b Jenner	30
R.G.D. Willis		not out	3
M. Hendrick		b Thomson	0
Extras	(b 8, lb 3, w 2, nb 5)		18
Total	(all out, 56.5 overs)		166

Bowling	O	M	R	W
Lillee	12	2	25	2
Thomson	17.5	3	46	6
Walker	9	4	32	0
Walters	2	2	0	0
Jenner	16	5	45	2

Jeff Thomson

'JUST FUCK AROUND,' Greg Chappell told me. 'Don't show the English batsmen what you can really do.' Playing for Queensland, the captain wanted me to remain Australia's secret weapon until the Ashes started, so I followed his instructions and just toyed around, bowled within myself in the warm-up game against England. I only picked up two wickets as we lost, but England had no idea I would be bowling at speeds of up to 100 mph and making the ball leap angrily off a length on my Ashes debut a few days later.

I was raring to go for the first Test at Brisbane. I was blitzing everybody I came up against in domestic cricket, including six wickets on my Queensland debut against New South Wales. So I just had to carry on bowling like that to surprise the English. I had played against Ian and Greg Chappell in the Sheffield Shield and if great batsmen like them couldn't handle my bowling, the Poms weren't going to either.

It was November 1974 and I had been called into the Australia side for the first time since my debut against Pakistan in January 1973. I have good and bad memories of that match. Obviously it was fantastic to get picked for Australia but because I was carrying a serious injury I under performed and wasn't selected again for almost two years.

I didn't find out I had been picked for my debut Test from the selectors, but from Tony Radanovic, the skipper of my club side, Bankstown. My mother and I had been visiting my sick uncle in hospital and when we got back at 11 o'clock at night, Tony was waiting on the doorstep.

He insisted on taking me down to the club for a few drinks but didn't tell me why we were celebrating. All my club-mates were there and Tony then informed me I had been selected for Australia. It was the biggest shock of my life.

Shortly before the Test I played in a Sheffield Shield match for New South Wales and bowled a short ball and heard my foot crack. Sometimes your knee or back cracks and you just get up and get on with it. I thought it was like that, but it transpired I had broken my foot.

Anyway, I arrived in Melbourne to play Pakistan and although my foot was sore I thought the pain would go away. Besides, I was playing for Australia and was determined to be fit. But throughout the match I couldn't walk on that foot, let alone bowl on it, so I took 0-90 and 0-20.

50

Some people criticised my performance, but I would love to see how many of them could have bowled 19 eight-ball overs with a fractured bone in their foot. I couldn't even walk back to the hotel at night. Our wicketkeeper Rod Marsh was upset with me because I shouldn't have played. I didn't actually know the bone was broken until I had an x-ray when I returned to Sydney after we beat Pakistan. It was a bit of a comedown after all the excitement of being selected, but I wasn't worried. It was no wonder I couldn't bowl if I had a broken foot.

When I got picked for the first Test of the 1974/75 Ashes series, I was really fired up because my debut was such a dud. I was bigger, better and more experienced now.

Australia's key players at that time were Dennis Lillee, the great fast bowler, and the Chappells, who were world-class batsmen. I was a wild card who could bowl at 100 mph, but nobody knew quite where the ball would go.

I loved Ian Chappell's captaincy because he was just so relaxed. He is like me, I'm not a panic merchant. If you bowl one bad ball or a couple, who cares? You're capable of bowling more better balls, so why worry about it?

Ian would tell you exactly what he wanted. In my case, that was usually five or six overs flat out, which meant I didn't have to pace myself over a long spell and could really let them go. Ian rightly recognised that when you've got the quickest bowler in the world, you don't use him as a stock bowler.

Behind the stumps, Marshy was an important figure in the team. We both told the other one what we wanted. He was good like that. I would tell him before an over what I was going to do, then give him a nod if the plan changed.

Also, he knew exactly how to rev up Dennis and me. He would make stupid comments and tease you to get you angry and take it out on the batsmen. He was a gorilla. That's why it was so hard to understand him coaching in England and becoming a Test selector there. He must have hated it!

Australia hadn't won an Ashes series since 1968, but I wasn't worried about the past because I'm not a historian. What happened to the blokes before me was their worry.

England's main batsmen were Brian Luckhurst, John Edrich, Dennis Amiss and the captain Mike Denness. I didn't know much about these blokes because I wasn't one to sit down and read about English county cricket – I couldn't care less about it. I didn't study the opposition way in advance, I just bowled a few balls and looked at them, very quickly saw what they liked and disliked. That's how you work it out.

We were all self-taught in those days. Nowadays all these guys run around with computers and that's rubbish. If you can't work out in five minutes what a batsman can and can't handle, you shouldn't be playing Test cricket. You don't need computers to tell you what's going on, you ask any bloke from our era.

Geoff Boycott didn't come on that tour, which obviously affected England. We were disappointed he wasn't there because he was a tough batsman and we would have been up for the challenge of getting him out. Fiery might have made a difference to the series, but we'll never know.

I had heard Edrich was pretty handy and knew Lillee rated him, but he was coming towards the end of his career and struggled against my pace. Besides, I loved bowling at left-handers because they were always likely to nick the ball, especially to a bloke like me who hit the deck and got the ball to jag in and away. I would get them going back and then toss one up, they would try to hit it but their feet wouldn't work, and all I then needed was for the slips to be alert.

I used to get really pumped up and angry before a match because I just wanted to get out there and bowl. Normally I was cool, calm and collected, but I hated hanging around and the adrenaline would get to me.

The night before the first Test, I had a drink or two in the hotel bar after our team dinner. 'If I've got a hangover,' I told Dennis, 'it makes me a bit crabby, so I'll take it out on these English blokes.' But I was joking and only had a couple, so I didn't get pissed.

We batted first at Brisbane and Ian Chappell's 90 was the top score in our total of 309. I played a few unorthodox shots and slogged a bit as I contributed 23 to an important last-wicket stand of 52 with fellow bowler Max Walker. It is always good to get a couple of runs as a bowler, it warms you up for the main event.

Before we took the field Ian told me I would be bowling the second over, with Lillee opening with the wind. Ian knew I could bowl quicker into the wind than anybody could bowl with it. Bowling into the wind never worried me like it did other bowlers because sometimes I built up a better rhythm that way. Besides, I couldn't wait to get going.

The crowd was behind me right from the start and I knew that if I performed against the Poms, I would be a hero. In those days there were no real regulations. People just got in the ground and didn't have to have a seat, so blokes were drinking and having a laugh, they had the best day of their lives.

I was lucky because I knew the Gabba like the back of my hand. Brisbane was now my home ground because I had transferred from New South Wales to Queensland at the beginning of the 1974/75 season. Queensland had promised me a game and employment with a local firm, which was an offer I couldn't refuse.

Just before I had left Sydney there was a big article about me in a cricket magazine that said I was a brutal killer and all that caper. A lot of it was blown out of proportion, but although it wasn't true to say that I enjoyed seeing batsmen twitching on the ground and bleeding all over the place after I had hit them, it probably didn't do my image any harm.

The Gabba pitch was nice and hard, which suited me, and it wasn't long before Luckhurst became my first Test victim, caught behind by Marsh to leave England 9/1. I am not that emotional about sport and I expected it to be the first of many wickets. That is not being big-headed, just confident.

One run later I had Amiss caught by Terry Jenner in the gully with a delivery that reared viciously at his chest off a length. The batsmen were clearly surprised by how quick I was. They thought, 'We'll keep Lillee out and then work on this bloke.' But they got the shock of their lives. I'm not being a smart-arse, that's obviously just what happened.

Most of them weren't too happy facing me but Tony Greig, the South Africa-born all-rounder, was one man who had a lot of guts. He came in and, alongside Edrich, helped England recover from 57/4 to 114/4 by the end of the second day.

The next morning I soon had Edrich caught at slip by Ian Chappell, which left England really struggling at 130/5. But Greig kept on taking the attack to our bowlers, driving hard if the ball was pitched up and slashing short deliveries over the slips. You have to have ability to do that because you can't just throw the bat and get away with it. He counter-attacked brilliantly, which was a hard thing to do, as a one-man band.

I didn't know Greig but realised some of the boys didn't like him. Dennis was trying to knock his block off and I followed the leader. We bowled too short to him and he just smacked us around. He wasn't a great bat but was a good striker of the ball. He guessed that we would bowl him a lot of bouncers, you didn't have to be too smart to work it out, and got a good hundred in the circumstances.

Greigy knew I wouldn't bite with his wind-up tactics. He could say what he liked and I wouldn't answer back. But he used to get to Dennis, doing stuff like going down on one knee and signalling a four if he hit him to the boundary. With the Chappells, Dennis and Greigy all giving each other grief, it was ego city out in the middle.

While they were really having a go at one another, I was the new kid on the block and just shut up and did my job. The problem for England was that Greigy stirred us up and it was then worse for his team-mates when they batted. Blokes like Luckhurst and Amiss copped a lot of flak.

Greig's 110 helped England to within 44 runs of our first-innings score and Ian was furious with Dennis and me for the way we bowled at him. 'You fucking pair of idiots,' Ian shouted, 'bowling that shit to him. What are you fucking trying to do? Anyone could see what was going to happen there.'

Then he turned to me and continued, 'You're the biggest idiot of the lot. You've got the best yorker going and you didn't even bloody bowl him one. The best thing you could do is hit him on the feet with the thing and bowl him out.' That stuck in my mind and I realised what an idiot I had been, just following Dennis.

My 3-59 in the first innings was a bit lean compared to what I should have achieved and I was far happier with my efforts in the second dig. I usually bowled better as the game wore on because I found rhythm and that meant I could send the ball down quicker than anyone.

We declared our second innings at 288/5 as Greg Chappell and Doug Walters made half-centuries. England's attack in that match consisted of seamers Bob Willis, Peter Lever, Mike Hendrick and Greig, plus Derek Underwood, the left-arm spinner. They were handy bowlers, but their job was very difficult throughout the series because England never made enough runs.

We weren't worried that England would reach the 333 we set them to win in the last day and a bit. We just had to get Greigy because he was the only one who would throw the bat. Nobody else was a real shot-maker, except Amiss, who was their best player on paper but didn't have a good series.

As we prepared to go out and field, Ian told me to bowl really fast and do the things we had worked on, especially with Greigy. I used to get the ball to move, usually late, and bounce sharply from a length, so it was just business as usual for me, a case of bowling to my field, which was four slips and a couple of gullies. That isn't hard to bowl to when you've got somebody on the back foot trying to fend the ball off.

Amiss described the last hour of the fourth day as 'the most frightening fast bowling I have ever seen.' Dennis was bowling really quick and I was letting them rip so that they really zinged through. When I got my rhythm it felt like everything was going in slow motion. It wasn't anything that I hadn't done umpteen times before, but the English were really caught unawares.

Other than raw pace, bounce was my biggest weapon. I could get it to lift from a length. It would just take off and that's very awkward because batsmen are used to bounce at a certain height and when it comes that bit higher it messes them up. You are not going to swing it bowling as quick as I did, but I used to hit the seam. That gave me a bit of deviation, which was always hard for batsmen to predict.

Many players also found it difficult to pick the ball up because of my slinging action, which meant the ball was hidden from view until the last second. My action was completely natural to me, I never worked on it; it was just the way I was. My old man bowled like that and I inherited it.

We bowled eight-ball overs in those days and I preferred that because I could really work on a batsman with those two extra balls, which were sometimes good to get a bloke out. If somebody bowled eight-ball overs now, they would probably think, 'Bloody hell, how long's this going on?' But it was what we were used to.

England started the last day on 10/0, with all three outcomes possible. We soon got into them as Dennis had Luckhurst caught by Ian Chappell and I bowled Edrich. Amiss batted with a broken thumb after I had struck him in the first innings – when I hit a batsman they usually broke something – and he was next to go. I got one to rise sharply and it flew off his bat handle for Walters to take a superb slip catch.

When the same combination got rid of Denness, England were staring down the barrel at 92/4. I had a lot of catches dropped off my bowling in my career, but in that series they seemed to stick, which makes a hell of a difference.

Greig came to the crease and I remembered how angry the captain had been that Dennis and I bowled so much short stuff at him in the first dig. So when he had made just two, I bowled Greig a yorker straight on his plates of meat and the ball flew on to the stumps. It was the funniest thing ever and we collapsed laughing. Ian and I were elated the plan had worked. It was a really quick yorker and soon became known as my famous 'Sandshoe Crusher'.

After Greig's dismissal, England were 94/6 and it was just a case of survival for the remaining batsmen, so we set really attacking fields. But Alan Knott showed some typical grit in the face of a vicious attack. Knotty was one I always wanted to get out because he was a pain in the arse. He would always get a fifty or something to hold you up and he had batted two hours for 19 on this occasion. He was a fighter, had a good eye because of being a wicketkeeper and played a long way back, which is a sensible ploy against quick bowlers. He wasn't a pretty batsman to watch, but he was effective and I always rated him.

So I was ecstatic to get my five-for by bowling Knotty with one that nipped back. That left England on the brink at 163/9 and it wasn't long before I bowled Hendrick to finish the match. He was almost walking before I sent the ball down and clearly didn't want to get hit. He might as well have said, 'There are my stumps, hit them!'

I remember walking off the ground and all the blokes patting me on the back because I had taken 6-46 as we won by 166 runs. We knew we had done some big damage in that match, mentally and physically, for the rest of the series.

It was the best feeling in the world to win the game and clinch my spot in the side, like scoring a couple of goals in soccer or tries in rugby. It was good to get wickets, but the most important thing was I had arrived on the Test scene. Anyone who didn't believe I could perform at the top level could get stuffed.

There was a lot of talk about the pitch being under prepared for that Test match because two days before the game there were storms in Brisbane and the ground was flooded. I am not covering myself here, but the pitch was fine. We declared at 288/5 in the second innings and Greg Chappell made 71. That was after scoring over 300 in the first dig, so the track can't have been that bad.

We had a drink with the English afterwards, which was something Ian insisted on. They came into our dressing room because we were on the field last. In those days you then used to go and mingle with the crowd and drink, get on the piss with them, so I remember having a good time. Everyone in our team was delighted with the victory. We were on fire and it never went out.

Because of injuries to Amiss and Edrich, England called up Colin Cowdrey who flew to Australia in time for the second Test at Perth. Cowdrey was a fine player but he turned 42 during the series, so it was a hard ask for him against Lillee and myself.

To Kipper's credit, he got in line, took the ball on the body and never winced. I got to know him pretty well and it might surprise people, because he was raised in

India and went to Oxford University, while I was just one of the boys, but we became good friends.

Kipper was one of my victims – the other was David Lloyd, who was caught by Greg Chappell – as I took 2-45 in England's first-innings total of 208. He went across too far to the off side and was bowled past his legs, which was a surprise because most of the others were going the opposite way, towards square leg.

Cowdrey had our respect because he stood up to us. The minute you see someone backing away, that's just a no-no, something we thought was pathetic. It was a game of balls back then, with no helmets or anything, so it was a macho thing.

Being able to bowl really fast makes you feel powerful, like you have something special. If you ask the blokes who played against me, they'll tell you I was far quicker than anyone around today. It was just something I could do and I don't know why people don't bowl as fast now.

I never went out there to maim anybody, but hitting people comes with the trade and if you get struck by a ball travelling at 100 mph, it's going to break something. You can't worry about that otherwise you wouldn't be a fast bowler.

Although Knotty put up his usual stout resistance, making 51, England's batsmen hadn't given their bowlers much to defend. The Poms had a handy attack, with the pace of Willis and Geoff Arnold backed up by Chris Old, Fred Titmus and Greig, but they just never got going because they didn't have enough to bowl at in this match or during any of the important times in the series.

Our batsmen took full advantage on the second day as Walters hit a magnificent century. Dougie was a fantastic bloke and a great player, although people in England never saw the best of him. He was unorthodox but had a really good eye.

Dougie loved a wager and on this occasion he bet he would get a hundred in the session between tea and stumps. He was on 97 as Willis ran in to bowl the last ball of the day and pulled a flat six through midwicket to the scoreboard to bring up his century.

We all went out on to the balcony and waved and applauded, though we realised he clearly was not a bloke you should bet against. When he came into the dressing room, we were all hiding in the showers so he started looking for us and we came out drinking beer and laughing.

From 352/4 overnight, we moved on to 481 all out on the third day as Ross Edwards, the Western Australia batsman, also reached three figures. England were facing a huge deficit of 273 and we felt they would struggle again. Their openers, Cowdrey and Lloyd, put on 52 before I hit Lloyd in the balls and he had to retire hurt. I nipped one back and it cleaned him up as he shuffled across the crease. It was a painful blow, but I'd rather have had him caught out than hit him on the old fella.

Just ten runs had been added after Lloyd's retirement when I trapped Kipper lbw. England finished the day on 102/1, but on the fourth morning I soon had Greigy caught in the slips by Greg Chappell, which brought Lloyd back to the crease. Their problems continued as Denness and Fletcher were both caught off my bowling with the score on 124. I had accounted for four of their top five batsmen, which is what you do if you're any good because it doesn't prove much just getting tail-enders.

Wickets fell regularly throughout the day, although Titmus (61) and Old (43) had a good thrash down the order before I caught Old. Ashley Mallett, the South Australia off-spinner, and I then polished off the tail, with him catching Arnold off my bowling. I finished with figures of 5-93 as we bowled England out for 293. That left us with a target of just 21, and we strolled to a nine-wicket victory.

The Perth success took us 2-0 up in the series, but we still weren't thinking about getting our hands on the Ashes, we were just taking it game by game. Although the third Test at Melbourne petered out into a draw, I continued my good form with four wickets in each innings. Then it was on to the Sydney Cricket Ground for a match I was really excited about because I was born in Sydney and this was the first Test I had played there.

I love the atmosphere of the SCG. I was a big rugby league and soccer fan and that was where all the internationals were played, so for me it was like walking out at Wembley for a Pom.

By this stage of the tour, Denness was like the commander of a sinking ship. His team were losing heavily and he had hardly scored a run. His batting style involved shuffling across, going nowhere, neither backward nor forward and just giving catching practice to the slips.

Denness dropped himself for the fourth Test and Edrich took over as skipper. We batted first and Rick McCosker and both the Chappells passed 50 as we headed towards a big total. All I wanted to do was get out there and bat in front of my home town crowd and my chance finally came on the second day with the score on 368/9.

As I went out to bat, Lillee crossed my path on his way back to the pavilion. He was spewing and he's not a bloke to talk to when he's like that. Greigy and Fletcher had been winding up the England bowlers to bowl bouncers at Dennis.

Usually batsmen walking past each other say good luck, but he grabbed me by the shirt and said, 'When you get out there to bowl I want you to get that bastard there and I want you to knock that bastard's head off.'

And he pointed at Greigy and Fletcher while I thought, 'What about saying good luck, Dennis?'

In fact, the biggest problem I had that day was getting away from Dennis Lillee. I eventually got out to the middle and smashed 24 not out in 23 balls as we posted a handy total of 405. When I came off, the rest of the team were ready to go out, while I had to change. But Lillee grabbed me by the neck again.

'When you get out there I want you to get that fucking Greig,' he ranted. 'Fuck off or I won't ever get out there, I need to get dressed,' I replied and all the boys burst out laughing.

When I was bowling to Fletcher, Lillee ran up to remind me how he wanted me to bowl. 'You'd think I had fucking Alzheimer's or something,' I told him. 'I know what the plot is. Now fuck off and leave me alone.'

I accounted for Cowdrey, Greig, Knott and Willis in my 4-74 as we dismissed England for 295. We then declared our second innings on 289/4, with Redpath and Greg Chappell both completing excellent centuries. Redpath used to wear down the openers and performed really well in that series, while Greg was at his best. England reached 33/0 by stumps on the fourth day, but still needed another 367 to win.

The crowd went berserk on the last day. You could drink as much beer as you liked at that time, so there were lots of pissed people. As I ran in to bowl, they chanted, 'Thommo! Thommo! Thommo!' Then when I got nearer to the stumps, it was, 'Kill! Kill! Kill!' It must have been pretty unnerving for the batsmen.

I was bowling well and picked up Lloyd, caught by Greg Chappell, to make it 68/1. When Fletcher came in England were 74/3 and it wasn't long before I made one take off from just short of a length. The ball flicked off his glove on to his head and ballooned to cover, where Edwards almost caught it.

Fletcher was out on his feet like a boxer, didn't know what day it was. Greg Chappell and I stood beside him but nobody else came near except Lillee, who gave him another barrage, following on from their spat in our first innings. I told Dennis he might as well be talking to a brick wall.

I got Fletcher soon after he resumed his innings when he diverted a full-length ball to Redpath in the gully. England never looked like reaching their target and only Greig passed fifty in a total of 228, while Mallett was our leading wicket-taker, with 4-21. I was a little bit down that I only got 2-74 in the second dig after picking up four wickets in the first. You strive to get a five-for, which is a benchmark for a bowler, and I didn't get that in my home Test.

But we won the match to go 3-0 up after four matches and that meant we had reclaimed the Ashes. The euphoria was something I hadn't experienced before. I was obviously happy that we had won the series, but the blokes who had played against England before and hadn't won the Ashes were absolutely jubilant.

People like Ian Chappell had been to England and drawn in 1972 after losing at home in 1970/71, both against teams captained by Ray Illingworth, so they were overjoyed to have finally beaten the Poms. We celebrated, really got on the piss.

We were going well in the fifth Test at Adelaide when I injured my shoulder and ended up missing the rest of the series. We batted first and made 304, with Jenner contributing 74 while Underwood took seven wickets. I then took 3-58 in England's reply of 172. Cowdrey, Denness and Fletcher were my victims, as my series total reached 33.

By the end of day three we were 111/2, already almost 250 ahead. So on the rest day, we went on the piss at the Yalumba Winery, up in the Barossa Valley. I was playing tennis and trying to serve like Andy Roddick when I jerked my shoulder.

It turned out I had pulled a tendon and torn muscles, so didn't play the rest of that match, which Australia won handsomely as Lillee picked up four second-innings wickets.

I also missed the sixth and final Test in Melbourne, when Fletcher and Denness both made big centuries and England won by an innings. I wonder how England got all those runs? Because I wasn't playing and Lillee only bowled six overs, that's the answer. I am not criticising England but it's quite obvious what the difference was.

We won the series 4-1 and I was thrilled to have taken 33 wickets. But those wickets came so easily that it just felt like playing Sheffield Shield cricket. Guys like Luckhurst, Edrich and Lloyd were dancing around against my bowling all series – it was the same for everyone I played against in those days.

Although some of the batsmen received nasty blows, I don't think the way Dennis and I bowled really compared with the Bodyline series of 1932/33. With Bodyline, you had all those fielders around the leg side. Imagine if we had done that, it would have been ridiculous. I am not having a go at Bodyline, though, because it was legal at the time and done for a reason.

Life was pretty good for me. A Brisbane radio station signed me up on a big contract and I had a great house on the river. I was into watersports and fishing and had a boat tied up to the jetty. A couple of mates lived with me for nothing because I didn't like being on my own and we had a great laugh, although the media fuss around me became a bit of a pain. They thought I was some sort of caveman because I was always one of the boys, wasn't your English gentleman.

One of my house-mates was a rugby league player and he used to go through all my fan mail and ring up the Sheilas to check them out. We had party after party. If you're young, single and successful, the girls get attracted. There was no problem with that.

It was all pretty relaxed and we always had time to unwind between matches. You didn't have anybody looking over your shoulder telling you what you could and couldn't drink and eat. If there had been, we would have thrown them in the river.

In our day, blokes used to play a winter sport like soccer or rugby. Playing other sports helped my cricket. I played soccer when I was young and could have made that a career. But I still played some soccer in Brisbane at the time when my Test career was taking off.

That is the problem with cricketers these days. These blokes just play cricket, so you see them dive for a ball and the next minute they're back in the dressing room, in traction, in physio, getting injuries treated. They are just not used to getting knocked around. Doing other sports made you tougher and less prone to injury.

I never wore the baggy green cap very much when I fielded. I wasn't one who glued it to my head like Steve Waugh. I don't have a shrine at home to my sporting ability. All my trophies are in boxes, not out on display. I played for my country and I know what I achieved, starting with that unforgettable first Ashes Test at Brisbane.

GEOFFREY BOYCOTT

Geoffrey Boycott – Third Test, Trent Bridge (Nottingham), 28 July to 2 August 1977

Boycott was, without doubt, one of England's finest opening batsmen. Total dedication and a never-say-die attitude were two of the Yorkshireman's key attributes. Such qualities came to the fore as Boycott hit seven of his 22 Test centuries against Australia. It is an indication of his longevity that Boycott made his first Ashes hundred at The Oval in 1964 and his last at the same venue 17 years later.

Right-handed batsman
Born: 21 October 1940, Fitzwilliam, Yorkshire
Test debut: June 1964 v Australia
Last Test: January 1982 v India
Test record: 108 matches, 8,114 runs at an average of 47.72

The state of play
England were already 1-0 up in the series, having won the second Test, when Boycott made a dramatic return to Test cricket – just what the Australians did not want to see. Boycott scored centuries here and in the fourth Test to help England to a 3-0 series win.

Scoreboard
Australia first innings

R.B. McCosker	c Brearley	b Hendrick	51
I.C. Davis	c Botham	b Underwood	33
G.S. Chappell		b Botham	19
D.W. Hookes	c Hendrick	b Willis	17
K.D. Walters	c Hendrick	b Botham	11
R.D. Robinson	c Brearley	b Greig	11
R.W. Marsh	lbw	b Botham	0
K.J. O'Keeffe		not out	48
M.H.N. Walker	c Hendrick	b Botham	0
J.R. Thomson	c Knott	b Botham	21
L.S. Pascoe	c Greig	b Hendrick	20
Extras	(b 4, lb 2, nb 6)		12
Total	(all out, 82.2 overs)		243

Bowling	O	M	R	W
Willis	15	0	58	1
Hendrick	21.2	6	46	2
Botham	20	5	74	5
Greig	15	4	35	1
Underwood	11	5	18	1

England first innings

J.M. Brearley	c Hookes	b Pascoe	15
G. Boycott	c McCosker	b Thomson	107
R.A. Woolmer	lbw	b Pascoe	0
D.W. Randall		run out	13
A.W. Greig		b Thomson	11
G. Miller	c Robinson	b Pascoe	13
A.P.E. Knott	c Davis	b Thomson	135
I.T. Botham		b Walker	25
D.L. Underwood		b Pascoe	7
M. Hendrick		b Walker	1
R.G.D. Willis		not out	2
Extras	(b 9, lb 7, w 3, nb 16)		35
Total	(all out, 124.2 overs)		364

Bowling	O	M	R	W
Thomson	31	6	103	3
Pascoe	32	10	80	4
Walker	39.2	12	79	2
Chappell	8	0	19	0
O'Keeffe	11	4	43	0
Walters	3	0	5	0

Australia second innings

R.B. McCosker	c Brearley	b Willis	107
I.C. Davis	c Greig	b Willis	9
G.S. Chappell		b Hendrick	27
D.W. Hookes	lbw	b Hendrick	42
K.D. Walters	c Randall	b Greig	28
R.D. Robinson	lbw	b Underwood	34
R.W. Marsh	c Greig	b Willis	0
K.J. O'Keeffe		not out	21
M.H.N. Walker		b Willis	17
J.R. Thomson		b Willis	0
L.S. Pascoe	c Hendrick	b Underwood	0
Extras	(b 1, lb 5, w 1, nb 17)		24
Total	(all out, 127 overs)		309

Bowling	O	M	R	W
Willis	26	6	88	5
Hendrick	32	14	56	2
Botham	25	5	60	0
Greig	9	2	24	1
Underwood	27	15	49	2
Miller	5	2	5	0
Woolmer	3	0	3	0

England second innings (target: 189 runs)

J.M. Brearley		b Walker	81
G. Boycott		not out	80
A.P.E. Knott	c O'Keeffe	b Walker	2
A.W. Greig		b Walker	0
D.W. Randall		not out	19
Extras	(b 2, lb 2, w 1, nb 2)		7
Total	(3 wickets, 81.2 overs)		189

Bowling	O	M	R	W
Thomson	16	6	34	0
Pascoe	22	6	43	0
O'Keeffe	19.2	2	65	0
Walker	24	8	40	3

Geoffrey Boycott

I HELD MY head in my hands. There was no booing or anything, just a deathly silence. I was under enormous pressure on my return to the England side after a three-year absence and couldn't have imagined anything worse than to run out Derek Randall in front of his home crowd at Trent Bridge. I felt I had to make it up to them after doing something like that. I had to make a hundred.

After the first Test against India in the summer of 1974, I told Alec Bedser, the chairman of selectors, that I was in no mental or emotional condition to play well for England.

Firstly, I was not happy playing under Mike Denness, whom I did not rate highly as England captain. But I was also under intense pressure back at Yorkshire, so I stayed out of Test cricket for the next three years and missed 30 Tests, including two losing Ashes campaigns.

When I played for England between 1971 and 1973, Yorkshire hardly won a game. I used to go to Yorkshire committee meetings and, as captain of the county, I would get the blame for the team's defeats – when I hadn't even been playing!

'But you are the captain,' they kept saying. And I replied, 'Yeah, but how do I get the blame when I'm not even there?'

So I said to the committee, 'What do you want me to do? Cut myself in half? There ain't bloody two of me, you know. I can only be in one place at a time.' The conversations were that stupid at committee meetings. They were idiots.

On the one hand, the Yorkshire committee used to want me to play for England. I would get a real ear-bashing about how I was the best player and should be playing for my country. But then when I didn't play for Yorkshire, they were poor.

And when I said, 'Okay, I've opted out, I'll stay with Yorkshire,' they then criticised me for not playing for England. 'Oh, you have to play for England,' they said. I couldn't win.

Now it's very difficult for people to believe but Yorkshire cricket was everything to Yorkshire people in the 1970s. You still had to be born in Yorkshire to play for them. In those days, you played two three-day county matches when a Test match was on. They would lose both matches and all hell would break loose in the local papers like the *Sheffield Telegraph*, the *Yorkshire Post* and the *Yorkshire Evening Post*.

However, the seasons of 1975 and 1976, when I didn't play any Test cricket, were probably the best two years of my life playing for Yorkshire. In 1975, we finished second in the County Championship after two seasons of not breaking into the top half of the table. We lost only one championship match all summer, which would have been unthinkable only a year before.

There were a lot of young players in the side, like David Bairstow, Graham Stevenson and Arnie Sidebottom, and they were a fantastic bunch to captain. These young lads kept telling me, 'Go on, go and play for England. You're the best player.'

I suppose that was one of a number of things that prompted me to make myself available for England again, although I knew it would be tough coming back. Ironically, what had done me good was in the winter of 1976/77 I went to Australia, where I played for Waverley in the Sydney leagues. I had a great season and got six hundreds. I also got plenty of good net practice against some pretty handy bowlers and gained a lot of confidence when I realised how much respect the Australians had for me, because they are pretty hard to please.

That is actually why I like them and maybe that is something we Yorkshiremen have in common with the Aussies. You have got to earn their respect and the best way to do that is with performances. So when I did well for Waverley, I realised, which I probably hadn't before, that they did respect me.

When I was playing out in Australia, people kept saying to me, 'Will you be playing for England? Will you be playing next year in the Ashes?' And, in the end, I realised the time was right for my return.

The selectors had been trying to persuade me to come back, but when I made myself available, they had to make a statement by not picking me. The team for the first Test of 1977 was settled before I announced I was happy to return, but they also left me out for the second. They did that on purpose. It was like a headmaster with a schoolboy, a case of, 'I'll just show you who's boss.' They treated me like a naughty boy, gave me a slap on the wrist, then let me play. Fine. Alright. They did that and I came back for the third Test at Trent Bridge.

I was very nervous on my return. Three years is a long time to be out of Test cricket and I knew it would be very difficult to step back up to that level after such an absence. The team hadn't done particularly well the year before against West Indies, losing the five-Test home series 3-0.

That was when Tony Greig had made his infamous comment about making the West Indies 'grovel'. But they struggled against all the bowlers, particularly Michael Holding, and Viv Richards made loads of runs. The year before, they had gone to Australia and lost 4-1 against the likes of Dennis Lillee and Jeff Thomson, so a lot of people were asking where the best batsman was during that time.

Some people obviously wanted me to succeed, while people who were entrenched as my enemies or just didn't like me were hoping I would fail, which added to the pressure. But I didn't really know how great it was until I went to the nets. We always used to practise at three o'clock on the Wednesday afternoon because we had that much county cricket that we were playing until the Tuesday night.

When we started going to the nets, which at Trent Bridge were right over the far side from the pavilion, where the new media centre is now, there were thousands of people watching. I got halfway and looked at the pitch. Then, when I started the last walk towards the nets, there was this eruption of applause.

'Bloody 'ell!' I thought to myself. All the players who were practising stopped to see what was happening as the supporters applauded me on my way over. It was embarrassingly nice, a tremendous wave of support and noise. But, by God, I was only walking to the nets. I thought then, 'Shit. This is big.'

I felt a great fear of failure. Letting yourself down comes bottom of the pile. But letting everybody else down, especially your supporters who believe that you're good, that you're in your rightful spot, that was unthinkable. So the pressure was huge.

At least there was nothing bad about coming back into the dressing room. Mike Brearley was an excellent skipper and treated me brilliantly. Right from the word go, he made sure I had all the quality practice I wanted. Then, after practice, he would say, 'You okay?' And I would say I was fine. He knew how to handle me perfectly.

We had the team meeting, but as a batsman, you're on your own. It is no different to when you're in a boxing ring. Joe Louis used to talk about how trainers and managers could stand up and spout for the opposition and how good they were and what they were going to do to him, but he used to say, 'Well, when we get in the ring, it's only him and me. The trainers and the managers ain't fighting.'

Cricket is like that: when you're batting, you're on your own. It is a test of skill but it's also a test of your mental strength and character.

I have great memories of Trent Bridge. The crowd was fantastic and lots of my supporters made the trip down from Yorkshire to witness my comeback.

On the first morning, Australia won the toss and batted. Their opening pair went along nicely until Derek Underwood had Ian Davis caught by Ian Botham with the score on 79. Botham was just a young man making his Test debut but he took five wickets as Australia were then dismissed for 243, with only opener Rick McCosker reaching 50.

We had no idea Botham would develop into such an important player for England. He took his first wicket in Test cricket with a long-hop. It was just an innocuous looser with no great pace and Greg Chappell, Australia's captain, went to pull it, got an inside edge, and it knocked the lot over. He just laughed, did Both, but that was the start of a great cricketer's Test career.

As the Australians discovered against Botham, Bob Willis and Mike Hendrick, it was a good pitch for fast bowling. There was some grass on it but it was concrete-hard. When I saw the Trent Bridge groundsman Ron Allsop the previous day I said to him, 'Hell, Ron, it'll be no picnic against their bowlers on this.' But straight away he replied, 'It's a good pitch for them that can bat. You'll get a hundred on it, you always get runs on my pitches.'

Still, I knew that Jeff Thomson and Len Pascoe, the Australian quicks, were going to bombard me with short stuff because I was returning to Test cricket at 36 years of age, when most people are finishing their international careers. But here I was coming back, with all the pressure and the baggage that came with having stayed out of the side.

So Pascoe and Thomson were going to test my resolve, find out whether I was still good at playing fast bowling. That is what fast bowlers do. They test your courage, your character, your mental strength, and that's why some people buckle.

When I wouldn't play and England were losing to the likes of Lillee and Thomson, and Holding and Andy Roberts, some people said, 'Well, Boycott's afraid to play.' People who don't like you and who can't get you to do what they want cast all sorts of aspersions. So the Australian bowlers naturally gave my technique and commitment a gruelling examination.

However, the verbal hostility you sometimes got from fast bowlers never bothered me because I never listened. I had the ability to switch off, so whatever they said to me was a waste of time. It was like talking to a brick wall. And I just never got involved in eye contact, ever.

Brearley and I survived a difficult little period on the first evening to make sure we started again the next day with all our wickets intact. But Pascoe dismissed Brearley and Bob Woolmer cheaply on the Friday morning, which brought Derek Randall to the wicket at 34/2.

We had taken the score on to 52 when I managed to run Derek out. This was the nightmare scenario, especially since Derek was a Nottinghamshire player and a real hero at Trent Bridge. It was tough enough with all the pressure, but then running out a guy who is a friend, a lovely lad, I just wanted to dig a big hole and jump in it.

I played a delivery from Thomson towards the non-striker on the on side and called for a quick single. But you don't expect anybody to be quite as nippy and athletic as they are finishing their follow-through as Thomson proved to be. Thomson was so agile that he quickly stepped to his right and sort of ran into Derek, who had to stop, hesitate and try and get round him. So Derek had no chance of running straight.

He was blocked, but within the laws. The bowler can go for the ball and batsmen have to avoid him. Derek couldn't get round Thomson, who threw the ball to Rod Marsh, their wicketkeeper, who demolished the stumps.

I felt awful. I have always had such great affection for the Nottinghamshire ground because I played my first Test there and got on great with the crowd. I think there were a lot of people wanting me to succeed, so it was quite a shock, seeing their idol run out. I was a hero but I had run out their local hero.

There was a part of me that just wanted to get off the field because I felt I had done something terrible. The easiest thing to do in that situation is to play a rash shot, get out, go and hide in the dressing room, but something inside wouldn't let me do that, I just didn't want to give in.

Derek was fine afterwards. My lasting memory was not long after I had run him out, when I was still feeling pretty bad and was getting bombarded by Pascoe and Thomson, I saw him by the pavilion with his wife and young baby. Derek was tossing the baby up in the air as if nothing had happened.

Normally I just switch off completely, but I can remember that as clear as a bell. That is the sort of fantastic fellow he was. We used to go out together on tour. He was amusing, easy natured, you just couldn't get anybody better to socialise with.

Derek always consoles me, saying, 'If I'd have run a bit straighter and truer, without hesitating, I'd have got home, Fiery.' He always says it wasn't my fault and I really appreciate that but I'm not taking it. He just has such a wonderful nature.

We weren't in a very good position and things soon got worse when Tony Greig and Geoff Miller fell in quick succession. We were really struggling at 82/5 when Alan Knott joined me at the crease and the fact that I was very tense didn't help things at first. When you're like that, it's very difficult to remain relaxed enough to hit the bad ball. That was the problem.

It took me about three hours to reach 20 because I was getting blitzed with short stuff, they were on top of us and just kept on coming. Apparently I was then dropped by McCosker at slip, off Pascoe, but I don't remember that, so I must have been totally caught up in what I was doing.

It was such hard work. Thomson was a terrific bowler, lightning quick. He had really made his mark on the Test scene – and English batsmen – in 1974/75, when England were thrashed in Australia. His partner in crime then was Dennis Lillee, but he missed this series tour because of back trouble.

Thomson took 23 wickets in 1977, so he was a very dangerous opponent. Pascoe was a good bowler as well. He didn't move the ball quite as much as Thomson, but was a good, honest trier and had great aggression and speed. He kept on coming at you all day long at around 90 mph.

Everybody focused on the two really quick bowlers because they are the ones who win Test matches, but Max Walker was a tough proposition as well. Walker was a good bowler who provided a great foil for the opening pair. He was 6ft 4in and could swing the ball and make it move off the seam.

Normally when you stay in and bat, it gets better. But this just kept getting worse. Where's the end? Where's the bloody silver lining? It would have been easy to say, 'I can't take this, I need to get out of here, this is too much for any human being to take.' But no, there was something inside me that said, 'I ain't getting out.'

Knotty helped by talking to me. I was pretty tense and he's a good friend of mine, so I listened to him and was able to get my feet and brain working again. On tour we used to have rooms next to one another so that we could nip into each other's room and chat. We weren't guys who went out a lot living it up, so we would have quiet dinners, talk cricket, which meant I knew him really well and that helped in this innings.

First of all with playing quality fast bowling, you've got to have a good technique. You have to get your body and your hands high and relax your hands when you play the ball out of your throat – as I did a lot against Thomson and Pascoe. You can make a statement by playing a fast delivery well, so that they look at you and think, 'I've bowled my best ball and this bastard ain't going anywhere.'

It is a mental battle. Normally, after a while, if a bowler keeps on peppering a batsman, the chinks will start to appear: the batsman plays and misses, he nicks it or he gets hit. But when that doesn't happen, you can slowly and surely see in their eyes that they're beginning to realise that the intimidation isn't working. Once you've done that, the game's over.

Thomson and Pascoe gave me a torrid time. They were testing my technique and my courage with a lot of bouncers, but eventually the runs came. Knotty started to get a few and we just talked together. We began to feel comfortable and then, slowly and surely, the confidence grew and the scoreboard started ticking over.

When you have been facing fast bowling for a long time, there is definitely a danger of losing your concentration when the spinner comes on. So we just had to hold it together. But after facing the quicks, I wasn't going to fall asleep when Ray Bright was bowling. I was going to perk up, not cock up.

There was a great sense of relief all around the ground when I hit Bright through the covers for four. I will always remember watching the highlights that night and Jim Laker, who was commentating, saying, 'Oh, he's hit a four!' That just about summed it up because the boundary was such a big surprise at that point.

Anyway, the shackles had been broken and I started to play. By stumps that night Knotty and I had taken the score on to 242/5. It never bothered me that I was within 12 of a century overnight because nobody can get hundreds all the time. I got out the odd time in the 90s, but most of the time, I got a hundred. I got 151 centuries in my first-class career, so I didn't miss out too often.

I fancied my chances of reaching three figures because I felt I had done the hard work. However, it's always a little bit difficult to begin again the next morning. Batsmen often get out when they start after lunch and tea and the next day, because they've got to get their feet moving and their concentration sharp again. But I didn't really have much of a problem and went to my century off Thomson. It was my best stroke, off the back foot, square of cover, and run like hell! It is as simple as that: head down and go.

Getting to a hundred was magic. Knotty helped me because he played fantastically well and that released a little bit of pressure. It was mental strength, then relief, to get through, to get us in a good position to win the game.

I got a marvellous ovation from the Trent Bridge crowd, who were great to me. They came to see if I was still the opening batsman I was before, but they also wanted to see Derek, the local lad. So there was a sense of mixed emotions when I ran him out, but when I went to my century there was great relief. It was joyous. It was fantastic.

The likes of Thomson and Chappell congratulated me. I have always found that the Australians are great sportsmen, true competitors. If you want to test yourself against people, the Aussies will test you, they will compete. It doesn't matter what it's at. They will play you at bloody marbles, never mind cricket or rugby or football.

They will knock your block off, they'll get you out any way they can. But if you can succeed, if you can get through the mill of what they have to throw at you in terms of mental toughness, fast bowling, aggression and verbal abuse, if you show that you deserve their respect, they will pay you that. And they will do so handsomely.

If they see a weakness in anyone as a player, they'll go for the jugular, but they admire people who stand up to them and perform. Yorkshiremen are the same. We played it hard in the days of Fred Trueman, Brian Close and Ray Illingworth, but we would always stand up and admit it if someone had played fantastically.

It is almost gladiatorial. You are in the arena and it's time to see what you're made of, to see how good you really are. And if you can come through it and succeed, they'll put their hands up and say you were terrific. Chappell was brilliant in that respect, everybody was.

There's no point in scoring a hundred if you don't win as a team. It is like scoring a hat-trick and the other side gets four. You might as well not have bothered.

I was brought up in a very hard school at Yorkshire where I was taught that winning is the object of the exercise. So for me to get from 82/5 to 242/5 at the end of the second day and then go on and get a hundred was more meaningful than ever. It resulted in success for me, but above all, it got England into a winning position.

My innings was a long, hard slog. There wasn't too much fluency as it took me six hours and 18 minutes to reach my century. It was just mind over matter, a wearing process rather than an aesthetically pleasing innings. It was a fight – within myself and against the opposition.

When I was eventually caught by McCosker off Thomson, I had made 107 of England's 297/6. It is always disappointing to be dismissed but Knotty's excellent 135 helped us to 364 all out, which meant a healthy first-innings lead of 121. The Aussies then made 309 in their second innings, with McCosker scoring 107 and Bob Willis taking five wickets.

Brearley and I then knocked off most of the 189 runs required, with an opening stand of 154. Mike wasn't a great batsman but he was a good man-manager and he was very knowledgeable. He had his own mind, his own ideas, but if he thought you had sound ideas, he definitely listened.

One of the good things about Brearley was that he didn't have an ego problem, which some people do when they're playing with other great players, with Botham, myself, Underwood and Knott. I think that's why he was successful, because he could talk to everyone. We all knew he was captain, in charge. Many people thought because he went to public school and to Cambridge, and I was just an ordinary bloody miner's son, maybe we were opposites. But in fact, we got on fantastically well.

It was a magic moment when Randall struck the winning run ten minutes after tea on the final day. It was great for such an ebullient character to get it, especially in front of his home crowd and after the run-out.

It was wonderful just to win and by seven wickets in my comeback match. When I got a hundred and 80 not out I became the first Englishman to bat on all five days of a Test, which made it really special. And Botham, the up-and-coming great player, got five wickets, which proved he had arrived on the scene.

We had champagne in the dressing room as we celebrated. There are pictures of me on the balcony and I was over the moon, but more than anything I felt total relief. I was proud to have got the ovation from the public, that's what mattered. I got cheered every time I touched the ball on the boundary. It was embarrassingly nice, but I'll take that rather than the opposite. I loved it.

Victory at Trent Bridge took us 2-0 up in the series. And by winning the following match at Headingley, where I scored my 100th first-class hundred, we secured the Ashes. Despite playing just three out of five Tests, I was the top run-maker in the series, with 442 at an average of 147.33.

It was special helping England win back the Ashes. I didn't want to get hundreds and not win because then they don't mean anything. It is like making a hundred on a flat pitch when everybody makes one and even number nine or ten makes a fifty. That doesn't really prove a lot and that's why I liked a challenge.

I was better when the pitches did something, better when I was up against it. It brought out the best in me. There were other players that could score quicker than me on flat pitches, but that didn't necessarily mean that their innings was going to win the match.

I didn't socialise a lot with the Australians. But I knew one or two through having been to Australia that winter and the Aussies would always come in and chat at the end of the day. I still have Chappell's cap because we swapped. I got Greg's because I thought he was a fantastic player and I've got Viv Richards's cap, so I picked my players. Greg said I was the best English batsman of the period and it's terrific that someone like him thought that.

That innings at Nottingham was the most important of my life. Just imagine if I had failed in both innings. That was always in the back of my mind because people would have said I was past it. All the doubters would have come out of the woodwork, saying, 'I told you he wasn't that good, I told you he couldn't play fast bowling, I told you he was over the hill.' There would have been reams written on it. That was the pressure I was under and why I couldn't afford not to succeed.

I played in many games, in strange, stressful situations, but never one more than that. I played against intimidating fast bowling, I played in matches where the clock is against you, I played under all permutations, but I think that innings was the finest I ever played.

Everybody talks about my 100th first-class hundred, but this century at Trent Bridge is the important one, with all the feeling, the tension, the emotion. This is what matters.

Test cricket is hard enough at the best of times. But the circumstances that were imposed on me – or self-imposed in some ways – and the tensions of coming back after three years, knowing some people wanted me to fail, then the Randall run-out and all that huge publicity, made it my hardest innings physically, mentally and emotionally. And the key for me is I didn't give it away. I got a hundred and we won.

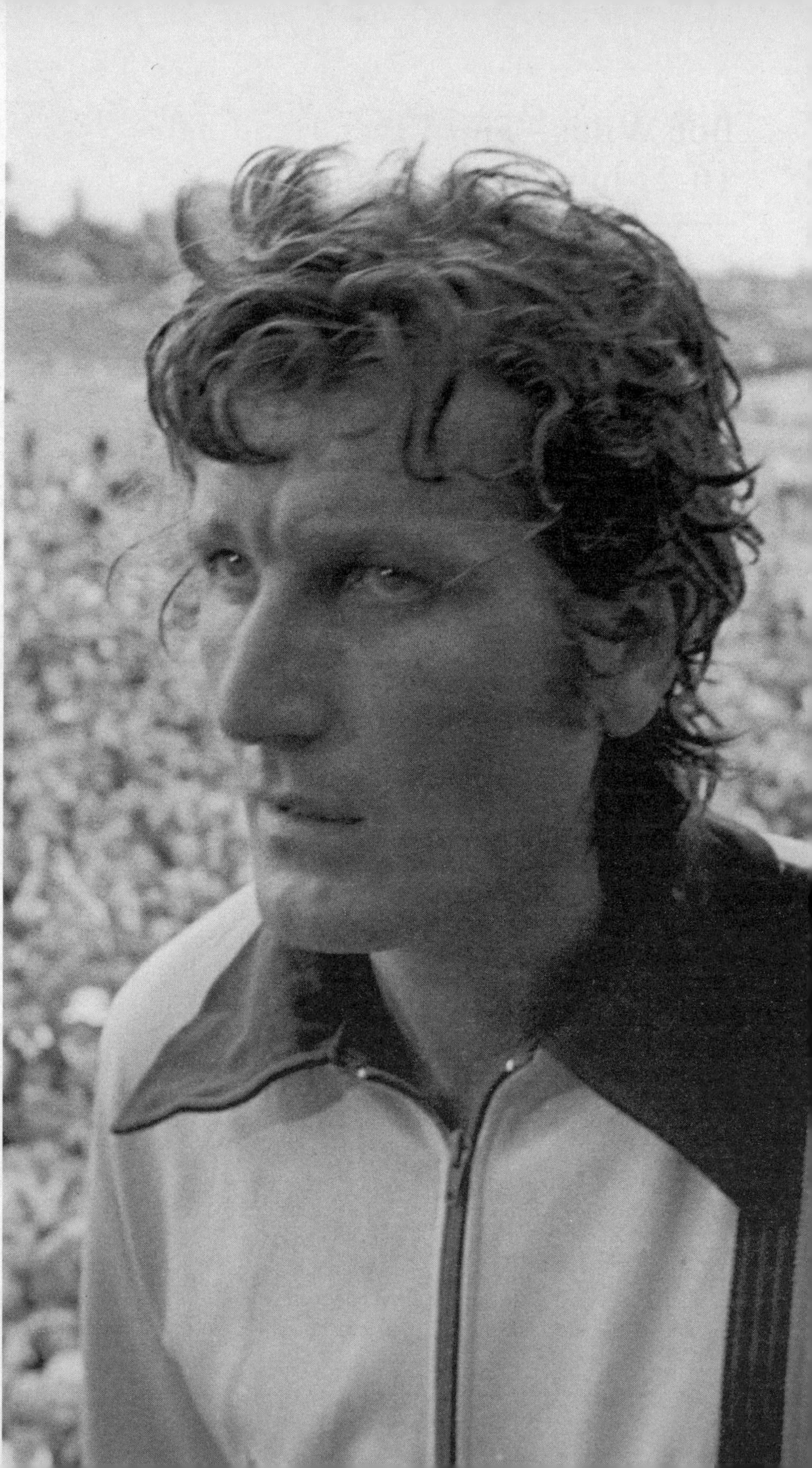

BOB WILLIS

Bob Willis – Third Test, Headingley, 16-21 July 1981

It is testament to Willis's courage and determination that he overcame several knee injuries to enjoy a long, successful England career. The lanky paceman wore his desire to play for England on his sleeve and saved his greatest performances for the Test arena. Willis's speed and aggression made him perhaps England's most intimidating post-war bowler. He captained England 18 times in the early 1980s, during which time England won series against India, Pakistan and New Zealand, but lost the Ashes to Australia in 1982/83.

Right arm fast bowler, right-handed batsman
Born: 30 May 1949, Sunderland, County Durham
Test debut: January 1971 v Australia
Last Test: July 1984 v West Indies
Test record: 90 matches, 325 wickets at an average of 25.20; 840 runs at an average of 11.50

The state of play
England were in disarray. They were 1-0 down in the series and contemplating defeat before Ian Botham and Bob Willis took charge at Headingley in a historic and series-changing victory.

Scoreboard

Australia first innings

J. Dyson		b Dilley	102
G.M. Wood	lbw	b Botham	34
T.M. Chappell	c Taylor	b Willey	27
K.J. Hughes		c & b Botham	89
R.J. Bright		b Dilley	7
G.N. Yallop	c Taylor	b Botham	58
A.R. Border	lbw	b Botham	8
R.W. Marsh		b Botham	28
G.F. Lawson	c Taylor	b Botham	13
D.K. Lillee		not out	3
T.M. Alderman		not out	0
Extras	(b 4, lb 13, w 3, nb 12)		32
Total	(9 wickets dec, 155.2 overs)		401

Bowling	O	M	R	W
Willis	30	8	72	0
Old	43	14	91	0
Dilley	27	4	78	2
Botham	39.2	11	95	6
Willey	13	2	31	1
Boycott	3	2	2	0

England first innings

G.A. Gooch	lbw	b Alderman	2
G. Boycott		b Lawson	12
J.M. Brearley	c Marsh	b Alderman	10
D.I. Gower	c Marsh	b Lawson	24
M.W. Gatting	lbw	b Lillee	15
P. Willey		b Lawson	8
I.T. Botham	c Marsh	b Lillee	50
R.W. Taylor	c Marsh	b Lillee	5
G.R. Dilley		c & b Lillee	13
C.M. Old	c Border	b Alderman	0
R.G.D. Willis		not out	1
Extras	(b 6, lb 11, w 6, nb 11)		34
Total	(all out, 50.5 overs)		174

Bowling	O	M	R	W
Lillee	18.5	7	49	4
Alderman	19	4	59	3
Lawson	13	3	32	3

England second innings (following on)

G.A. Gooch	c Alderman	b Lillee	0
G. Boycott	lbw	b Alderman	46
J.M. Brearley	c Alderman	b Lillee	14
D.I. Gower	c Border	b Alderman	9
M.W. Gatting	lbw	b Alderman	1
P. Willey	c Dyson	b Lillee	33
I.T. Botham		not out	149
R.W. Taylor	c Bright	b Alderman	1
G.R. Dilley		b Alderman	56
C.M. Old		b Lawson	29
R.G.D. Willis	c Border	b Alderman	2
Extras	(b 5, lb 3, w 3, nb 5)		16
Total	(all out, 87.3 overs)		356

Bowling	O	M	R	W
Lillee	25	6	94	3
Alderman	35.3	6	135	6
Lawson	23	4	96	1
Bright	4	0	15	0

Australia second innings (target: 130 runs)

J. Dyson	c Taylor	b Willis	34
G.M. Wood	c Taylor	b Botham	10
T.M. Chappell	c Taylor	b Willis	8
K.J. Hughes	c Botham	b Willis	0
G.N. Yallop	c Gatting	b Willis	0
A.R. Border		b Old	0
R.W. Marsh	c Dilley	b Willis	4
R.J. Bright		b Willis	19
G.F. Lawson	c Taylor	b Willis	1
D.K. Lillee	c Gatting	b Willis	17
T.M. Alderman		not out	0
Extras	(lb 3, w 1, nb 14)		18
Total	(all out, 36.1 overs)		111

Bowling	O	M	R	W
Botham	7	3	14	1
Dilley	2	0	11	0
Willis	15.1	3	43	8
Old	9	1	21	1
Willey	3	1	4	0

Bob Willis

I WAS LIKE a sailor walking the plank during the third Test at Headingley in 1981. I realised that if I didn't perform, I might not get picked for England again. Playing for my country meant a hell of a lot to me and I wanted to keep my place in the side, especially since I had fought my way back from a series of injuries. Little did I know I would end up playing a leading role in what has become known as the 'Miracle of Headingley'.

Injuries had often interrupted my career and I had to return early from England's 1974/75 tour of Australia because of a knee problem. After a period of rehabilitation, I tried to play a practice match at the start of the 1975 English season and broke down. Then I had extensive operations on both knees and missed virtually the whole of the campaign.

The injury curse returned during the 1981 tour of the West Indies when I was forced to come home early. But by that time surgery had improved significantly and I had an arthroscopy, so I was jogging just ten days after the operation. That meant I was fit for the start of the 1981 English season and, without too much difficulty, won back my place to face Australia.

We went into the Ashes following back-to-back series defeats to the formidable West Indies. You weren't likely to beat a side that included Clive Lloyd, Viv Richards, Malcolm Marshall and Michael Holding, but our form still wasn't as good as it should have been given the players available, like Geoff Boycott, Ian Botham, Graham Gooch and David Gower.

Our poor run continued when we lost the first Test at Trent Bridge. It was a low-scoring game and the Aussies got home with four wickets to spare. Their fast-bowling duo Dennis Lillee and Terry Alderman claimed 17 wickets between them in the match, showing that they would be a force to be reckoned with throughout the series.

Then, during the latter stages of the drawn second Test at Lord's, it became clear something had to give regarding Ian Botham's captaincy. Ian made a pair in front of a stunned Lord's crowd and we realised from talking to him and to some of the selectors that he wasn't going to be captain for the next game. Ian will always say he resigned and told the selectors he didn't want to do the job any more, but the fact was they weren't going to ask him to continue as skipper.

I felt sorry for Ian because he only captained England for two complete series, both against the West Indies at their best, so it was a tough baptism for him. The trip to the West Indies was particularly difficult because the assistant tour manager Kenny Barrington died of a heart attack during it. Ian has always said Kenny, who scored almost 7,000 Test runs for England, was his greatest hero in the game.

Although Ian had an excellent cricket brain, there were facets to that job that basically made it a management role. And because he prepared for cricket in a different way to everybody else, it was difficult for him to manage the team in that way, not necessarily on the field during matches, but off the field during practice and preparation.

The selectors decided to appoint Mike Brearley, who had overseen England's 1977 and 1978/79 Ashes victories, as Ian's replacement. Mike received a great welcome back from all of us who had played under him, including Ian.

Brearley wasn't a particularly demonstrative character but was a terrific man-manager and usually quite placid, although if he got irate about something he wasn't slow to tell people. He was the complete opposite of Ian: much calmer and less gung-ho. Ian would be all instinct on the field whereas with Mike you could almost hear the cogs whirring in his brain as he worked out what tactic to employ next.

It was certainly a fun dressing room because even though people like Brearley and Boycott were senior figures and revered in the game, they wouldn't be outside the mickey-taking philosophy that existed in English cricket at the time.

I wasn't originally selected for the third Test at Headingley because I had flu during the Lord's match and didn't play in the subsequent round of county fixtures. But I called Alec Bedser, the chairman of selectors, to say I was only missing the Warwickshire game to make sure I was fit for Headingley, so he rang Derbyshire and told them to intercept my replacement Mike Hendrick's invitation to play against Australia. That is the only reason I even played at Headingley.

Brearley quite rightly didn't want anybody in the team who wasn't 100 per cent fit because the momentum was clearly with Australia and the press were on our case. But I was senior enough to say if I was fit or not, so I played a second XI game at Warwickshire to prove my fitness and then went up to Leeds.

The Australians batted first at Headingley and I didn't take a single wicket as they racked up 401/9 declared over the first two days, with John Dyson making a century. Botham's fifty was the only high note as we slumped to 174 all out in our reply and by the close of play on the Saturday night we were already 6/1 following on. We were staring at a humiliating defeat and most of the older players thought that was the end of their Test careers, that the selectors would turn the page and look for younger players. I was 32 and feared I could be on my way out.

Ian was living up in Humberside at that stage and during every Headingley Test, no matter what was happening in the game, he would invite both teams to a barbecue at his place on the Saturday night. He was always that type of sociable character. It was something he picked up when he went to play in Australia as a youngster on the Whitbread Scholarship, in 1976/77.

Because the Aussie clubs didn't have clubhouses, the players stayed in the dressing room and drank beer together after the match. So during Ashes series in Australia Ian would leave the ground, still in his whites, at around nine o'clock in the evening after beers with the opposition.

Personally, I found being at a cricket ground a draining experience. From the moment I walked through the gates, that was the start of my working day and I just wanted to get away from there at the end of the day so the gap between leaving the ground and returning the next morning was as long as possible. But once I was away from the ground I was always happy to socialise.

At Ian's barbecue, we didn't talk in any great detail with the Australians about the match we were playing, there was no 'you're giving us a drubbing here' or anything of that sort. You didn't chat like that and the Aussies were on a long tour so wanted to get away from talking about cricket.

A lot of us stayed at Ian's place and came back to Leeds on the Monday morning to check out of the hotel, thinking the match would end that day. It looked like we were right when we were reduced to 135/7, still 92 behind, on the Monday afternoon, but it was then that Botham began a death-or-glory assault on the Aussies in the company of Graham Dilley.

At the start of Ian's dramatic innings, to very attacking fields for the seam bowlers and against some not very good bowling, there were a lot of thick outside edges, with fours flying down to third man and behind point. Even Ian admits his innings began as a slog. It wasn't a patch on the hundred he would get at Old Trafford, which was absolute class. But as he progressed, he played better, while Dilley made an unlikely 56.

The pair shared a magnificent stand of 117 before Dilley was bowled by Alderman. By that stage, we had a tiny lead of 25, with two wickets remaining, but Ian went into overdrive. He smashed the ball to all parts of the ground to bring up an astonishing century in just 87 balls.

When Ian was batting with Chris Old and myself at the end of the innings, most of his shots were pretty orthodox and he was really commanding. He told me to try and hang in there and we would get as many as we could.

Ian always kept his cricket fairly simple, didn't theorise too much, so there wasn't a great deal to be said, just the usual mickey-taking of my batting style. He pointed out that trying to play Australia's seam bowlers off the front foot wasn't always the right technique!

The whole culture of our generation was about taking the mickey. But there wasn't a lot of banter with the Australians. I guess when they got down to me they thought at least they were going to roll us over, and they weren't far wrong. I never experienced a lot of sledging or banter out in the middle playing Australia. I know there was plenty, but not during that game.

Not being captain definitely took the pressure off Ian and by stumps on the fourth day he had made 145 of our 351/9. He certainly felt a lot happier coming off at Headingley that day than when he crept off at Lord's in the previous match after his pair.

Australia's captain Kim Hughes was a thoroughly decent guy but he made a major tactical error by not bowling their spinner Ray Bright earlier. The seamers – Lillee, Alderman and Lawson – had taken all the wickets, but at first Ian hit almost everything in the air and the pace of the seam bowlers ensured the ball carried over the catchers. Against the slow bowlers, with the field spread, Ian might well have got 50 or 60 just as rapidly, but he would almost certainly have perished to a catch.

I don't think some of Australia's senior players thought much of Hughes as a captain. On occasions, Lillee or Rod Marsh would step in and say, 'Hang on a minute, you can't have this field to this batsman.'

Life was a bit different then and during Headingley Tests four or five of us used to go to a pub in Otley, outside Leeds, have a few pints and then go back to the hotel for a meal and off to bed. And it was no different on this night.

On the final morning, I soon fell when Allan Border caught me off the bowling of Alderman. Still, I had kept an end up for long enough for us to add a crucial 37 runs, of which I made two. Ian remained 149 not out from 148 balls, a tremendous innings which included 27 fours and a six. Despite his heroics, Australia's target was just 130 and we didn't really feel we were in the game.

Brearley didn't give any up-and-at-them team talk saying we could still win the Test. He preferred to do his preparation before the game, with quite a lot of in-depth discussion of our opponents.

Mike gave Ian the new ball and he had Graeme Wood caught behind early on, but Australia got to 56/1 before there was any shift in the balance of power. Ian had played a long innings so I was surprised he opened the bowling with Dilley. I was the fourth person to bowl after Old and didn't understand why Mike had left me out of the attack for so long. When he did bring me on, it was from the Football Stand End, when I should have been bowling from the Kirkstall Lane End.

Bowling uphill and into the wind, I struggled for rhythm and pace, so I persuaded Brearley to let me swap ends. By this stage, I was driven by anger because I felt I should have bowled earlier and from the other end. Also, the press were giving us a hard time and I thought I would show everybody what I could do bowling down the hill. I had nothing to lose and playing for England meant so much to me, so I ran in really hard and fast.

As the final day progressed, if you pitched the ball just full of a bouncer length, you didn't really know how much it would bounce. Some deliveries were rising alarmingly and that is not what you want to see when you are waiting to bat. I managed to hit that length all the time. I was bowling some no-balls, but Mike told me to forget about that and keep running in and bowling as fast as I could.

The match was turned on its head when I took three quick wickets just before lunch. I got Trevor Chappell, the younger brother of Ian and Greg, with a vicious bouncer that reared up at him and all he could do was present a simple catch to Bob Taylor behind the stumps. Hughes was then brilliantly caught by Botham at third slip, making it 58/3, before Graham Yallop flicked one to Gatting at short leg. Close fielders are much better protected now than they were then and you were going to take some blows, but we would always say Gatting had plenty of natural padding. So Australia were four down at lunch and required another 72 to win, which meant the pressure was shifting on to them. After the break I stayed in a cocoon of concentration, avoiding distractions like excessive celebrations or setting the field.

Border was Australia's best batsman at the time, so it was a pivotal moment in the match when he played on to Old, leaving Australia 65/5. Just three more runs had been added when I picked up the wicket of Dyson, who had scored half Australia's total up to that point. He was caught behind hooking, a pretty injudicious shot considering the state of the match. Bowling him a bouncer was a calculated gamble on my part. I was prepared to give away a boundary in the hope of getting a wicket, and it worked.

With Dyson gone and Australia languishing at 68/6, we were probably favourites. But Marsh had scored more than one hundred against us so his was an important wicket. He also got out to a short ball, brilliantly caught by Dilley at long leg as he ran back towards the boundary. Graham looked back to the rope as soon as the ball was in his hands, but he was safely inside the boundary, and I had my fifth wicket. The sixth soon followed as Geoff Lawson was caught behind.

So Australia were 75/8, with 55 more runs required, when Lillee came to the crease. Up until that point I hadn't felt under any pressure to get my line and length right despite bowling with five slips, a gully and a short leg. But Lillee was a thinking cricketer and improvised brilliantly. The runs had pretty much dried up in the middle of Australia's innings and he started stepping away and hitting the ball over and around the slip cordon.

Lillee played well enough to get Australia within 20 runs of victory with two wickets standing, and I realised that since he was scoring off the short ball, I had to bowl a much fuller length. So I pushed one a lot further up and Dennis lobbed it towards mid-on. At first I thought it was going to drop short of Gatting. The ball was travelling up the hill, Gatt was coming down it, and I never thought he was going to get there, but he clung on to a fine diving catch.

Even so, I feared we would be denied at the last when Alderman was twice dropped at slip by Old off Botham's next over. But Alderman's insecurity probably persuaded Bright to try and play shots to get the remaining runs for victory, and that helped our cause.

After getting Lillee out pitching the ball up, I decided to bowl a full length to the remaining batsmen and I got my of reward when Bright's middle stump went flying out of the ground. We had won by 18 runs after appearing dead and buried for much of the match. I felt elation mixed with relief. All kinds of different emotions went through my head, including, selfishly, that by taking 8-43 I had salvaged my Test career.

In my post-match television interview, I made some criticisms of the way the team was being covered by the press. It was pretty immature of me to detract from that performance by talking about the press. I really regret the tone of the interview now, but they were forever trying to hit little wedges between friends in the team. They started when Ian was made captain against the West Indies in 1980, taking quotes out of context. But as the years went by, I learnt you've just got to ignore that.

A lot of people said I should have got the man of the match award, but I never saw a lot of kudos in that sort of thing. Besides, there wouldn't have been any 8-43 if Ian's innings hadn't taken place, so it was absolutely right he got the award.

There were the usual photos of us spraying champagne on the balcony. The champagne had actually been delivered to the Australian dressing room for their celebration, so we sent our attendant, a South African called Ricky Roberts, who is now Ernie Els's caddie, to retrieve it.

But we didn't really celebrate the victory because we all had to get off for a round of Gillette Cup one-day games the next day. By the time Brearley, Ian and I had done the press conferences and TV and radio interviews, more than half the side had gone, so I had a couple of pints of bitter with Ian and his father-in-law in the dressing room before heading off.

I didn't find out until days later that Marsh and Lillee had placed a wager on England to win at 500-1 when an Australian victory seemed the only possible outcome. Their bus driver put it on for them and I remember Bob Taylor seeing the odds and trying to get a bet on, but couldn't. Dennis has since pointed out that small bets by players weren't that unusual during this age of innocence before anyone had really heard of match-fixing and he joked that if he had known the result in advance through a set-up, he wouldn't have bet just £10, he would have put his house on it!

I liked beating Australia but the match was on such a knife-edge that I don't know whether enjoyment was my first emotion. Test cricket was an exhausting experience for me because of bowling with a pretty unorthodox action and a very long run-up, and in those days we went straight back into a demanding county programme, so there was very little recovery time after a Test match.

Fortunately, I had found ways of keeping fitter and relaxing away from the game. In the winter of 1976/77, we went on a very long tour of India before playing Australia in the Centenary Test at Melbourne, arranged to celebrate the 100th anniversary of the first ever Test between England and Australia. We were all exhausted and I certainly ran out of steam as we lost to the Aussies, although at least the Ashes weren't at stake.

After that match I met a hypnotherapist called Arthur Jackson, who hosted a barbecue which I attended with Mike Brearley, Tony Greig and one or two others. Arthur recommended hypnosis, which helped me wind down from the tour, and put me on to a running regime because I wasn't properly fit to do the job of a fast bowler. From then on, apart from the knee problem in the West Indies and a sort of whiplash injury I sustained dodging bouncers from Pakistan's Imran Khan in 1982, I hardly had any injuries at all.

I gained a lot from hypnosis. I would recommend it to anybody despite being sceptical before I tried it. I had never been a very good sleeper because of moving around a lot, staying in different hotels and sharing rooms with team-mates on tour, but hypnosis helped me relax and sleep. I also used it for motivation and for visualising being successful.

Our victory at Headingley squared the series at 1-1 with three to play and we felt the momentum was on our side. But we thought Headingley was a freak result until we went to Edgbaston for the fourth Test and history repeated itself.

Again Australia were chasing a small target in the last innings when one of our bowlers, Ian Botham, made a dramatic intervention. It was an amazing match because although it wasn't a bad batting pitch, nobody on either side scored a half-century. We made 189 and 219, while Australia scored 258 in their first innings.

So the Aussies needed just 142 more runs to win when they resumed on 9/1 on the fourth morning. I bowled a ferocious, long spell from the City End and trapped Dyson lbw before having Hughes caught, hooking, on the square-leg boundary by John Emburey. My efforts reduced Australia to 29/3 but by the time they had progressed to 114/5 it looked as though they would easily make the remaining 37 for victory.

That was when Ian Botham produced a blistering spell in which he took five wickets for one run in 28 balls. Through a mixture of appalling shots and very good deliveries, Australia were bowled out for 121. Botham's victims were Martin Kent, Marsh, Bright, Lillee and Alderman, so it was a case of Goldenballs strikes again! His very presence by then was intimidating our opponents.

We couldn't believe we were now leading the series 2-1. We were the cat that got the cream because the balance in the series had well and truly shifted. We felt Australia couldn't ever recover from such agonising back-to-back defeats. They were gutted.

The Edgbaston match finished on a Sunday and afterwards Marsh and Lillee were good enough to attend a function for my benefit season. It was really special that they made an effort after losing another Test they should have won. Obviously the Australians were pretty low and it was probably not the thing they most wanted to do.

The England boys managed more of a celebration that night than we had at Headingley because the game was over in four days, giving us a day off. We had a pretty good time and at least one of the Australians was able to put aside his woes for the evening. Dennis and I ended up in a nightclub in Birmingham and it was light by the time we stumbled out.

By the end of the second day of the fifth Test at Old Trafford, England were well in the ascendancy. Having posted a first-innings total of 231, mainly thanks to half-centuries from Chris Tavare and debutant Paul Allott, we dismissed Australia for a paltry 130. I was delighted with my own figures of 4-63 from 14 overs as I picked up the wickets of Dyson, Hughes, Yallop and Marsh. I had also contributed with the bat, making 11 in a crucial tenth-wicket stand of 56 with Allott.

But in our second innings, a real all-rounder took over. Ian Botham's 118 from 102 balls, which included 13 fours and six sixes, was probably the best innings he ever played. It was remarkable, a much more measured innings than he produced at Headingley. The steam was certainly coming out of Lillee's ears as he ran in and bowled a bouncer, only to see the ball disappear for six into the railway, now tram, station. There are some great pictures of Ian with his eyes closed playing that shot.

Ian received some great support, especially from Tavare, who batted seven hours for his 78, as we piled on the runs. Our 404 all out meant Australia could only keep the series alive by scoring 506 to win or surviving a day and two sessions for a draw.

The pitch went very flat so we had to work hard for the wickets to win the game. Yallop and Border responded valiantly to the challenge, each scoring a century. Allan's effort was particularly courageous as he made 123 not out with a broken finger, but the avalanche was on the move and there was no way back for Australia. I claimed the wickets of Marsh, Bright and Mike Whitney as we bowled them out for 402 to win the match by 103 runs and take an unassailable lead in the series. The sixth and final Test at The Oval was then drawn as we won the series 3-1.

Ian Botham was rightly named man of the series for his tremendous contribution of 399 runs and 34 wickets, and I was elated with my own haul of 29 wickets. Australia's best performers were Alderman and Lillee who took 42 and 39 wickets respectively, while Border scored 533 runs.

There are a lot of comparisons between the 1981 and 2005 series. They both ebbed and flowed and Australia didn't really play to their potential on either occasion. Our celebrations were very low-key compared with 2005, I don't think there was even a celebration dinner. But in 2005, there was the enormous relief of having regained the Ashes after waiting almost 20 years. So you can understand the outpouring of emotion.

Winning the Ashes is the pinnacle of success in English and Australian cricket. I was lucky to have a very early taste of it on my first tour in 1970/71, when Ray Illingworth's side won 2-0 Down Under. As a teenager playing cricket in the garden, I would pretend to be Colin Cowdrey, John Edrich or Illingworth, and there I was, six years later, playing alongside them. I was only 21 and to be part of an Ashes victory at that age made a lasting impression. Having watched him in awe, I always wanted to emulate what John Snow did in that series, when his pace and aggression brought him 31 wickets. I am happy to say that with 29 wickets in 1981, I achieved that ambition.

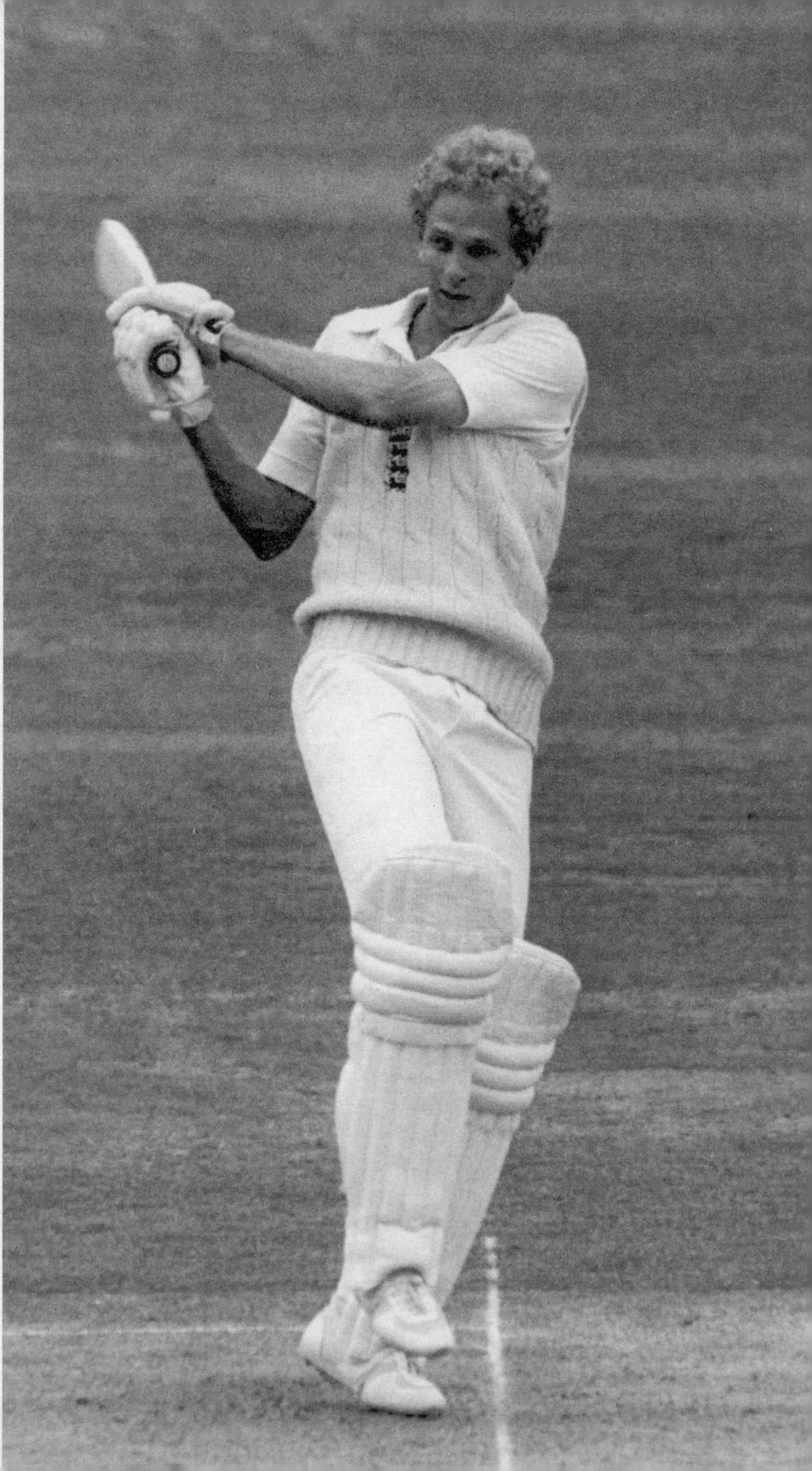

DAVID GOWER

David Gower – Sixth Test, The Oval, 29 August to 2 September 1985

David Gower pulled his first ball in Test cricket for four and when he retired 14 years later he had scored a total of 8,231 runs, at the time more than any other Englishman. The left-handed batsman delighted a generation with his grace and style at the crease. He once said he batted with Bollinger in his veins, but others were exasperated with his languid approach. As England captain he won in India and regained the Ashes in 1985, but won only five of his 32 Tests in charge and suffered successive whitewash series defeats to the West Indies. He is now a presenter on Sky Sports.

Left-handed batsman
Born: 1 April 1957, Tunbridge Wells, Kent
Test debut: June 1978 v Pakistan
Last Test: August 1992 v Pakistan
Test record: 117 matches, 8,231 runs at an average of 44.25

The state of play
England were 2-1 up going into the final Test of the six-match series so knew that they just had to avoid defeat to regain the Ashes, whereas a victory for Australia would have seen them retain the urn with a 2-2 series draw. England did what was necessary, winning by an innings and 94 runs.

Scoreboard
England first innings

G.A. Gooch		c & b McDermott	196
R.T. Robinson		b McDermott	3
D.I. Gower	c Bennett	b McDermott	157
M.W. Gatting	c Border	b Bennett	4
J.E. Emburey	c Wellham	b Lawson	9
A.J. Lamb	c McDermott	b Lawson	1
I.T. Botham	c Phillips	b Lawson	12
P.R. Downton		b McDermott	16
R.M. Ellison	c Phillips	b Gilbert	3
P.H. Edmonds	lbw	b Lawson	12
L.B. Taylor		not out	1
Extras	(b 13, lb 11, nb 26)		50
Total	(all out, 118.2 overs)		464

Bowling	O	M	R	W
G.F. Lawson	29.2	6	101	4
C.J. McDermott	31	2	108	4
D.R. Gilbert	21	2	96	1
M.J. Bennett	32	8	111	1
A.R. Border	2	0	8	0
K.C. Wessels	3	0	16	0

Australia first innings

G.M. Wood	lbw	b Botham	22
A.M.J. Hilditch	c Gooch	b Botham	17
K.C. Wessels		b Emburey	12
A.R. Border		b Edmonds	38
D.M. Wellham	c Downton	b Ellison	13
G.M. Ritchie		not out	64
W.B. Phillips		b Edmonds	18
M.J. Bennett	c Robinson	b Ellison	12
G.F. Lawson	c Botham	b Taylor	14
C.J. McDermott		run out	25
D.R. Gilbert		b Botham	1
Extras	(lb 3, w 2)		5
Total	(all out, 84 overs)		241

Bowling	O	M	R	W
I.T. Botham	20	3	64	3
L.B. Taylor	13	1	39	1
R.M. Ellison	18	5	35	2
J.E. Emburey	19	7	48	1
P.H. Edmonds	14	2	52	2

Australia second innings (following on)

G.M. Wood		b Botham	6
A.M.J. Hilditch	c Gower	b Taylor	9
K.C. Wessels	c Downton	b Botham	7
A.R. Border	c Botham	b Ellison	58
D.M. Wellham	lbw	b Ellison	5
G.M. Ritchie	c Downton	b Ellison	6
W.B. Phillips	c Downton	b Botham	10
M.J. Bennett		c & b Taylor	11
G.F. Lawson	c Downton	b Ellison	7
C.J. McDermott	c Botham	b Ellison	2
D.R. Gilbert		not out	0
Extras	(b 4, nb 4)		8
Total	(all out, 46.3 overs)		129

Bowling	O	M	R	W
I.T. Botham	17	3	44	3
L.B. Taylor	11.3	1	34	2
R.M. Ellison	17	3	46	5
J.E. Emburey	1	0	1	0

David Gower

IT WAS like that scene from *Monty Python's Life of Brian*. Standing on the upper balcony of the pavilion at The Oval, high above the thousands gathered on the pitch, I was holding aloft a trophy that was only four and a half inches high. Down below you could imagine the throng of people saying, 'Where is it? Can you see anything? What is he doing up there?'

Despite the mild farce, this was the climax to a truly wonderful summer. I had captained England to the Ashes and helped myself to a lot of runs in the process. The easiest question I am ever asked is what was the best year of my life. It will always be 1985.

When England won the Ashes in 2005 it felt like a unique and ground-breaking experience, but during the late 1970s and early 1980s the urn was frequently passed back and forth between the two countries. We won down in Australia in the 1978/79 series, then retained it in 1981 with Botham's Ashes, only for Australia to swipe it back 16 months later.

On the 1982/83 tour we didn't start quickly enough, losing both the second Test in Brisbane and the third in Adelaide. After winning at the MCG by only three runs we had a chance to claw it back at the end. We needed to win the final Test in Sydney to retain the Ashes, but we never recovered after a key decision went against us during Australia's first innings. Bob Willis ran out their opener John Dyson before he had faced a ball by almost half the length of a cricket pitch, but somehow the umpire decided he had made it back. He went on to score 79, which helped Australia get the draw they needed.

Yes, it was frustrating to leave Australia without the Ashes, especially as one felt that there was not a huge gulf between the sides, and on this occasion we had simply been a bit unlucky. On a purely selfish note I had been rather pleased with my own form by scoring 441 runs, including a century in Adelaide, at a respectable average of 44.10.

After serving as a stand-in on three occasions, I succeeded Bob Willis as England captain on a permanent basis in the summer of 1984. Unfortunately my first assignment could not have been more daunting: a series against the awesome West Indies side of that era including the likes of Greenidge, Haynes, Richards, Lloyd, Marshall, Roberts, Garner and Holding.

To be honest, I was all at sea during that summer. I was the leader but one with little confidence in my ability to come up with a plan that could threaten the strongest side I have ever played against. I even managed to become the first England captain since 1948 to declare and lose a Test, and we would lose each of the five matches in that infamous 'Blackwash' series. It was a terrible trial for everyone.

I learned there is very little you can do against a far stronger side, no matter what approach you take. Sadly, I wasn't even able to lead by example and scored just 171 runs in the five matches. At the end of a hard summer, I cast an eye over my dispirited side and wondered whether I should continue as captain.

Three and a half months in India resurrected my self-belief. We won a hard-fought series there to prove that things were not as bad as they had seemed at the end of the summer. I was particularly proud because not many of my predecessors had managed to return from India with a win. Despite losing the first Test in Bombay and being without Ian Botham, who was out of action that winter, we showed character to come back and win the series 2-1.

This was all achieved amid a climate of political unrest. Three hours after arriving in the country the Indian Prime Minister Indira Gandhi was assassinated and only three weeks later, the morning after we had attended a drinks party at the Deputy High Commissioner's residence in Bombay our host, Percy Norris, was shot dead on his way to work. It shook us all but we stayed and got on with the job with the team showing all the required resilience and I regained some confidence in my own abilities as a captain.

At the start of the following summer the return of Graham Gooch and John Emburey after serving three-year bans for taking part in a rebel tour to South Africa made me feel even better. There was no resentment towards the pair, none at all; they were old friends who I remained close to while they were in exile. Botham was also available again and returned looking refreshed and hungry to get at the Aussies.

It meant we now boasted an exceptionally strong batting line-up with Gooch, Tim Robinson, myself, Mike Gatting, Allan Lamb and Botham. Gooch's return meant Graeme Fowler, who had scored a double century months earlier in Madras, was dropped. Having to tell Graeme he was out was a very tricky moment.

The top six in our batting order would remain the same throughout the series, but it was a different story with our bowling attack. You could say it evolved during the summer. We used a total of nine bowlers; Emburey, Phil Edmonds, Paul Allott, Richard Ellison, Les Taylor, Jonathan Agnew, Norman Cowans, Neil Foster and Arnie Sidebottom. It was an era where the selectors were ready to make quick changes. If you do this and it doesn't work you can end up in disarray as in 1989, but in 1985 it brought success.

As captain I always sought to treat my players as adults and allow them as much freedom as possible. In team meetings I preferred everyone to be involved and wanted them to contribute. Other regimes I can think of worked all too simply on the basis that the captain and coach would do all the talking and merely hand down plans as if talking to a bunch of prep school kids. If you hand players a long list of rules and orders, they feel like children. Treat them like Test players and they will perform like that.

I was always careful not to over-clutter the players' minds with information about our opponents. I wanted them to concentrate on their own game. Primarily we looked after ourselves. But this approach wasn't without its faults. There were times when I left people too much to organise themselves when maybe they needed more direction and encouragement. Subsequently maybe that is where I failed, but it worked in this series.

The Australian touring party of 1985 was in a state of transition. At the end of the 1982/83 series Greg Chappell, Dennis Lillee and Rodney Marsh had all retired and a set of players, including Terry Alderman, who had taken 42 wickets against us in 1981, defected to join their own rebel tour of South Africa.

Undoubtedly these hefty blows affected their team spirit, but when you prepare for the first Test of an Ashes series you know the Aussies will be giving everything. We certainly were not going to underestimate them. The moment you start thinking something will be easy, you are likely to be in for a shock. Australia had more than enough good players, including their captain Allan Border, a tough cookie and an outstanding player, David Boon, Greg Ritchie, Craig McDermott and Geoff Lawson, that if we slipped up, they could give us plenty of problems.

Despite winning in India, there were still doubts abroad about whether I would keep the captaincy because of my continued poor form with the bat. I had managed only 167 runs in five Tests in India, which extended my wait for a Test century to 18 innings.

As the Ashes drew closer, I began to feel under more pressure after we lost the first two one-day games to Australia and I could only manage a grand total of three runs in the two innings. The newspapers were suggesting I should at least drop myself down the order from number three, but I felt if I were to do that, I might just as well not be there at all.

I arrived at Lord's for the third and final game obviously desperate to improve my form. The catalyst for this came in the field when I found myself under a really high chance from David Boon. I had more than enough time to think as the ball made its way down. 'Oh, please catch this,' I muttered to myself. Catching it seemed to be the only fillip I needed and when it came to batting suddenly it seemed all was well again; my 102 off 118 balls helped us to victory by eight wickets.

In the first Test at Headingley the Australians began rather well, making 331, but we made that look small with our reply of 533. It was pleasing to see Tim Robinson help himself to a large maiden Ashes century of 175, and Botham put the fear of God in to the Aussies with a nice reminder of what he could do, scoring a quick 60, which included 12 boundaries.

We had immediately exposed some glaring weaknesses in the Australian attack. One of the biggest was the once great Jeff Thomson, who had conceded 166 runs, then the most ever by an Australian fast bowler in a Test innings. This wasn't the Thommo of the mid-1970s; he was clearly past his best and missing much of his old pace and menace.

Australia made a fight of it in their second innings, scoring 324, but it still meant we only needed 123 to win. I was out to Simon O'Donnell for only five as we fell to 110/5, but we were never seriously in trouble. Victory was confirmed when Allan Lamb hooked the ball high towards the boundary. Attempting to catch it, Geoff Lawson was engulfed by fans running on the pitch. Understandably he was not amused but even he would have to admit it didn't make a jot of difference to the final result.

There really wasn't much of a party to celebrate our win. There was a warm glow and a glass of something cold, but that's about it. In those days we all had county games the next day, so afterwards it was almost a question of, 'Well done, lads … now could someone order me a taxi?'

On to Lord's for the second Test where I seemed to rediscover a bit of form with a very enjoyable 86 in our first innings. It was unfortunate that the rest of the side then chose this moment to lose their form, no one else got past 50 and we were all out for 290.

We were then forced to watch the Australians make 425, which was chiefly the work of Allan Border, who made a brilliant 196 over the course of seven and a half hours. It was galling that we literally threw away the chance to get him out. When Border was on 87 he was caught by Gatting at short leg, but Gatt began to celebrate too soon and succeeded only in throwing the ball away. The law is very clear: if you don't have control over the further disposal of the ball it is not out. If you try to throw it up and it goes straight down then you don't have control.

In our second innings the Australian leg-spinner Bob Holland took five wickets as we were all out for 261. It left Australia needing 127 to win, a total just three less than the one they famously failed to reach at Headingley four years earlier. Memories of that must have come flooding back when we had them 65/5 and Both was busy whispering 'Headingley' in their batsmen's ears. But Border guided Australia to victory with an unbeaten 41 and once again they had triumphed at Lord's. I appreciate it is meaningless to manipulate the figures, but one cannot help but muse that if Gatt had caught Border in the first innings we might well have won this Test and gone 2-0 up rather than being pulled back to 1-1.

On the first morning of the third Test in Nottingham I decided to unveil my secret weapon: a ten franc coin. Up until then I had a dreadful record with tosses, losing six on the trot, but ten francs did the trick and we decided to bat on what looked a splendid pitch. And so it proved as I scored 166, my first hundred for 16 months. It was a great relief, and to be honest, once I hit my stride it felt easy. It was a good flat Trent Bridge pitch and it would have been an awful shame not to make runs on it. Gatt and I shared a third-wicket partnership of 187 to help us to a first-innings total of 456.

Unsurprisingly the Australians also took full advantage of the pitch by reaching 539 as Graeme Wood and Greg Ritchie scored big centuries. At 300/5 we thought we had Ritchie when Phil Edmonds caught him at third man with a brilliant diving effort during a very quick spell from Botham, operating as a strike bowler. However, the umpire, Alan Whitehead, called it a no-ball.

Both was incensed as he bowled so few of them in his career and his mood further darkened when Alan pulled him up for bowling too much short stuff and then for running on the pitch. Now I had two strong characters clashing and I did my best to placate both of them. I thought I had done a pretty good job on that front but it did not prevent Ian being reported to the cricket authorities. In our second innings, Gooch and Robinson helped take us to 196/2 as the match finished in a draw. We were still locked at 1-1 with three Tests to play.

At the fourth Test at Old Trafford I put the Australians in and watched as Botham and Edmonds, with four wickets each, restricted them to 257. Craig McDermott, aged just 20, took eight wickets in our reply, but they came at a price as we declared on 482/9. We hoped to inflict an innings defeat on the Aussies, but the Manchester rain, which constantly interrupted play, and Allan Border, who made an unbeaten 146, helped them reach the safety of 340/5 as the match finished in another draw.

Frustration was beginning to creep in. After winning the first Test of the summer we had failed to win any of the next three. At this stage, no one was saying this was a bad Australian side. We had reached a stalemate and it was proving to be bloody hard; they couldn't get us out and we couldn't get them out.

The Australians went in to the fifth Test at Edgbaston knowing victory would see them retain the Ashes. On the eve of the first day's play at our normal post-dinner team meeting I had prepared some rousing words to inspire the troops. Having said thank you and goodnight to the selectors I rose to my feet but before I had said a word bread rolls and small plant pots were flying through the air towards me. I got the message; a speech wasn't necessary. The spirit was still very good and we just wanted to get on with it.

For this Test we replaced Paul Allott with Richard Ellison, and this was immediately made to look like a masterstroke as the Kent seamer took 6-77 to help get Australia all out for 335. Due to plenty of rain delays their innings lasted until the Saturday morning.

On the same morning I was also confirmed as captain for the winter tour to the West Indies, these being the days when they only appointed you series by series if you were lucky. Maybe this gave me a bit of a lift because by the close of play I was unbeaten on 169, and would eventually finish on 215. On another flat track, I enjoyed myself against a stuttering Australian attack, finding plenty of space around the ground. I was regularly cover-driving Thommo and hitting Bob Holland, who wasn't a bad bowler but was still no Shane Warne, all over the place. McDermott was aggressive, but the pitch took the sting out of him.

I brought up my double century with a drive through extra cover off McDermott, which was a very special moment. Fifteen runs later and after seven and a half hours at the crease I was caught by Border off Lawson. Strolling off I felt rather proud of what was my highest ever Test innings, especially as it had also carried me past Denis Compton's record of 562 runs for a home series against Australia. In my wake Tim Robinson and Gatt both scored centuries before we declared on 595/5, a tidy 260 ahead.

It got even better for us late on the fourth evening when Ellison took four wickets for just one run in the space of 15 balls to leave Australia 36/5. I will never forget the ball he got Border out with, it was as sweet as you like. As the wickets fell you could feel the atmosphere rolling down from the stands as the crowd realised they were watching an object lesson in how to put a side under pressure.

Now only the weather could save Australia. On the final morning my agent, Jon Holmes, rang me from his home in Nottinghamshire at 8.30am to find out what the weather was like in Birmingham. The forecast wasn't good and he was desperate for an on-the-scene update. I was still in bed with the curtains drawn. 'I don't know, I haven't really looked yet,' I muttered. He was, to say the least, surprised that the one man in England whose day would depend on the weather had yet to heave himself out of bed. Anyway I dragged myself from my pit, peered out of the window and passed on the bad news, 'Well, I'm sorry to say, it's not great. It's drizzling.'

When we got to the ground the first man I saw was Allan Border, who was just giggling, loving that drizzle and now highly optimistic the weather would rescue him. At 2.30pm, however, play finally began to wipe the grin from Border's face, but it reappeared as his side continued to frustrate us. With an hour remaining, they hadn't lost another wicket and were looking comfortable on 113/5. Their wicketkeeper, Wayne Phillips, was playing his shots and had progressed from one to 59 when he hit a ball from Edmonds straight on to the instep of Allan Lamb's foot at short leg. The ball looped up and landed in my hands. Thank you very much.

There were plenty of witnesses to this course of events; I saw it, our wicketkeeper Paul Downton saw it and Lamby certainly felt it on his foot. It hadn't hit the ground. The umpires, David Constant and David Shepherd, conferred and gave Phillips out. The Aussies, however, were convinced it wasn't out and will maintain this until their dying day. 'Nah, mate, you did us there,' is their attitude. If they want to stick to their story, fine, but our story is the one history has recorded. Just look at *Wisden*. It is there in black and white: Phillips was out!

That was the crucial turning point. The Aussies' resistance disappeared and they were soon all out for 142. We had won by an innings and 118 runs to go 2-1 up.

'Thank God' was our overwhelming emotion. We could handle drawing the previous two Tests, but it was essential we won here, and we had. Just.

For the first time since 1953 an Ashes series in England would be decided by the final Test of the summer. A win or a draw would see us retain them, but if Australia triumphed at the death they would disappear back home with them for another 16 months.

At The Oval I felt that normal first morning thrill, which continued when I won the toss for the fourth time in the series and decided to bat on a typical Oval belter. I was in quickly after Tim Robinson had fallen with the score on 20 and I nearly joined him back in the dressing room when I got a high one from McDermott which took the shoulder of my bat but luckily just carried over third slip.

I then played as well as I had done for a long, long time. In truth, it was probably the best innings I have ever played. I could be modest and brush over it, but it was a knock when everything came together both technically and mentally. Time and time again, I kept hitting the ball sweetly and finding the gaps. There was one shot when I hit David Gilbert on the up through cover, which was as sweet as it gets. I will play that shot in my mind for the rest of my life.

The Australian selectors had dropped Thommo and Holland and replaced them with Gilbert, a brisk but not rapid bowler, and Murray Bennett, who wasn't a patch on our slow left-armer, Phil Edmonds. I am happy to say the new pair, along with Lawson and McDermott, were hit to all parts of the ground.

I reached my century off just 123 balls before going on to reach 157. It felt rather good to be leading from the front; as a captain it does not get much better than this. Gooch, who would make 196, helped me put on 351 for the second wicket before I was caught by Bennett off McDermott. I can't say I was that annoyed with myself – I might have been if we were 250/7 – but we were in a dominant position and I had made the most of the conditions and bowling.

As I made my way from the field, we were 371/2 and I just knew we would now win this Test. There were some kind words and appreciative nods on my return to the dressing room – precious little back-slapping and very few high fives in those days!

I was happy to settle for 376/3 at the close of play, but the Aussies began the second day much better and bowled us out for 464. Still, our bowlers rose to the occasion and all took at least one wicket as we knocked over the Aussies for 241. It was a classic balanced attack that did the job for us; Botham bowling at pace, Taylor hitting the bat hard, Ellison swinging it and the spinners, Edmonds and Emburey, keeping absolute control.

We then had a healthy debate about whether we should bat again or enforce the follow-on. Interestingly we were pretty evenly spilt; some feared they would get back in the game if they made 400, but I had the final decision. 'No, lads, let's bowl them out again.' Once you have a side on the rack you don't loosen the straps.

On the Saturday night this decision was vindicated as Australia slumped to 62/4. Despite the state of the match and series, I seem to remember Both and Border having dinner together that night. It was symptomatic of the good spirit in which the series was played, not that any quarter was given or expected on the field. Mind you, Border's approach was to be entirely different four years later when he hardly spoke to any of us until the Ashes were won and the most I got from him for weeks was the word 'tails' at the toss.

It didn't take too long to polish off Australia and by 12.35pm on the fourth day they were all out for 129. They had no answers to Ellison as he took four wickets. But it was Les Taylor who took the final wicket of the series when he caught and bowled Bennett to confirm that we had regained the Ashes. These were the days when the crowd were allowed on the pitch at the end of a match, so we made a sharp exit feeling rather good about ourselves.

The crowd gathered in front of the pavilion to watch as I was presented with the Ashes. Despite the difficulty they might have had actually seeing that take place on the balcony, it was at least a magic feeling for me to get my hands on the urn, a moment to cherish for all time.

As soon as we came off the balcony Steve Pearson, the BBC's floor manager, approached me. 'Can I have the urn back now please?' he said. I was utterly bemused. 'What on earth do you mean?' I had been looking forward to bringing it in to the dressing room, passing it around the boys and taking some pictures before placing it on my mantelpiece at home. 'Sorry I've got to give it straight back to Lord's, it is one of their replicas,' he told me. And I went back to the dressing room empty-handed.

Any disappointment about the absent urn did not last long. Back with the team in front of the dressing room and a bit closer now to that crowd, Gatt sprayed me with champagne, while Both gave me a XXXX shampoo by pouring a whole can of it over my head.

Compared with the mass celebrations of 2005 I am afraid ours were rather muted. We lingered for some time in the dressing rooms, had more than a few drinks, but once again we all drifted off in our separate directions afterwards.

There was of course never any talk of an open-top bus parade or a trip to Downing Street. Yes, I suppose I was envious of the celebrations Michael Vaughan's team enjoyed in central London, but we could never have even envisaged such a thing. Anyway, it would have killed me if I had drunk through the night like Freddie Flintoff.

I will say that I found it strange that the 2005 team all found themselves with MBEs in the next honours list. None of the 1985 team was honoured at the time, indeed Ian Botham and I, who both were eventually awarded OBEs, had to wait until virtually the ends of our careers, and I believe that is how it should be. If I had been given an award every time England won the Ashes during the course of my career I would be in the House of Lords by now.

As well as my leadership of the team, I was able to look back with pride on my performances with the bat. It was easily my most productive summer, with a total of 732 runs at an average of 81.33. At the end of the series the former England captain and my first captain at Leicestershire, Ray Illingworth, declared, 'David is no longer the easy-going boy wonder. He is a man.' It was a good line and there was some truth to it. Ray had known me since I was an 18-year-old at Leicestershire and had helped transform me from a gifted amateur in to a good professional. He was right, I had grown up, and I enjoyed every moment of that summer.

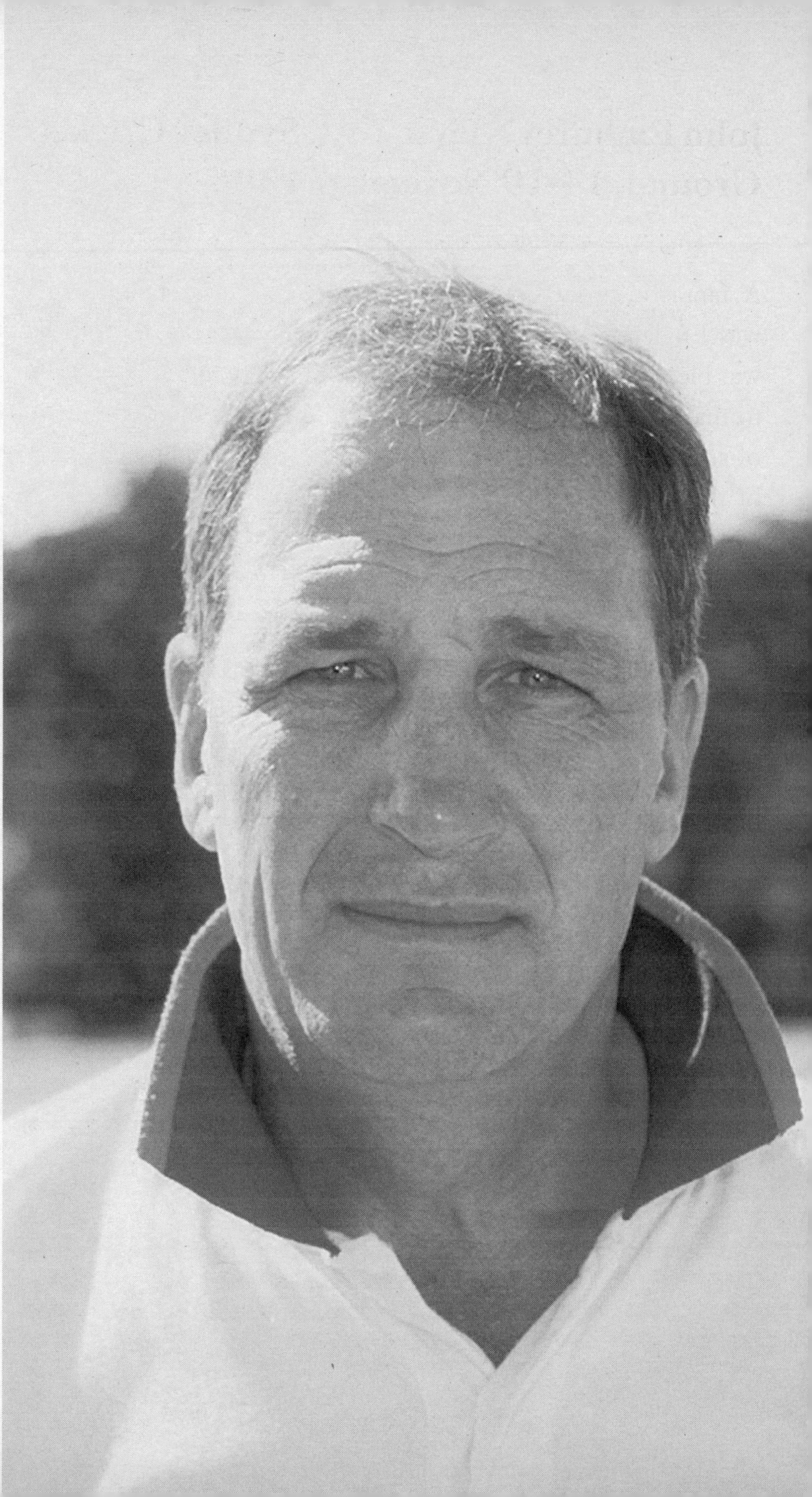

JOHN EMBUREY

John Emburey – First Test, Sydney Cricket Ground, 14-19 November 1986

A fantastic professional who relished Test cricket, Emburey was England's premier off-spinner throughout the 1980s. He was blessed with a safe pair of hands and would often improvise to make useful runs down the order. Emburey enjoyed plenty of success in Australia, as England won five and lost only two of the nine Ashes Tests in which he played on the 1978/79 and 1986/87 tours. The Middlesex man was also a member of England's 1981 and 1985 Ashes-winning sides.

Right-arm off-spinner, right-handed batsman
Born: 20 August 1952, Peckham, London
Test debut: 1978 v New Zealand
Last Test: 1995 v West Indies
Test record: 64 matches, 147 wickets at an average of 38.40; 1,713 runs at an average of 22.53

The state of play
Australia were firm favourites to win back the Ashes on home soil, but England cast aside their recent poor form as the old guard turned on the style at thet start of a series triumph Down Under.

Scoreboard

England first innings

B.C. Broad	c Zoehrer	b Reid	8
C.W.J. Athey	c Zoehrer	b C.D. Matthews	76
M.W. Gatting		b Hughes	61
A.J. Lamb	lbw	b Hughes	40
D.I. Gower	c Ritchie	b C.D. Matthews	51
I.T. Botham	c Hughes	b Waugh	138
C.J. Richards		b C.D. Matthews	0
J.E. Emburey	c Waugh	b Hughes	8
P.A.J. DeFreitas	c C.D. Matthews	b Waugh	40
P.H. Edmonds		not out	9
G.R. Dilley	c Boon	b Waugh	0
Extras	(b 3, lb 19, nb 3)		25
Total	(all out, 134 overs)		456

Bowling	O	M	R	W
Reid	31	4	86	1
Hughes	36	7	134	3
C.D. Matthews	35	10	95	3
Waugh	21	3	76	3
G.R.J. Matthews	11	2	43	0

Australia first innings

G.R. Marsh	c Richards	b Dilley	56
D.C. Boon	c Broad	b DeFreitas	10
T.J. Zoehrer	lbw	b Dilley	38
D.M. Jones	lbw	b DeFreitas	8
A.R. Border	c DeFreitas	b Edmonds	7
G.M. Ritchie	c Edmonds	b Dilley	41
G.R.J. Matthews		not out	56
S.R. Waugh	c Richards	b Dilley	0
C.D. Matthews	c Gatting	b Botham	11
M.G. Hughes		b Botham	0
B.A. Reid	c Richards	b Dilley	3
Extras	(b 2, lb 8, w 2, nb 6)		18
Total	(all out, 104.4 overs)		248

Bowling	O	M	R	W
DeFreitas	16	5	32	2
Dilley	25.4	7	68	5
Emburey	34	11	66	0
Edmonds	12	6	12	1
Botham	16	1	58	2
Gatting	1	0	2	0

Australia second innings (following on)

G.R. Marsh		b DeFreitas	110
D.C. Boon	lbw	b Botham	14
D.M. Jones	st Richards	b Emburey	18
A.R. Border	c Lamb	b Emburey	23
G.M. Ritchie	lbw	b DeFreitas	45
G.R.J. Matthews		c & b Dilley	13
S.R. Waugh		b Emburey	28
T.J. Zoehrer		not out	16
C.D. Matthews	lbw	b Emburey	0
M.G. Hughes		b DeFreitas	0
B.A. Reid	c Broad	b Emburey	2
Extras	(b 5, lb 6, nb 2)		13
Total	(all out, 116.5 overs)		282

Bowling	O	M	R	W
Botham	12	0	34	1
Dilley	19	6	47	1
Emburey	42.5	14	80	5
DeFreitas	17	2	62	3
Edmonds	24	8	46	0
Gatting	2	0	2	0

England second innings (target: 75 runs)

B.C. Broad		not out	35
C.W.J. Athey	c Waugh	b Hughes	1
M.W. Gatting	c G.R.J. Matthews	b Hughes	12
A.J. Lamb	lbw	b Reid	9
D.I. Gower		not out	15
Extras	(b 2, nb 3)		5
Total	(3 wickets, 22.3 overs)		77

Bowling	O	M	R	W
C.D. Matthews	4	0	11	0
Hughes	5.3	0	28	2
Reid	6	1	20	1
G.R.J. Matthews	7	1	16	0

John Emburey

'THERE ARE ONLY three things wrong with England; they can't bat, they can't bowl and they can't field.' That was the damning assessment of Martin Johnson of *The Independent* after we lost a warm-up match against Queensland. Although we drew against Western Australia and beat South Australia in the other state games before the first Test at Brisbane, it was true we weren't exactly scaring our opponents.

We hadn't actually won a Test match since overcoming Australia at The Oval 14 months earlier when we reclaimed the Ashes 3-1 under David Gower's leadership. But the English winter and summer of 1986 were a huge struggle. We lost 5-0 in the Caribbean against a formidable West Indies side, although too many of our players, including myself, were in awe of stars like Viv Richards and Malcolm Marshall.

Things got worse when we lost home series against India and New Zealand. The Indians had some good players, including the great all-rounder Kapil Dev, while New Zealand were at the top of their game, with Richard Hadlee, another legendary all-rounder, leading the way.

But when we played Australia, it was totally different. We felt we were going to win all the time, something you can't often say about an Ashes series. I had only known success against the Aussies after we beat them in 1978/79, 1981 and 1985. Of course I missed the 1982/83 defeat because I was banned from Test cricket for three years after going on the rebel tour to South Africa in 1981/82.

On the tour to the West Indies there were protests against those of us who had been to South Africa; Peter Willey, Graham Gooch and myself. It was particularly severe at Trinidad, as we made our way into the ground and even outside the dressing rooms, but there were no problems in Australia.

Despite our lack of form going into the series, the atmosphere in our camp was fantastic. We had some good young players like fast bowlers Phil DeFreitas and Gladstone Small, and Ian Botham had returned after an operation earlier in the year. Both probably wasn't back to his best and I think he would admit he got by on brute force and reputation for the next three or four years. But he was so wholehearted it felt like having 12 players in your team.

The media changed in the mid-1980s. Botham was writing for the *Daily Mirror* and all of a sudden there was jealousy from rival papers, which led to aggressive coverage of the team. A lot more news writers started to follow us around, looking for off-field sensations, and that created a certain amount of pressure. You probably weren't able to enjoy touring as much as when I first went away, but you still had a good time.

When your preparations for a big match haven't been perfect, you look for a little bit of inspiration, and this is where Micky Stewart played a crucial role. It was the first time England had had a proper coach/manager and Micky was absolutely fantastic in the way he dealt with the players. He talked to us individually about our roles and how we were performing, controlled the younger players and let the senior players have their freedom.

Micky only played a few Tests himself in the 1960s, but he had captained and later managed Surrey with success. So to have someone with his knowledge of the game was invaluable. He provided great support for Mike Gatting on his first tour as skipper, helping him lead the side very well.

Our performances in the state matches and the Tests were chalk and cheese. When we got to the first Test in Brisbane, we were able to turn it on straight away. We went in first, and Bill Athey, realising we needed runs at the top of the order, batted a long time to see off the new ball after Chris Broad fell early. Bill took about 72 overs to get 76 and although it was slow going, he developed important partnerships with Gatting and Allan Lamb, who got 40. So we were 198/2 at stumps on the first day.

Gatt made a half-century at number three as Gower dropped down the order. Officially, that was because he had struggled in the warm-up matches and had got a pair against Western Australia just prior to Brisbane. But really Gower was in the toilet and Gatt had his pads on, so when we lost a wicket Gatt took responsibility and batted at number three.

It worked out well because David made a half-century on the second day after we had lost Lamb and Athey without adding to our overnight score. Gower shared in an important partnership of 121 with Botham and they had taken the score on to 316 when David was the fifth man out, caught by Greg Ritchie off the bowling of debutant Chris Matthews.

We were in a good position until Jack Richards got out cheaply and I made just eight, as we went from 316/5 to 351/7. But Daffy DeFreitas came in and turned it around with Ian. He was a young 20-year-old and swiftly took to Test cricket.

He made 40 in good time and by playing a couple of big shots, kick-started Botham, who went into overdrive. Ian realised that a partnership could develop and he started hitting the seamers back over their heads, pulling and cutting, and playing these big shots. Ian even took 22 off one over from Merv Hughes.

Botham's brilliant 138 included 13 fours and four sixes and took the game away from Australia. A score of 456 all out put us in a great position. Once you have runs on the board and two good spinners, myself and Philippe Edmonds, who are going to give you control, the confidence grows.

Australia had a very young bowling attack and they showed their inexperience. Seamers Hughes, Bruce Reid and Chris Matthews had played just nine Tests between them before Brisbane. Strangely, Geoff Lawson, a very good fast bowler, was 12th man and Craig McDermott, who had played throughout the 1985 series, was left out altogether.

The Australians felt under pressure from the way their media had built them up and said we were one of the worst touring teams ever to come out of England. The thing is, they say that about every England team.

We really squeezed Australia when we bowled. We took our catches and everyone chipped in as we dismissed them for 248 on day three. Graham Dilley got five wickets, Botham and DeFreitas grabbed a couple each and Edmonds claimed the prize scalp of their captain Allan Border. Phil and I bowled steadily, even though I didn't take a wicket in 34 inexpensive overs.

So we made Australia follow on at home in an Ashes Test for the first time in 21 years and this time I managed to get some wickets. Australian pitches didn't spin a great deal but they were hard and because I was tall they gave me bounce, which made me awkward to play. My strength was that I exerted pressure by keeping things very tight and placing close catchers around the bat, so I got many of my wickets in the series with bat-pad catches.

It didn't take long for us to make inroads on the fourth morning when Botham trapped David Boon lbw. That brought Dean Jones to the crease at 24/1 as I began a marathon spell. Jones was a very dangerous player who had made a double century in a tied Test against India at Chennai earlier in the year, so his was a key wicket. He played spin well and was always aggressive, using his feet and never letting you settle.

Jones was looking in good touch when he came down the wicket to me and played over the top of one, making it into a yorker. It was a very difficult stumping for Jack Richards because he had to stay down when it would have been easy to come up. But he held his low body position, the ball went straight into his gloves and he whipped off the bails. Getting rid of Jones for just 18 was a huge bonus because he had made the error. We were thrilled.

Allan Border was next in. He was Australia's real danger man and always produced his best form against England. Allan had scored over 500 runs against us in both the 1981 and 1985 series despite being on the losing side each time and this was a feat he would almost repeat in 1986/87.

But at Brisbane I developed a plan of attack that we would use against him throughout the series. It was one of the first times I bowled over the wicket to him and really tucked him up, which he didn't like at all. He preferred the off-spinners to bowl around the wicket because he could free his arms and with the ball drifting in, play his little fine sweep shot.

I bowled a leg-stump line and if there was a bit of spin, I had a chance of picking up a wicket because he couldn't kick the ball away since it might go straight on and get him lbw. Allan tended to push hard at the ball rather than letting it come to him, so there was always the possibility of getting him caught close to the wicket. After jamming at the ball several times off my bowling, he eventually squeezed a catch out to Lamb at silly mid-off.

The Australian captain was gone for 23 and they were struggling at 92/3, still 116 runs behind. But their resilient opener Geoff Marsh was still there and he took the score on to 205 with Ritchie before DeFreitas trapped Greg lbw. Greg Matthews, the New South Wales all-rounder, followed not long after when he was caught and bowled by Dilley, leaving Australia 224/5.

Marsh batted a long time for his century and we needed his wicket badly because he was holding us up, keeping everything together and developing little partnerships. At the end of the fourth day, Australia had a lead of 35 with five wickets standing. Marsh was on 108 and Steve Waugh had 12.

The next morning we kept at them and DeFreitas soon bowled Marsh for 110, which he had made in just over six and a half hours. Waugh didn't last much longer as he became my 100th Test victim. Like Jones, he tried to use his feet but just turned my delivery into a yorker which bowled him.

Waugh had just come into the side but looked a very solid player for his 28. He was someone you really had to get out because he was in the Border mould and would never give his wicket away. Steve got some useful runs in the series, some 60s and 70s, and showed he could play.

I then got Chris Matthews lbw for a second-ball duck and we were on a roll, with Australia 266/8. Because Marsh had gone and I had dismissed Jones, Border and Waugh, there was nobody to play with their long tail. So we kept chipping away, knowing the end was in sight.

DeFreitas bowled Hughes for a duck and I removed Reid to claim a five-for. I don't remember that one very well but he was caught by Broad so he must have had a slog! Australia lost their last five wickets for only 58 runs as they collapsed to 282 all out and I finished with figures of 5-80 from my 42.5 overs. Then it was just a matter of getting the 75 runs to win, which we did for the loss of three wickets, with Broad and Gower there at the end.

After the match, a lot of us went out for dinner while some stayed in the hotel bar. In those days, the bowlers wound down at the end of a Test match by getting absolutely pissed. I got my first experience of this in Sydney on the 1978/79 tour.

Chris Old and Mike Hendrick had had a few drinks and came and sat down with me, my fiancée, Susie, and her parents. But Chris and Mike started abusing my future in-laws because they thought they were a couple of old Aussies giving us an ear-bashing, when in fact they were ex-pat Brits. I was shaking my head, but they kept on taking the piss. I explained to them afterwards that those people were my future parents-in-law, so Chris and Mike apologised to them.

We also socialised with the opposition a lot. If we were in the field all day, they would come in to our dressing room at the end of play and bring a few cans of beer. Then we would reciprocate the following day if they were in the field. Needless to say the greatest socialisers were Botham, Gower, Lamb, myself and Gatt. From the Aussies, it was Border, Hughes and Dirk Wellham. There was a great sense of camaraderie and you got to know your enemy.

That was something that had changed when I came back and played the one Test in 1993, against Australia at Edgbaston. Because of all the sledging, the younger batsmen didn't want to mix with the Australians. But I think you are better off getting to know them by having a drink and a chat afterwards. You are not in awe of them that way.

We didn't appreciate how much excitement our victory had sparked back in England. All we knew was that there had been a lot of criticism in the media of our performances leading up to the first Test. But when you face difficult times, you tend to get closer together, so the critics only succeeded in galvanising us.

Gower and Lambie went off to a nightclub with Kerry Packer, the Australian media tycoon, during the first Test and didn't get back until the small hours. After that Lambie got out very early on the second day and the media found out where he had been. I was vice-captain and part of the management team and we didn't know they were out until a couple of days later, when it was reported in the paper. Micky Stewart had a word with David and Allan about their responsibilities.

The fact we had some characters who liked to go off to parties could have meant we became a bit fragmented, but the Brisbane victory and the criticism we endured beforehand meant everybody supported one another.

The game has become more professional than it was then. We still enjoyed ourselves off the field, we would go out to dinner and have a bottle or two of wine between three of us. There would be occasions when we had a bottle each, and it wasn't a problem because we would get up the next day and perform.

The morning preparations were very relaxed and probably a bit of a joke, in the sense that some of the guys didn't really believe in them. We had a physio who took our warm-ups but we didn't have training regimes as such and didn't always have access to a gym.

But that wasn't to say the boys weren't exercising when they weren't playing. We played golf and tennis and swam, so we were maintaining a certain fitness level. There was no such thing as watching your diet, it probably consisted of beer and pies.

We didn't have dieticians or nutritionists, there was none of the support staff and structure there is nowadays.

After winning the first Test, we got T-shirts printed which read, 'Can't bat, can't bowl, can't field.' There was a lot of humour in the dressing room by this stage and it was a very good environment to be in.

We batted really well at Perth, in the second Test. Broad, Gower and Richards got hundreds as we amassed the whopping score of 592/8 declared on a very flat pitch. Border then hit a century in Australia's reply of 401, during which I took 2-110, and we declared our second innings at the end of the fourth day, setting them a target of 391 in three sessions.

Some huge cracks appeared in the pitch and I got Marsh lbw with a ball that Muttiah Muralitharan would have been proud of. But the cracks weren't generally as helpful as we had hoped and Australia held out comfortably for a draw.

In terms of tactics and the way he dealt with people, the outstanding skipper I played under for England and Middlesex was Mike Brearley, the brains behind our 1978/79 and 1981 Ashes triumphs. Mike Gatting was totally different because he was very up-front and took a challenge head on, while Brears was more laid back.

Gatt would give us a rollicking if we weren't performing, really let us know what was required. He had already had three years of captaincy experience at Middlesex, so wasn't daunted by the reputations of great players like Botham and Gower.

Between the second and third Tests, we played Victoria in a state game. We got to the ground and started practising before realising our captain wasn't with us, so Gower had to toss up while Broad went back to the hotel to look for Gatt. Chris found him stretched out on his bed after being out all night on the piss.

Mike eventually got to the ground at about 11.30am, after the start. I asked, 'Where the bloody hell have you been?' He said something and the smell of alcohol on his breath was unbelievable, but he went out and took four wickets with a Botham-like performance.

Ian enjoyed himself just as much off the field as he did on it and his generosity was a great part of touring. He always wanted to go places and do things and wanted everyone to come along with him, probably to help him home!

On one occasion, Lambie, Gower, Botham and I went to a do in Fremantle, in Western Australia, as guests of Harold Cudmore, who was skipper of one of the crews in the America's Cup, which was taking place at the time. Ian had a skinful and fell off his chair so we had to get him straight back to the hotel.

If anyone was going to play pranks it was generally Botham, cutting players' socks or the bottoms off their ties. But you dared not do it to him because the shit would hit the fan then.

Both sides batted well again in the third Test at Adelaide. David Boon made a century before I had him caught by James Whitaker, as Australia declared their first innings at 514/5. In our reply of 455, Broad and Gatting hit centuries, and I made 49.

Then Border dug in for his second hundred of the series and Australia set us a target of 261 on the final day. Unfortunately the rain fell and we had little chance to chase the runs as the match petered out into a draw. But we were still 1-0 up in the series and knew that with two Tests to play, we just needed to avoid defeat in one of them to retain the Ashes.

We spent Christmas in Melbourne ahead of the fourth Test, which started on Boxing Day. Our celebrations consisted of a lunch, to which all our wives were invited, and a fancy dress party. DeFreitas won the prize for the best fancy dress by coming as Diana Ross, but my costume was dreadful. I had to dress up as a character beginning with the letter R and couldn't think of anything else, so I got a big brown cloak and a black wig and went along as the Russian mystic Rasputin.

It was a fun occasion but we had business to do the following day, so we were careful what we drank. We knew Christmas was over when we got a hostile reception at the MCG the next morning. There were about 65,000 people in the ground and we realised we had to match the Australians from the outset.

The first time I played there, in 1978, the noise and banter from the Southern Stand were incredible and rather than someone fielding down there for a whole session, we had to change positions every half hour because it got so intense.

It is more abuse than anything else. They piss in beer cans and say, 'D'you wanna cold beer, mate?' Some of the boys would have a drink on the boundary, but the ring had to still be attached to the can. If it felt slightly warm in your hand, you definitely didn't have it.

I played a lot of club cricket in Melbourne and got a mixed reception. Some guys shouted out, 'Embers, when are you going to play for St Kilda?' Others just gave you downright abuse, swearing at you, saying, 'What are you doing here? Why aren't you at home? Who's shagging your missus?' They obviously didn't realise my missus was with me in Melbourne.

They tried to upset you and get a cheap laugh in front of up to 20,000 people in that one stand. It was a very intimidating ground, more so than any other in Australia, but we quietened the crowd on the first day. Botham and Small took five wickets each as Australia were skittled out for 141. Ian got wickets more through bravado than great bowling, with the way he ran in and hit the deck hard. He still had the ability to make something happen, get a batsman to play a false shot.

We had a good relationship with the Australians. Out on the field, there was some banter, backwards and forwards stuff, nothing serious. Merv used to give the players a bit of verbal but it was all good-humoured. We would laugh and tell them to piss off or something stronger occasionally. It was all in jest, there was nothing serious on the sledging side. A lot of it was meant to put you off, but it was seen more in fun because we knew each other so well.

However, there was one incident between Phil Edmonds and their wicketkeeper Tim Zoehrer during England's innings of 349 on the second day at Melbourne. Phil and I shared a profitable ninth-wicket partnership of 30, to which I contributed 22, after Broad had made his third century in as many Tests.

NEIL HARVEY – 1948
FOURTH TEST, HEADINGLEY

The pull shot was one of my most productive strokes in my innings of 112 at Headingley.
Here I am pulling Ken Cranston to the boundary (left) and hitting another four watched by
England wicketkeeper Godfrey Evans (right)

Sam Loxton congratulates me on reaching my maiden Ashes century.
He seemed even more pleased than I was!

RAY ILLINGWORTH – 1970/71
SEVENTH TEST, SYDNEY

Umpire Lou Rowan warns John Snow for intimidatory bowling after Terry Jenner was struck on the head. But Snowy's delivery was never a bouncer and I ask the umpire why he is warning my bowler

Snowy pours the champagne for the injured Geoff Boycott as I toast our Ashes success in the dressing room at the SCG. Winning back the Ashes in Australia was the absolute highlight of my cricket career

JEFF THOMSON – 1974/75
FIRST TEST, BRISBANE

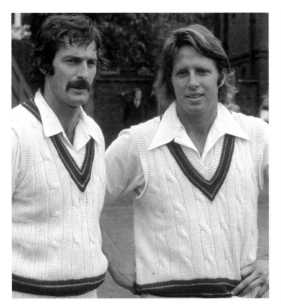

*Deadly duo: Dennis Lillee and I took 58 wickets
between us in the 1974/5 series*

*If great batsmen like Ian and Greg
Chappell couldn't handle my bowling,
the Poms weren't going to either*

*(Left) Rod Marsh and I celebrate victory in the fourth Test at Sydney, in which I took
six wickets. Marshy knew how to rev up Dennis and me so we took our anger out on the
opposition. My action (right) was completely natural; I never worked on it. My father bowled
like that and I inherited it*

GEOFFREY BOYCOTT – 1977
THIRD TEST, TRENT BRIDGE

I get away with hitting one in the air during my comeback at Trent Bridge

A rare moment of fluency (left) during an innings that really tested my courage and technique, and (right) acknowledging the crowd after reaching my greatest-ever century

Derek Randall and I receive a great ovation from the Trent Bridge crowd after steering England home. I was delighted Derek was there at the end, especially since I ran him out in the first innings

Champagne moment: I celebrate victory at Trent Bridge, but my overriding feeling was relief

BOB WILLIS – 1981
THIRD TEST, HEADINGLEY

I'm determined to keep my concentration despite Gatting's excellent catch to remove Graham Yallop during my match-winning 8-43 on the final day

No time to celebrate as we rush from the pitch after I bowled Ray Bright to win the match

DAVID GOWER – 1985
SIXTH TEST, THE OVAL

Everything came together for me both technically and mentally at The Oval. In my mind I will play shots from this innings for the rest of my life

Raising my bat to celebrate scoring a century on the first day. I can honestly say I have never played any better than this

As we watch Allan Border return to the pavilion during Australia's second innings, we are certain the Ashes will soon be ours

Ian Botham and Mike Gatting shower me and wicketkeeper Paul Downton in champagne as we celebrate regaining the Ashes. This was the climax to the best summer of my life

JOHN EMBUREY – 1986/87
FIRST TEST, BRISBANE

All together now: there was a fantastic team spirit throughout the 1986/87 tour of Australia

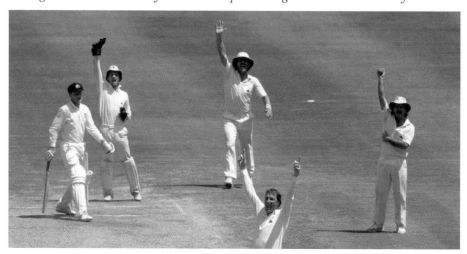

The Australian pitches gave me plenty of bounce so most of my wickets came through bat-pad catches. Here, Allan Lamb catches Peter Taylor off my bowling in the fifth Test at Sydney

All the bowlers played their part in our success. Here, Botham, Gatting and Richards congratulate Gladstone Small on his 5-75 at Sydney

(Right) The captains Allan Border (left) and Mike Gatting chat over a beer. We always enjoyed a drink with the Aussies at the end of play; it was part of the camaraderie of that era

MARK TAYLOR – 1989
FIRST TEST, HEADINGLEY

After being stranded on 96 at stumps and suffering a sleepless night, it was a great relief to reach my maiden Test century. Headingley gave me a great reception

After reaching my century I played the best cricket of my innings before I was out for 136. Here I am hooking Phil Newport to the boundary

Geoff Marsh and I leave the field after making 301-0 on the first day of the fifth Test at Trent Bridge. It was the first time a wicket hadn't fallen on a full day's play in a Test in England

MERV HUGHES – 1993
FIRST TEST, OLD TRAFFORD

Goochie and I were made to dress up in these ridiculous costumes on the eve of the first Test

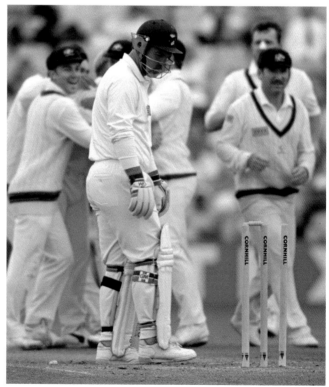

Poor Mike Gatting is in a state of shock after being bowled by the ball of the century from Warney. I would have loved to have been a fly on the wall as panic broke out in the England changing room

*I didn't say a word
to Graeme Hick after
getting him out for
the second time in the
match. I just screamed
in his face so he would
have me on his mind
the next time he came
out to bat*

*It's my turn to get
Gatting out with
an in-swinging ball
that surprised the
bejingers out of him
during England's
second innings*

JUSTIN LANGER – 2002/03
FOURTH TEST, MELBOURNE

Hitting a six to bring up my century and (right) raising my arms aloft to celebrate. It was simply the most exhilarating moment I have ever had on a cricket field

Tired, but happy, I have just realised my childhood dream by scoring 250 in the Boxing Day Test at the MCG

(From left) Me, Tugga and Gilly are smiling at the SCG because we have retained the Ashes with a 4–1 series victory. While we lost the fifth Test, it witnessed Steve Waugh's incredible century, one of the great moments in Australian sporting history

GLENN McGRATH – 2005
FIRST TEST, LORD'S

Marcus Trescothick trudges back to the pavilion as I celebrate my 500th Test wicket with my team-mates and (right) raise the ball to the crowd to mark the achievement. I was both proud and relieved

To have my family with me at Lord's really made this the perfect Test. Here I carry my daughter Holly as my son James proudly wears my Man of the Match medal around his neck

Warney holds a nick from Simon Jones off my bowling to give us victory in the first Test of what would prove to be an epic summer

ASHLEY GILES – 2005
FIFTH TEST, THE OVAL

On the final day at The Oval, I celebrate reaching my fifty with Matthew Hoggard. That told the real story of Ashley Giles and, whatever the doubters had said earlier in the series, they couldn't take that away from me

It doesn't get any better than this! We leap around at The Oval having regained the Ashes after 16 long years. The bond between the players who won this series will remain forever. (Right) I enjoy a beer and a smooch with the urn back in the dressing room

MIKE HUSSEY – 2006/07
SECOND TEST, ADELAIDE

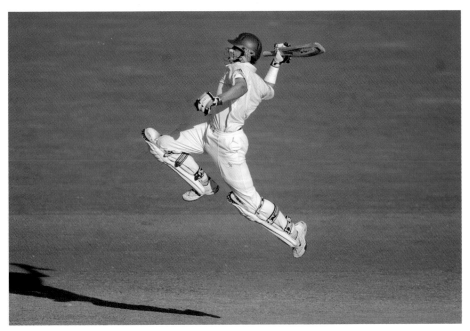

*When I hit those winning runs at Adelaide I was consumed with this incredible sensation, a
surge of emotion...I let out a scream, ran down the wicket and jumped in to the air*

*Here I am celebrating with my captain Ricky Ponting after the Test. It felt like a miracle, a bit
of a dream. I looked around and thought, 'It will never get any better than this.'*

PAUL COLLINGWOOD –2010/11
FIFTH TEST, SYDNEY CRICKET GROUND

The England captain Andrew Strauss and I celebrate with the Ashes after winning at the SCG. It felt like the perfect end to the perfect tour

I could not have imagined a better way to bow out of Test cricket than sitting in the dressing room of the SCG holding the Ashes and a nice cold beer

But while we were batting, Zoehrer kept talking behind the stumps, so Philippe went up to him at the end of one over and said, 'Don't give me all that shit, I don't need it. If you've got a problem, we'll sort it out.'

Zoehrer didn't say a word but Philippe mentioned what happened to Frances, his wife, who was a writer, and she wrote a little poem poking fun at Zoehrer. We made sure this got into the Australian dressing room and, of course, the Aussies saw the funny side and ribbed Zoehrer, so we didn't hear a peep from him after that.

The England players didn't really sledge, but if someone was out and they didn't walk, we might say a few words. In Australia's second innings, Marsh punched me to silly mid-off but didn't walk, and the umpire gave him not out. It was unbelievable, he made clear contact with his glove as he played a forward defensive and we got stuck into him so much that he ran himself out three balls later. He then got a few more words on his way back to the pavilion.

Marsh's dismissal left Australia 153/4, still more than 50 runs short of avoiding an innings defeat. I then bowled Greg Matthews without addition to the score. He tried to pad up but the ball flicked the top of his front pad and deflected off his arm on to the stumps. Edmonds was taking wickets at the other end, including his mate Zoehrer, and when I bowled Craig McDermott with my arm ball, Australia were 189/9.

We held on to some stunning catches throughout the tour, especially during the fourth Test. I took a good one myself at third slip to get Border off Small and break a key partnership between the Australian captain and Marsh in the second innings. It was made more difficult because Botham was fielding two and a half yards in front of me at second slip and I wasn't sure if he was going to go for it.

We wrapped up the match by an innings and 14 runs when Gladstone caught Hughes in the deep on a slog-sweep off Edmonds's bowling. Elton John had been touring Australia and came into the dressing room to help us celebrate retaining the Ashes. He had this silk suit on, God knows how much it would have cost, maybe £5,000, but the champagne was going round and Gatt sprayed him with all this bubbly.

We had a great party back at the hotel that night. Elton John came along but wasn't too happy we were playing a lot of his songs, so he sent his driver back to the Hilton to get his music collection and Elton became the DJ for the evening.

George Michael came to another party we had on that tour, in an apartment just by Bondi Beach, in Sydney. I didn't have a clue who he was. He came in, put a bottle of red wine on the table, said hi and flitted around. I opened the bottle and drank some, unaware it was his, and he came over and said, 'Do you think I could have a glass of wine?' So I poured him one, not realising it was his bottle or who he was. They didn't tell me until afterwards!

The fifth Test at Sydney was a great game for me personally as I made runs and took wickets. We reduced them to 236/7 on day one, but Jones was still there at stumps and his 184 not out really turned the game around, taking Australia to 343 all out the next day. Infuriatingly, we believed we had him out twice. The first time was caught down the leg side, off the face of the bat, when he was on 11. The other was my lbw shout when he was in the 90s.

We were then bowled out for 275. There were some very soft dismissals, including when Botham chipped one up to midwicket off the off-spinner Peter Taylor, who was a virtual unknown. Everyone said the Australian selectors had called up the wrong Taylor, it was meant to be Mark Taylor. But Peter got the call and played a huge role in the match, taking 6-78 in our first innings.

I batted three and a half hours for 69, an important knock in the context of the game. Despite suffering a painful groin strain, I found batting easy as I worked the ball around and didn't feel any particular bowler was going to get me out. I played some good shots and some unorthodox ones, including slog-fall-over-sweeps against the spinners, which brought a bit of amusement from the Australians, and some sledging!

My 7-78 in Australia's second innings was probably my best ever bowling performance, although I felt I could actually have taken more wickets. I accounted for all their last seven batsmen. Jones, Wellham, Waugh, Sleep and Taylor were all caught, while I trapped Zoehrer leg before and bowled Hughes.

But Taylor had made 42 crucial runs, helping Australia set us a target of 320 in a little over a day. We were 233/6 when I joined Richards at the crease on the last afternoon and we were still determined to try and win the match. But when Jack and Phil Edmonds fell to consecutive Sleep deliveries with the score on 257, all I could do was try to survive.

I had backed myself to play out the overs for a draw, but with only seven balls remaining, Sleep bowled me with one that kept low. I was trying to work the ball for a single, to get to the other end and face the last over from Reid rather than leaving that job to Dilley, who had just come in.

I felt a huge sinking feeling when I got out and we lost because we were on top for much of the match. I had never been the last man out in a Test, to lose the game, and I didn't like it. It was as if my whole world had caved in.

Taylor was named man of the match for his eight wickets and useful second-innings runs, which took a lot away from me. Had we won the game, I might have got the award for my overall contribution of seven wickets and 91 runs.

Although I was disappointed with the outcome of the final Test, we had won the Ashes in fine style and had another big party back at the hotel. Elton John paid for all the food and drink, which was amazingly generous.

We got back to the hotel quite late after the match and one of the guys knocked over a fire hydrant in the underground car park without realising it. While we were partying upstairs, the bloody fire engine's sirens were going. We didn't know the fire hydrant was flooding the car park.

Our families met us at the airport when we returned to England, and one or two people cheered and said well done. I was involved in four series wins against Australia and there was never anything more than a pat on the back. MCC gave you a gift for every tour you went on, things like MCC cufflinks and cut glasses with your name and the tour inscribed on them, but there were no grand dinners or receptions.

I can't think of any time when I didn't enjoy the 1986/87 tour. The cricket was brilliant and we all just lived to play. Everyone made a contribution. Broad and Gower scored 487 and 404 runs respectively, but I also chipped in with 179 at an average of 35 from my position at number eight.

After the first Test, I don't think we dropped a catch and we took some real stunners. I was the highest wicket-taker in the series, and I only got 18, so the likes of Dilley, Small, DeFreitas, Botham and Edmonds put in good performances as well. As you grow up, Australia are the team you most want to be successful against and in that series we produced our very best cricket when the Ashes were at stake.

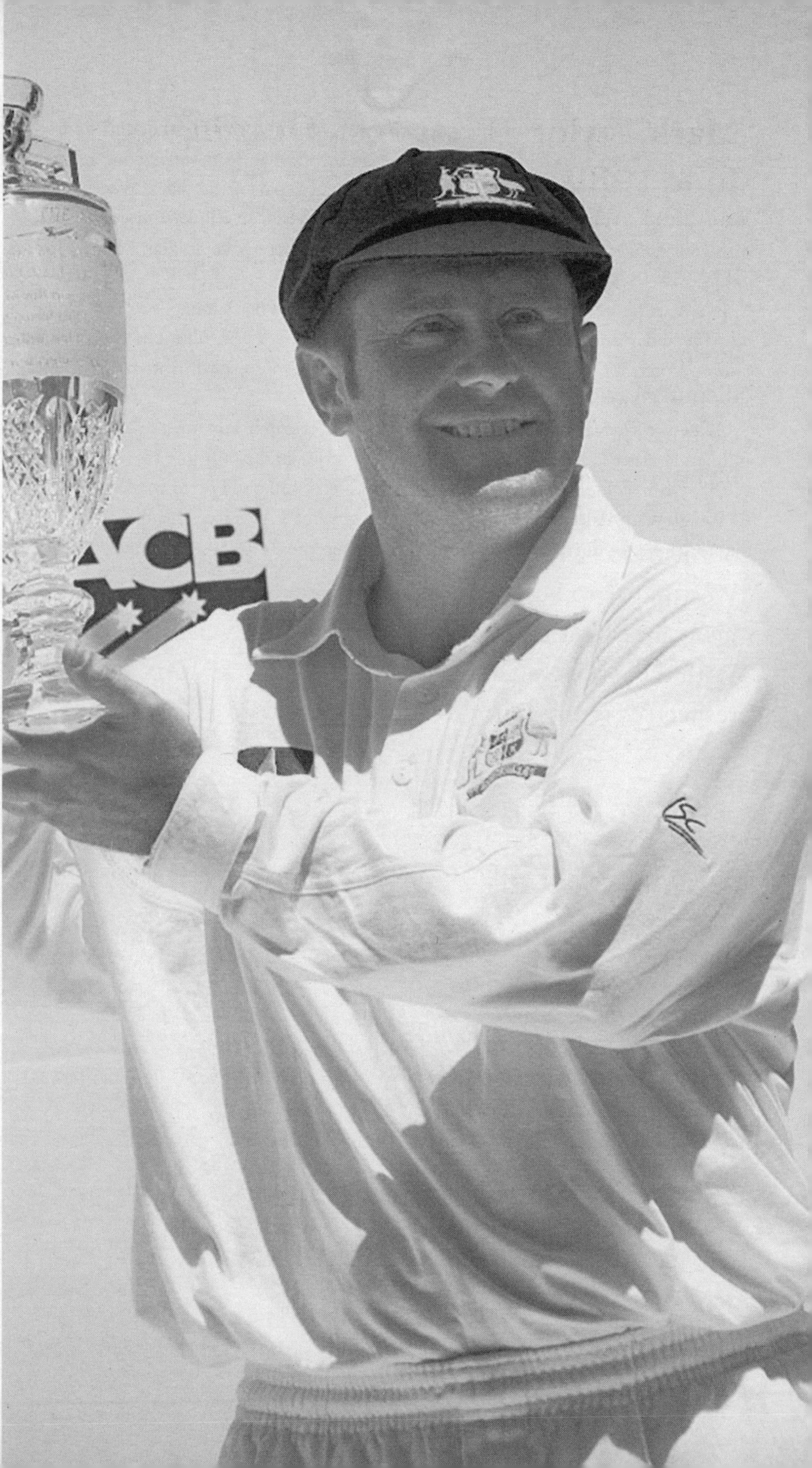
ACB

Mark Taylor – First Test, Headingley, 8-13 June 1989

'He's a limited player with limited shots … I don't think he's going to be a great player,' declared Geoffrey Boycott after Mark Taylor's Ashes debut at Headingley. A decade later no one could dispute Taylor's greatness as either an opening batsman or a captain. He scored 7,525 runs and equalled Sir Don Bradman's highest ever score for an Australian with 334 not out against Pakistan, and in 1994 succeeded Allan Border to become one of Australia's most popular captains. After quickly toppling the West Indies to become the best Test team in the world, he led his country with flair and invention for five successful years. With the Ashes safely retained in 1999 he retired to become a respected commentator for Channel Nine.

Left-handed batsman
Born: 27 October 1964, Leeton, New South Wales
Test debut: January 1989 v West Indies
Last Test: January 1999 v England
Test record: 104 matches, 7,525 runs at an average of 43.49

The state of play
On his Ashes debut Mark Taylor scored his maiden Test century to set Australia on their way to winning the series 4-0 and regaining the Ashes in England for the first time for 55 years.

Scoreboard
Australia first innings

G.R. Marsh	lbw	b DeFreitas	16
M.A. Taylor	lbw	b Foster	136
D.C. Boon	c Russell	b Foster	9
A.R. Border	c Foster	b DeFreitas	66
D.M. Jones	c Russell	b Newport	79
S.R. Waugh		not out	177
I.A. Healy		c & b Newport	16
M.G. Hughes	c Russell	b Foster	71
G.F. Lawson		not out	10
Extras	(lb 13, w 1, nb 7)		21
Total	(7 wickets dec, 178.3 overs)		601

Bowling	O	M	R	W
DeFreitas	45.3	8	140	2
Foster	46	14	109	3
Newport	39	5	153	2
Pringle	33	5	123	0
Gooch	9	1	31	0
Barnett	6	0	32	0

England first innings

G.A. Gooch	lbw	b Alderman	13
B.C. Broad		b Hughes	37
K.J. Barnett	lbw	b Alderman	80
A.J. Lamb	c Boon	b Alderman	125
D.I. Gower	c Healy	b Lawson	26
R.A. Smith	lbw	b Alderman	66
D.R. Pringle	lbw	b Campbell	6
P.J. Newport	c Boon	b Lawson	36
R.C. Russell	c Marsh	b Lawson	15
P.A.J. DeFreitas	lbw	b Alderman	1
N.A. Foster		not out	2
Extras	(b 5, lb 7, w 1, nb 10)		23
Total	(all out, 121.5 overs)		430

Bowling	O	M	R	W
Alderman	37	7	107	5
Lawson	34.5	6	105	3
Campbell	14	0	82	1
Hughes	28	7	92	1
Waugh	6	2	27	0
Border	2	1	5	0

Australia second innings

G.R. Marsh	c Russell	b Foster	6
M.A. Taylor	c Broad	b Pringle	60
D.C. Boon	lbw	b DeFreitas	43
A.R. Border		not out	60
D.M. Jones		not out	40
Extras	(b 2, lb 5, w 9, nb 5)		21
Total	(3 wickets dec, 54.5 overs)		230

Bowling	O	M	R	W
Foster	19	4	65	1
DeFreitas	18	2	76	1
Pringle	12.5	1	60	1
Newport	5	2	22	0

England second innings (target: 402 runs)

G.A. Gooch	lbw	b Hughes	68
B.C. Broad	lbw	b Alderman	7
K.J. Barnett	c Taylor	b Alderman	34
A.J. Lamb	c Boon	b Alderman	4
D.I. Gower	c Healy	b Lawson	34
R.A. Smith	c Border	b Lawson	0
D.R. Pringle	c Border	b Alderman	0
P.J. Newport	c Marsh	b Alderman	8
R.C. Russell	c Healy	b Hughes	2
P.A.J. DeFreitas		b Hughes	21
N.A. Foster		not out	1
Extras	(b 4, lb 3, nb 5)		12
Total	(all out, 55.2 overs)		191

Bowling	O	M	R	W
Alderman	20	7	44	5
Lawson	11	2	58	2
Campbell	10	0	42	0
Hughes	9.2	2	36	3
Border	5	3	4	0

Mark Taylor

I WAS THERE when Australia regained the Ashes in England for the first time since 1934. I had the best view in the house as David Boon played a rare sweep shot off Nick Cook to win the fourth Test at Old Trafford by six wickets and give us an unassailable 3-0 lead in the series. Not bad for a side branded the worst ever to tour England just three months earlier. I grabbed a couple of stumps and hugged Boonie before we raced from the field. I could see Allan Border and the rest of the team punching the air on the balcony.

A year earlier I had been playing for Greenmount in the Bolton League in Lancashire. I had thought it would be my last chance to spend a summer playing in England before I returned home and buckled down to a nine to five job as a surveyor. When else was I going to get the chance to play in England with someone else footing the bill?

I had sought refuge in this corner of northern England after a disappointing third season with New South Wales. To begin with it had gone well. I had enjoyed a wonderful first season, making my debut in October 1985, just two days before my 21st birthday, and had scored over 900 runs as we won the Sheffield Shield. My second season was not quite as good, but I still averaged just over 40.

But in my third season my form deserted me and I endured a hard time. I averaged below 20 for most of the campaign and had to wait until March for my first century. I was on the brink of being dropped and began to have doubts about whether I was good enough to be a professional cricketer. Maybe those first two seasons had simply been beginner's luck.

In my early years in state cricket I was also studying to be a surveyor at the University of New South Wales, so as my form got worse, I knew I had something to fall back on. I graduated from uni in January 1988 during my difficult third season, so at 23 I was beginning to think I would have a career in surveying rather than cricket. That was fine by me, I had enjoyed some good times in state cricket, but maybe it was time to move on.

In April 1988 I flew out to spend five months playing for Greenmount. I wanted to have some fun before starting work, and they gave me a £3,000 contract and paid my return airfare. I enjoyed my time as their club pro, making some good friends and rediscovering a bit of form. As their leading player I had to force the pace of games, often on some challenging uncovered pitches. We won the League and I scored six centuries, a club and league record. I felt like myself again.

On my return to Australia I knew I was at a crossroads. To become a registered surveyor I needed two years of practical experience and to sit some exams, but I felt I owed myself one final chance with cricket. If it didn't work I would have to accept I really wasn't good enough and concentrate on the surveying.

Five months later I was a Test player. After starting the 1988/89 season with a flurry of runs for NSW, most notably against the touring West Indies and Pakistan sides, in January 1989 I was called up for the last two Tests of the summer against the West Indies. I had scored 82 and 49 for NSW against them, but I quickly learned they had only been playing at a gentle half pace.

In the Test arena they went for the jugular. By the fourth Test in Sydney they were 3-0 up and had already won the series. I was petrified about facing their bowling attack of Curtly Ambrose, Malcolm Marshall and Courtney Walsh, who were a lot scarier than in the tour game. This was the real deal, and it got brutal at times. I made just 25 and 3 in Sydney, and 3 and 36 in the fifth Test at Adelaide.

It wasn't the most impressive start in Test cricket, but I returned to NSW feeling great and scored three centuries to finish top of the first-class runs table with a total of 1,241. I thought this had to be enough to get me on the plane for the Ashes tour later in the year. On the morning the squad was announced I was driving through Sydney's Eastern Suburbs and pulled over to listen to the radio. At 11 o'clock my heart jumped as I heard my name read out. To be part of an Ashes tour is the ultimate ambition of every Australian cricketer, and now after just two Tests I was going on one.

On the flight to London the legend of David Boon drinking 52 cans of beer was born. He isn't a nervous flyer, he just likes his beer. The rest of the team acted as pacers, we would take turns to sit next to him and have a couple of beers and a chat, then make up some excuse and someone else would jump in and take over. There is no way I could have sat through the whole session!

Arriving at Heathrow, he managed to stagger off the plane with some help from Geoff Marsh. He then got through customs and the press conference OK, and even training the next day as well. But two days later he said the booze and the jet-lag really hit him and he felt dreadful. I don't think he's ever tried it since.

Our coach Bobby Simpson was far from happy. Just before leaving he had given us a big talk about how becoming a more professional side would help us regain the Ashes, and then Boonie steps off the plane completely smashed. Simmo didn't really see the joke. Boonie's behaviour would be even more frowned upon these days, so he doesn't need to worry about anyone beating his record. I reckon it will stand forever.

As soon as we arrived in England the English press dismissed us as the worst Australian side to ever tour the country. Tony Greig called us 'Border's Pussycats' while Jeff Thomson said, 'I wouldn't give a XXXX for Australia's chance of regaining the Ashes.' This was clearly rubbish, but it was true we were a developing side. Looking down a list of the names in our squad England wouldn't have been too worried.

For a start, my own Test record didn't reflect what I could do, and the bookies in England clearly thought I wasn't up to much, having me on longer odds than Merv Hughes or Tom Moody to score the most runs in the series. Simmo picked me on a bit of a whim; he could see the merits in having a left-hander who could field a bit, but the truth is I was a bit of a punt. It was the same with Steve Waugh, who averaged only 30 and had yet to make a century in 26 Tests, but they stuck with him because they recognised his potential. Ian Healy was another guy the English wouldn't have known much about, he had only played about eight Tests at that point. The three of us played over 100 Tests each, so we can't have been too bad.

The English press were especially unimpressed by our bowling attack. Their attitude was, 'Who on earth is going to take your wickets?' Our guys, Terry Alderman, Geoff Lawson, Merv Hughes, Trevor Hohns and Greg Campbell, were considered not good enough or over the hill. It is true our bowling in the build-up to the series had been sound rather than brilliant, but our fielding was improving. Simmo started an era that lasted until the late 1990s when we were a brilliant fielding side. We clung on to just about everything.

England had won the last two Ashes series and were favourites to make it three in a row. Their batting line-up included guys like David Gower, Allan Lamb, Graham Gooch and Chris Broad, who had always made runs against Australia. It was going to be tough to get these guys out. On the other hand, I wasn't too concerned by their bowling attack, who looked solid rather than deadly, especially after just facing the West Indies.

I thought those bookies might be right about me after all as I suffered a slow start to the tour; a mere 23 was the highest score of my first eight innings. I remember sharing a beer with Ian Healy in a London pub and telling him, 'I don't think I'm good enough to make runs at this level.' I was too slow and my feet just wouldn't move the way I wanted them to.

Finally, I found some form against Somerset, hitting the ball really well and scoring 97 and 58. Maybe I could do something on this tour. I had a few concerns they might open with Boonie and Swampy [Geoff Marsh], but my name was read out as part of the 12 before training on the eve of the first Test at Headingley.

The Yorkshire ground held some bad memories for the older guys in our team; AB [Allan Border], Henry Lawson [Geoff Lawson] and Terry Alderman. They all still carried the scars of Australia's dramatic loss to England there in 1981. On the first morning David Gower won the toss and put us in, but rain wiped out the first hour of play. It was still overcast when we started, so I expected the ball to swing all over the place. A total of 150 might prove useful in these conditions.

I always liked being sent in to bat, believing it immediately put pressure on the bowling side. And so I felt pretty good heading out for my maiden Ashes innings. At first it looked to be a bowler's day, so I just wanted to hang in there. That is how I played it until AB joined me at 57/2. Our captain wasted no time in getting at England as he made a quick 66.

This pushed me into action. I started to look for the ball more and soon reached my first half-century in Test cricket. I enjoyed the moment, but the truth was, I was still just tagging along with AB. He had moved us on to 174/3 when he was out. With the stage to myself, I took up where he had left off and began playing a lot more shots.

England had made a mistake picking four identical bowlers in Phillip DeFreitas, Neil Foster, Derek Pringle and Phil Newport. None of them were particularly quick, but because they could all swing the ball they assumed they would easily take wickets. But because they bowled at the same pace once you got in you were well set and didn't have many problems. Foster was probably the best of the bunch, while Newport, who had taken wickets against us for Worcestershire, actually looked nervous.

As we approached the close of play, I was on 89, when I got a ball that bounced up the hill wide of off stump and I pushed it in to the hands of Gower at gully. Fortunately he dropped it. As the overs got fewer, I was in no rush to reach my century. Of course, I didn't want to be stranded in the 90s overnight, but more importantly, I didn't want to get out forcing the issue. I couldn't throw it away now. Get to stumps and forget about the century.

At the close of play I was 96 not out and we were 207/3. Afterwards I was whisked off to speak to the press. I had never had that sort of attention. No one in England had wanted to talk to me before, they assumed I wouldn't play, and if I did, I wouldn't make runs. They had only wanted to speak to AB, or the team larrikins Merv Hughes and Dean Jones.

Despite the interest, I hadn't actually got that century yet. That night I went out for dinner with my parents, who had come over for the Test. It was a bit of a disaster. They seemed to make me more nervous, asking me a thousand questions about why I hadn't made four more runs. My Dad even ordered a bottle of champagne, but I didn't want that, I still had to score those runs to earn it. By the time I got up from the table I was a nervous wreck!

Afterwards I couldn't get to sleep. I was wide awake at 2am, tossing and turning, waiting for 8am to come around so I could get on with the day. It was a relief to finally walk through the gate on the second morning. Early on I got a full toss from DeFreitas, which broke my bat and the ball trickled to cover. I had to change my bat and all of a sudden the ball was getting harder to hit and I couldn't see any gaps.

At 11.20am Pringle bowled to me about leg stump and I glanced the ball down to the boundary. I thought I was only going to get a single, so I started running, but halfway down the wicket, Dean Jones shouted, 'Tubs, you've got it.' It had gone for four and I had scored my maiden Test century on my Ashes debut. I was so happy, I didn't know what to do, but I took my helmet off and raised my bat. I felt a bit sheepish about it, but got a great reception from the English crowd.

Once I had my hundred I began play with abandon. For the next 50 minutes, I played my best cricket of the whole innings until Foster got me out lbw for 136. It was a terrible shot to get out to, but for that moment I had got carried away and thought I was good enough to hit anything.

Next in was Steve Waugh, who was determined to out-do me. We had been locked in a friendly battle to score more runs than the other ever since we first played for NSW. A few years earlier after I had got 118, my first ever first-class century, against South Australia at the SCG, Steve went in and wouldn't let the captain declare until he had made exactly 119 not out. So when we passed each other on the field at Headingley, I said to Steve, 'Getting a century is easy, mate.' I had got one after three Tests, while he had been waiting three and a half years. For the rest of the day I watched Steve finally get there as he made his way to 177 not out. When he reached 137 he looked up to the dressing room, gave me a little wave and shouted, 'Gotcha.'

We turned the screw by batting in to Saturday morning before finally declaring on 601/7. England fought back with 420, but we were always in control and again they couldn't bowl us out as we declared our second innings on 230/3. I contributed 60 playing a lot better than I had for my century. AB wanted us to force the issue, so we could set England a target far beyond their reach, so I was a lot more expansive, really going for it with lots of boundaries.

On the fifth morning we set them an impossible 402 to win and hoped we could get ten wickets in the space of 83 overs. Goochie put up a fight with 68, but once he was out the rest collapsed and were all out for 191. We had won by 210 runs. Our bowling wasn't unplayable, but it was consistent and in the right spot.

Alderman took another five wickets to add to his five in the first innings, and would take more than 40 wickets on this tour to match his achievements of 1981. In this series he was a very different bowler to the quick of eight years earlier and now was bowling nothing above medium pace. He just bowled straight, wicket to wicket, stump to stump, and kept the pressure on.

The Australian beer XXXX was our tour sponsor, so plenty of that got drunk and sprayed around the changing room. England knew they were in a tough series now. All that talk about us being the worst team ever was shown to be nonsense.

The England guys didn't join us for a beer after the Headingley Test. AB didn't encourage much socialising between the sides. He wanted to make the point that we were here to win Test matches rather than make friends. AB had been stung by the criticism that he was too close to Ian Botham and David Gower in 1985 when he had captained Australia to a 3-1 defeat. Any suggestion he wasn't a tough competitor hurt, so he wanted to let blokes know he wasn't going to be Mr Nice Guy any more. That didn't mean there was any ill feeling between the sides, we had a few drinks on the night before rest days, but it certainly wasn't as jovial as the 2005 series. The second Test at Lord's was another beauty. I was just excited to be there, walking around like a sightseer. Australia always play well here because there's the feeling you may never get the chance again, so you make the most of it. We did just that, scoring 528 in reply to England's 286. I made a good 62, but I was overshadowed by Steve Waugh who got 152 not out, and even Henry Lawson swung the bat to make 74.

England made some good runs with 359, but it still meant we only needed 118 to take a 2-0 lead. We got there with the loss of four wickets. I was one of them, out for 27, caught by Goochie off the bowling of Foster. It went low to his left, and I wasn't completely convinced he had caught it. These days players would stand there, but back then the feeling was if a guy said he caught it you walked off. That was the way I was taught to play.

After we had sunk a few beers and Boonie had conducted our team song, 'Under the Southern Cross', we had a more few in the pub next to Lord's before stumbling in to Langan's, which was then the best restaurant in London. We were noisy and treated the other diners to another rendition of our team song. I don't know how we weren't kicked out.

Rain ruined the third Test at Edgbaston. We eventually finished our first innings on the Saturday morning with 424 before bowling England out for 242. We ran out of time on 156/2 in our second innings, knowing we would have won without the poor weather.

England had brought Ian Botham back for the third Test, but he was nowhere near the player he was in 1981. He was probably bowling about three yards slower. None the less, AB was always worried Both would suddenly rediscover his form and rise up to lead England to another unlikely victory. It never happened and in three Tests he scored just 62 runs and took three wickets.

There was added pressure before the fourth Test at Old Trafford, knowing a win here would regain the Ashes. We were 2-0 up, but AB was desperate to kill them off. He wanted a win, as even a draw gave them a chance of drawing the series 2-2. Henry Lawson bowled brilliantly to take six wickets and blast out England for 260. In our reply I made 85 before being stumped by Jack Russell off the bowling off Emburey. I was furious not to get a hundred. I had a great summer, but I often think of the missed opportunities here and at The Oval when I made 71. When I was playing at my absolute best I never made the really big scores.

On the fourth morning news filtered through that several England players would be taking part in a new rebel tour to South Africa. If morale was low in the England changing room this took it through the floor. David Gower knew the game was up now.

Russell and Emburey showed some belated fighting spirit with a seventh-wicket partnership of 142 in England's second innings over the course of the final two days. There were a few worries they might pull off a miracle and get away with a draw, but we eventually got them all out for 264.

We needed just 78 to regain the Ashes, and I was there on 37 not out when Boonie hit the winning runs. The Ashes were ours again. It was pandemonium back in the changing room. The party had already started by the time we got back. Merv Hughes had a terrible habit of spraying bottles of champagne over the balcony, so our tour manager Lawrie Sawle had to rescue several. I kept telling Merv if he wanted to spray something, use the XXXX. AB was presented with the urn, but we weren't allowed to throw it around the changing room. I don't think I even got to touch it.

We had a county game in Nottingham the next day, so we had to quickly hop on a bus, but we carried on the party with a few beers on the motorway. As soon as we reached the hotel, it was a case of 'right, up to rooms and see you in 15 minutes'. We grabbed our keys, chucked our gear in our rooms and headed out for the night. Out until the early hours, it all got a bit messy. A couple of blokes somehow got anti-vandal paint all over their hands, while Tom Moody went over on his ankle.

We were desperate to sleep off our hangovers, but we had to be up early for the game against Notts at Trent Bridge. AB ducked out to leave Swampy in charge of a bunch of guys who felt absolutely awful. During the match we slept in the changing room when we could, but as bad as we felt we actually won that game. I honestly have no idea how we did it.

A week later we returned to Nottingham for the fifth Test. I was delighted when AB won the toss and gave us the chance to bat on a flat pitch that looked full of runs. On just three I nicked a ball from Angus Fraser between first and second slip. After surviving that Swampy and I indulged in a bit of a run riot. This was Devon Malcolm's debut, and though he would develop into a fine bowler, he was still raw here. I played a lot of shots off him, which really got my footwork going and probably damaged his confidence. He got worried about bowling too short and couldn't get his length right at all.

Together Swampy and I got to 100, then 200, and the first inkling we had that this was a historic day was when we got past 201. The ground announcer told Trent Bridge we had just set a new record for an Australian opening partnership in an Ashes series, overtaking Bobby Simpson and Bill Lawry at Old Trafford in 1961. We gave Simmo a little wave after snatching his record.

'Let's see if we can do something special and get to stumps,' I told Swampy halfway through the last session. We knew we had a good chance as England were absolutely shot. Already 3-0 down and with an exodus of players headed for South Africa, they were a mess. Most of these guys had never experienced the frustration of going through a day without taking a wicket, and we just made it worse by keeping going.

I cramped up a bit in the last over, but we got through it and finished on 301/0 for the day. It was the first time a wicket hadn't fallen on a full day's play in a Test in England. I was on 141, and Swampy was on 125. That night the two of us went out for an Indian meal with our wives. It was a magnificent feeling as we reflected on the day. Simmo and Lawrie Sawle had thrown us together as an opening partnership earlier in the year because they wanted a left- and right-handed combination. We had done OK, but this really showed what we could do in tandem.

The next morning we wanted to do it all over again, but it ended in the first session when Swampy was out for 138. We had put on an opening stand of 329, the highest ever in England and the fifth-highest in the history of the game. I was joined by Boonie, who had spent the whole of the previous day with his pads on, and alongside him I made my way to a double century. I started tightening up again around 180, thinking about milestones rather than the ball and twice nearly got out, but I survived to bring up my 200 by cutting Eddie Hemmings for four.

At lunch on the second day, when we were 370/1, the two teams had lunch together. I will never forget David Gower ordering a bottle of champagne. We all looked at him a bit puzzled. 'I'm celebrating our wicket,' he explained as he poured himself a glass.

My innings came to an end when I charged down the wicket to Cook, only to miss the ball and be stumped by Russell. After spending nearly ten hours at the crease and facing 461 balls, I was out for 219. 'Well done, but you're a bloody idiot,' was the first thing AB said to me. 'Mate, you might never have a better chance of making a triple century.'

We declared on 602/6 on the third day before twice bowling England out, for 255 and 167, to win by an innings and 180 runs. We were 4-0 up with just one to play. With the Ashes already safe, AB didn't mind the England players having a beer with us now. I remember David Gower saying, 'You have absolutely stuffed us, no question about it.'

So we arrived at The Oval for the final Test. Four months earlier I was just hoping to get a game and do OK, but by this stage I was seeing the ball as big as a watermelon and greedily thinking about getting more hundreds. So I was annoyed only to get 71 in the first innings and 48 in the second on the best wicket of the series.

We wanted to finish on a high and go home with a 5-0 win, but once again it was the weather, and not England, that stopped us. After scoring 466, fuelled by a Dean Jones century, we bowled England out for 285. We made a quick 219/4 declared to set England a target of 403, and they were looking uncomfortable at 143/5, but rain had spoiled the game and we ran out of time.

After some tense months we were looking forward to enjoying ourselves. We had a big dinner at the Grosvenor House Hotel on Park Lane with our wives and girlfriends, all getting dressed up and arriving in old Jags. Back home there was a ticker-tape parade through the streets of Sydney from Circular Quay to Darling Harbour. I never expected that for mere sportsmen, but the streets were packed with people. I couldn't believe so many people turned out for us winning a Test series. We were also given the keys to the city. I own this big key now, I'm not really sure what you are supposed to do with it. That Ashes series changed my life. I arrived in England as an anonymous guy who had played two matches and left four and a half months later as an established Test player. I made 839 runs at an average of 83.90, and I reckon I should have got more. It placed me second behind Sir Don Bradman's record of 930 runs on an Ashes tour in 1930. It was an honour and rather strange to be mentioned in the same breath as The Don.

I was lucky enough to play for Australia for the next decade, but no tour came close to matching that first one. On future tours we had to be careful not to keep going on about how great it was back in 1989. I returned for the Ashes in 1993, but we were expected to win that, and in 1997 I was the captain when we won again, but I was under pressure and it was hard work.

The 1989 tour was part of a golden age before cricket changed; it was spread over nearly four months with six Tests including rest days, and imagine this, only three one-day games. There was time to stop and smell the roses and have a game of golf. We played about 20 rounds in 1989 in the light English summer evenings, whereas Ricky Ponting told me his guys were lucky to get two in during the 2005 tour.

These days tour schedules are a lot tighter; there are no rest days, fewer county games and more one-day internationals. The cricket world has got a lot smaller, and they just fly in, play as many games as possible and get on to the next place as soon as possible. In my day the money wasn't as good, but I reckon the experience was better. I do feel sorry that today's guys will never know a tour like 1989.

In my study at home I have three prints on the wall from that tour, the 'Wizards of the Willows' with all the batsmen, 'The Destroyers' with all the bowlers, and 'The Tacticians' with AB, Simmo and our support staff. I just have to glance at them and the memories of that unique summer come flooding back.

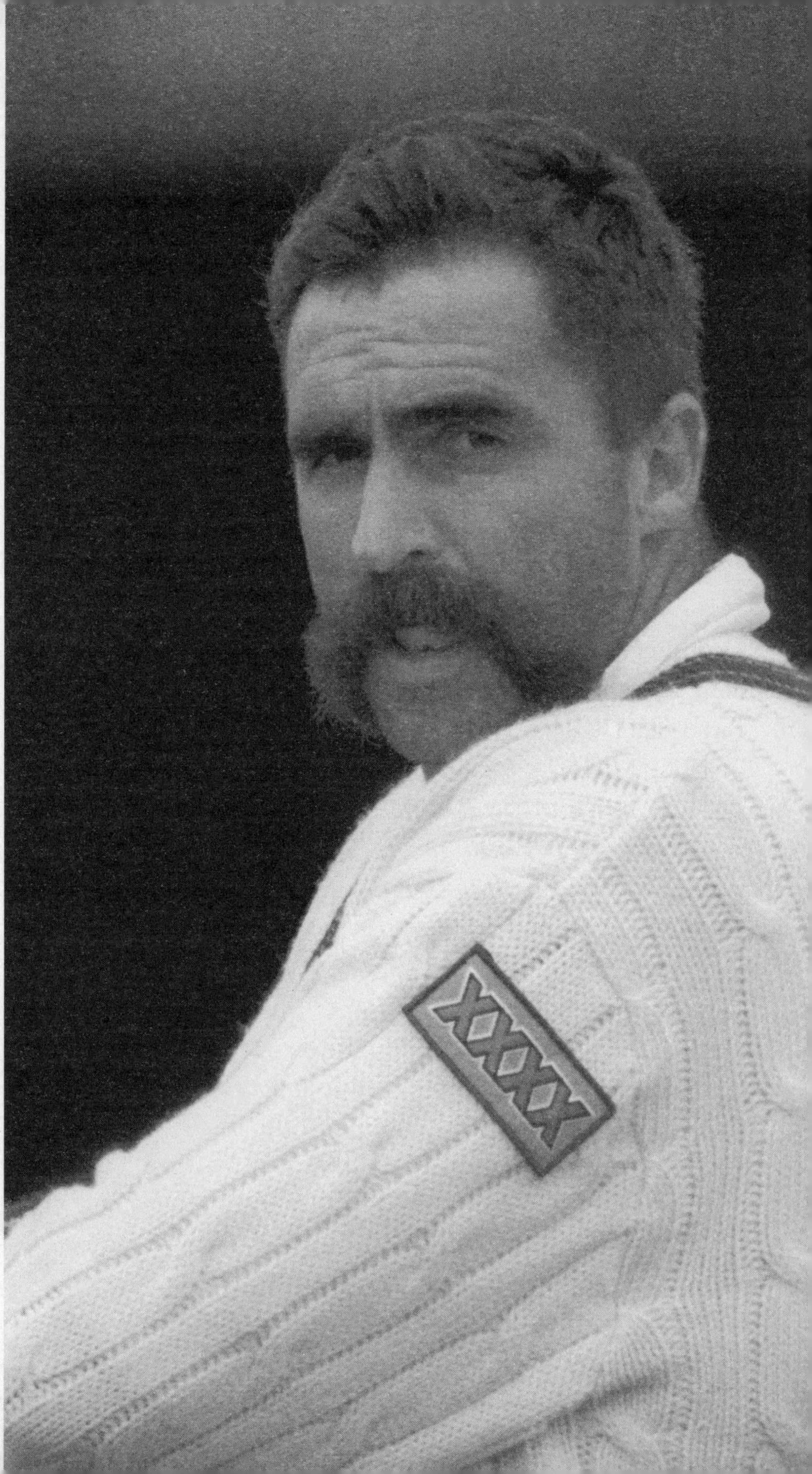

MERV HUGHES

Merv Hughes – First Test, Old Trafford, 3-7 June 1993

Beyond his famous bushy moustache and a reputation as a bit of a larrikin was a brilliant fast bowler, who is one of only 11 Australians to take more than 200 Test wickets. A cult hero for his sense of humour and obvious passion for the game, Hughes played a major role in reviving Australian cricket in the late 1980s and early 1990s. His finest moment came on the 1993 tour to England where despite battling with a serious knee injury he took 31 wickets to help Australia retain the Ashes.

Right-arm fast bowler
Born: 23 November 1961, Euroa, Victoria
Test debut: December 1985 v India
Last Test: March 1994 v South Africa
Test record: 53 matches, 212 wickets at an average of 28.38; 1,032 runs at an average of 16.64

The state of play
In a match that included *that* ball from Shane Warne to dismiss Mike Gatting, Australia kicked off the Ashes series with a comprehensive victory by 179 runs with Merv Hughes contributing eight wickets. Australia would go on to win the series 4-1.

Scoreboard

Australia first innings

M.A. Taylor		c & b Such	124
M.J. Slater	c Stewart	b DeFreitas	58
D.C. Boon	c Lewis	b Such	21
M.E. Waugh		c & b Tufnell	6
A.R. Border	st Stewart	b Such	17
S.R. Waugh		b Such	3
I.A. Healy	c Such	b Tufnell	12
B.P. Julian	c Gatting	b Such	0
M.G. Hughes	c DeFreitas	b Such	2
S.K. Warne		not out	15
C.J. McDermott		run out	8
Extras	(b 8, lb 8, nb 7)		23
Total	(all out, 112.3 overs)		289

Bowling	O	M	R	W
A.R. Caddick	15	4	38	0
P.A.J. DeFreitas	23	8	46	1
C.C. Lewis	13	2	44	0
P.M. Such	33.3	9	67	6
P.C.R. Tufnell	28	5	78	2

England first innings

G.A. Gooch	c Julian	b Warne	65
M.A. Atherton	c Healy	b Hughes	19
M.W. Gatting		b Warne	4
R.A. Smith	c Taylor	b Warne	4
G.A. Hick	c Border	b Hughes	34
A.J. Stewart		b Julian	27
C.C. Lewis	c Boon	b Hughes	9
P.A.J. DeFreitas	lbw	b Julian	5
A.R. Caddick	c Healy	b Warne	7
P.M. Such		not out	14
P.C.R. Tufnell	c Healy	b Hughes	1
Extras	(b 6, lb 10, nb 5)		21
Total	(all out, 74.5 overs)		210

Bowling	O	M	R	W
C.J. McDermott	18	2	50	0
M.G. Hughes	20.5	5	59	4
B.P. Julian	11	2	30	2
S.K. Warne	24	10	51	4
A.R. Border	1	0	4	0

Australia second innings

M.A. Taylor	lbw	b Such	9
M.J. Slater	c Caddick	b Such	27
D.C. Boon	c Gatting	b DeFreitas	93
M.E. Waugh		b Tufnell	64
A.R. Border		c & b Caddick	31
S.R. Waugh		not out	78
I.A. Healy		not out	102
Extras	(b 6, lb 14, w 8)		28
Total	(5 wickets dec, 130 overs)		432

Bowling	O	M	R	W
A.R. Caddick	20	3	79	1
P.A.J. DeFreitas	24	1	80	1
C.C. Lewis	9	0	43	0
P.M. Such	31	6	78	2
P.C.R. Tufnell	37	4	112	1
G.A. Hick	9	1	20	0

England second innings (target: 512 runs)

G.A. Gooch		handled the ball	133
M.A. Atherton	c Taylor	b Warne	25
M.W. Gatting		b Hughes	23
R.A. Smith		b Warne	18
G.A. Hick	c Healy	b Hughes	22
A.J. Stewart	c Healy	b Warne	11
C.C. Lewis	c Taylor	b Warne	43
P.A.J. DeFreitas	lbw	b Julian	7
A.R. Caddick	c Warne	b Hughes	25
P.M. Such	c Border	b Hughes	9
P.C.R. Tufnell		not out	0
Extras	(lb 11, w 1, nb 4)		16
Total	(all out, 120.2 overs)		332

Bowling	O	M	R	W
C.J. McDermott	30	9	76	0
M.G. Hughes	27.2	4	92	4
B.P. Julian	14	1	67	1
S.K. Warne	49	26	86	4

Merv Hughes

IT WAS THE first time I had got in trouble with my wife for NOT going out. Earlier that day we had retained the Ashes with a big victory over England in the fourth Test at Headingley. We had celebrated in the changing room, and back at the hotel, and then the plan was to meet our wives and girlfriends at a nightclub in Leeds. But I never made it. The rest of the team headed out to continue the party, while I retired to my bed. I had been bowling for three solid days; my right knee, which caused me problems throughout the tour, was in real pain and my whole body was aching. I was happy, but exhausted, and by midnight I was fast asleep.

Headingley was the 49th Test of my career, which was pretty good because eight years earlier I thought I would only play once for Australia. In December 1985 I played in my first, and I assumed last, Test against India at the Adelaide Oval. After being out for a duck after only five balls in our first innings, I then finished with match figures of 1-123 from 38 overs. It had been a big step up for me, clearly too big. The Indians made 520, with Sunil Gavaskar finishing on 166 not out, and I could do nothing to stop them. I was dropped for the rest of the series and overlooked for the tours to New Zealand and India. I thought my international career was over.

But 11 months later, after a good start to the domestic season with Victoria, the selectors decided to give me another chance against England in the first Test at Brisbane. The Poms were favourites to retain the Ashes with an experienced team, while we were still rebuilding after the departure of several players on a rebel tour to South Africa. By the time England had reached 198/4 in their first innings at the Gabba, I had trebled my total of Test wickets by claiming Mike Gatting and Allan Lamb and was feeling pretty good about myself. Then Ian Botham arrived at the crease.

The England all-rounder gave me a terrible mauling, hitting me everywhere. I had no answers. If I pitched it up he just hit through the ball, if I bowled short he would hook or pull it. My inexperience was being ruthlessly exposed. A couple of his sixes went a long, long way. 'Merv, these are going so far they might get frequent flyer points,' laughed Dean Jones as he went to fetch them.

It got ugly when Botham made 22 runs from a single over, scoring 2, 2, 4, 6, 4 and 4 off me. I am embarrassed to say it was a record for the most runs off an over in an Ashes Test. I would later check the record books, desperately hoping some poor soul had been worse than me, and while I found there was once 24 scored off an over, it was from an eight-ball over. I was stuck with the record for a six-ball over.

Steve Waugh finally brought Botham's run spree to an end after he had reached 138. At tea on the second day I was sitting outside our changing room watching the rain come down and trying to understand what had just happened when Botham came out of England's room and sat next to me. 'You probably don't remember me,' I said to him. 'But I was at a coaching clinic you did at Benalla when you played grade cricket here back in the 1970s.' He remembered the clinic, but not me.

'Did I give you any good advice?' he asked. 'Well, I told you I wanted to be a fast bowler, but you said I should take up tennis or golf because they were more enjoyable and you could make better money.' He got up to leave, turned to me and said, 'You should have listened to me.'

I would think about those words during the next six years as I cemented my place in the Test side. I took 8-87 against the West Indies at Perth a year after being humbled in Brisbane, and then regained the Ashes in 1989 against an England side containing Botham. I like to think I proved him and a lot of the doubters wrong. I was good enough to play for Australia.

By the end of 1992, after over 40 Tests and 170 wickets, I was beginning to feel a bit worn out. I was only 31, but I felt older as I struggled with both my weight and fitness. We were facing the West Indies that summer and I remember the great Courtney Walsh saying I looked as though I might be over the hill. He could see the pain on my face during each day's play. My right knee was constantly aching and my injuries weren't healing as quickly as before.

I got through against the West Indies OK, but I still had a tour to New Zealand to navigate before having surgery. Our physio Errol Alcott said I couldn't do any more damage; it was just a case of dealing with the pain. However, my weight was putting my knee under even greater strain, so Errol and our team manager Ian McDonald brought a pair of scales over to New Zealand to monitor it. I refused to get on. They told me I had to; it was in my contract and for every kilo I was overweight I would be fined. I asked if I lost some would I get a rebate? They weren't amused and kept asking me to jump on, so I thought, 'Right, I'll do just that.' I took three steps and jumped on. The scales disintegrated and that was the end of them.

Again I gritted my teeth to get through three Tests and five one-day games against the Kiwis. On my return home I finally had an arthroscopy, which is minor keyhole surgery to clean up my knee. I hoped this would be enough to get me through the long Ashes tour of 1993. Already saddled with a sore knee, I was made to feel even more ancient with so many young guys, including Shane Warne, Michael Slater, Matthew Hayden, Damien Martyn and Brendon Julian, in the squad bound for England.

After arriving it wasn't long before my knee began to bother me, and I knew it was going to lurk around for the entire tour. In those early weeks I didn't train much, instead spending a lot of time getting treatment with Errol. However, this didn't stop me heading off to watch a rugby league final at Wembley with Wayne Holdsworth. Afterwards we had a few beers and made our way to a nightclub where, to my horror, my knee locked up on the dance floor. Then a few weeks later I was walking on to the field at Northampton and it happened again. It is frightening when you suddenly can't walk. The very next day we saw a specialist in London, who told me while I could carry on playing, my knee would only get worse on the tour.

At the start of June the Ashes began with the first Test at Old Trafford. England won the toss and decided to put us in. Our openers, Tubs [Mark Taylor], with 124, and Slats [Michael Slater], with 58, got us off to a great start, but the rest of the guys failed to match that and we were all out for 289.

Early in England's reply Michael Atherton nicked me through the slips. 'In four years you've got no fucking better,' I snarled. 'And I see in four years you haven't got any new lines, Mr Hughes,' he replied. Don't worry about Michael Atherton, he gave as good as he got. His sledging was always more subtle and intelligent than my basic stuff. It would often take me about three overs to understand what he meant. 'What's he fucking talking about?' I would think. But I won the first battle of the summer when I got him out for 19 to leave England on 71/1.

After this tour Atherton said it was obvious I didn't respect him because of the way I sledged him. He was dead wrong. If I didn't think Atherton could play, I wouldn't waste my breath on him. He was one of the toughest competitors I have ever faced. His performances against Australia in that series were sensational, he stood up to us and gave it a go. If you wanted someone to bat for your life, you would give him a call.

Towards the end of my opening spell, England were 80/1 when Allan Border decided to bring on Shane Warne at the other end. With his very first delivery, Warney produced an unbelievable ball, later called the ball of the century, to dismiss a shocked Mike Gatting. I was down at deep backward square leg and as Gatt trooped back I walked in and asked Ian Healy, 'What did that do?' 'It pitched off and hit off,' he said. I thought Gatt had payed for the spin and it had gone between bat and pad. I turned around and watched a replay on the big screen. Heals smirked, 'Well, OK, it might have pitched outside leg.' I couldn't believe what I had just seen.

This was only Warney's 12th Test, and he had done OK so far, but we had seen nothing like this. He had just got Gatting, hailed as a great player of spin bowling, with the most incredible ball. Poor Gatt had absolutely no idea what had happened. I would have loved to be a fly on the wall in the England changing room as panic broke out. They must have all thought if Warne can do that against our best player of spin, what is he going to do to the rest of us?

There hadn't been too many quality leg-spinners around for a while, and most of the ones on the scene would give you at least one or two bad balls in each over to hit, but Shane's accuracy baffled batsmen. He would build up pressure because he couldn't be hit with any ease. Anyway, Shane knows that spin bowlers are only as good as the pace bowlers at the other end.

I played in Warney's Test debut against India at the SCG in January 1992. He got 1-150, and I was delighted to meet someone who had worse bowling figures on their debut than me. I had known him since he had got in to the Victoria team with me, and I quickly realised he had a rare talent. I was fascinated to see how far he could go, but while I knew he was good, even in 1993 I don't think anyone realised what he was going to do in Test cricket: take over 700 wickets and become one of the game's true legends.

As a fellow Victorian, I took Warney under my wing on the tour to England. He wasn't one of those young guys who sticks with other youngsters, he was the life and soul of the party, and liked to mix with the old blokes too. He likes a good time, but when it comes to playing cricket he switches on and he is the best there is. A lot of people get caught up with off-the-field activities, but he is a supreme professional.

While I looked out for him, that didn't make him immune to the odd joke. During his second Test in January 1992 we were sharing a room in Adelaide. Around midnight we ordered some sandwiches and drinks from room service. After polishing them off, I told Warney to roll the service trolley down the corridor and leave it outside someone else's room, so none of the team management knew we had been stuffing ourselves. He got out of his bed naked, and as soon as he was out the door I locked it. You should have heard him pleading for me to open it. I think he had to get someone from reception to let him back in.

At Old Trafford, everyone talks about Warney's ball to Gatting, but I'll also never forget the one he got Graham Gooch with to leave England 123/4. Goochie had been working really hard to keep Warney at bay, but then he was bowled a high full toss that he hit straight to Brendon Julian at mid-on.

While I didn't have much joy sledging Atherton, I got right under the skin of another target, Graeme Hick. He really copped it. It wasn't his fault, he was just a victim of circumstance. When he played for Queensland in the 1990/91 season he was compared with Sir Donald Bradman because of the amount of hundreds he had already scored in county cricket back in England. That really riled Australians. How could this bloke who had never played a Test be spoken about as if he was as good as Bradman? Earlier in the tour he made 187 against us playing for Worcestershire, so that got our backs up even further. We were going to get him.

I would shout all sorts of crap at Hick to unsettle him. It was old-fashioned sledging, just simple verbal intimidation. If you can get the batsman more worried about what you are saying rather than the next ball then you are halfway to winning the battle. That happened with Hick, and I put him off his game. When he was finding his rhythm and feeling comfortable he made runs, but it was my job to stop that.

Sledging had always been a crucial part of my armoury. When I was running in to bowl I hated the batsman. If you were facing me then you were the person I hated most in the whole world. Summoning up that feeling helped me whether I was playing for Footscray or Australia. Sledging put me in control, and it got me inside the batsman's head.

In England's first innings Hick never looked at ease as I went at him. On 34, it all got to him and he cut a ball straight to Border at point. He was mine. I also picked up the wickets of Phil Tufnell and Chris Lewis to finish with figures of 4-59. England were all out for 210, still 71 runs behind.

We stretched our lead far beyond that with Ian Healy making a century as we declared on 432/5 in our second innings to set England a target of 512. They were never going to get close, so it was more a case of us having 127 overs to take ten wickets.

Warney took care of Atherton for 25, but Gatt and Goochie moved England on to 133 as we neared the end of the fourth day. I had been giving Gatt a fair bit of the short stuff, so with the very last ball of the day he was expecting more of the same when I produced a full in-swinging ball that hit his pads and went on to his stumps. It surprised the bejingers out of him and England were two down. That lifted all of us, at only one down it would still be tricky, but now we had a real chance.

On the final morning Warney got rid of Robin Smith, but Goochie was proving difficult to shift. The England captain had made 133 and guided England to 233 with the loss of three wickets. We were getting a bit tense, knowing he was the type of guy to stick around. I came in and got the ball to rear up at him, and as it was looping towards his stumps he knocked it away with his hand. As soon as Goochie had done it, he looked like a schoolboy who had just broken a window. He knew he had done something wrong. I didn't know who to appeal to, the umpire at square leg or at the non-striker's end? Either way, he was given out and I was pleased to see the back of him.

It was only later that I learned Gooch had been given out handled the ball. That wasn't right, it should have been my wicket. Shane Warne and I both finished the match with eight wickets, and they gave him the man of the match award. I was robbed! I should have had nine wickets and that award!

Only seven more runs had been added when I had Hick caught behind by Heals. It was obvious I had cast a spell on him. Just a bit of sledging and he immediately looked uncomfortable. After that wicket I went up really close and shouted right in his face. There is a famous picture of it, so people ask, 'What did you say?' But I didn't say a word, I just yelled at him, it was one big 'ahhhhhhhh'. I wanted that to be his lasting memory of me, so when he next came out to bat he would have me on his mind.

I grabbed the last two wickets of the game, Andy Caddick and Peter Such, to finish with 4-92, and we won by 179 runs to go 1-0 up. After sitting in the dressing room for a while, we went back to the Copthorne Hotel for a party with our family and close friends. Once that had ended a group of guys headed in to the Manchester night for some more fun, but I was too knackered to join them. In 1989 I would have been one of the first ones out to the pub, but now I was too shattered and just happy to get an early night.

I was relieved to get some more rest when we won the toss and decided to bat in the second Test at Lord's. It turned out to a long rest too as we accumulated 632/4 declared right in to the Saturday morning. It was great to see Tubs, Slats and Boonie [David Boon] make hundreds. When Mark Waugh was on 99, I was poised with my camera to get a picture of the scoreboard. It would have been the first time in Test history the first four in the order had scored centuries. I never got the picture, as Mark was bowled by Tufnell without adding to his score.

A lot of people didn't understand why we batted so long, but at tea on the Friday we were about to declare when we found Craig McDermott on the floor of the shower area. He was curled up in the foetal position, really crook in the guts. We didn't know whether it was food poisoning or something more serious. He was rushed to hospital where they discovered a twisted bowel. He was on his way home and out of the series.

It meant you had the strange sight of me opening the bowling with Mark Waugh. I pounded in for 51 overs over the course of more than two days. Believe me, it was hard work. In the first innings I gave Goochie a short ball that he top-edged with a hook that Tim May took at fine leg. I also got Graeme Hick again, and Alec Stewart, as England posted just 205. It had been a hell of an effort from all the bowlers.

Allan Border enforced the follow-on and we had to take a deep breath and go again. I bowled 31 overs in the second innings, but didn't get a wicket this time as the spinners shared them, though I did provide the throw for Atherton's run-out on 99. England were all out for 365 to lose by an innings and 62.

The extra workload wasn't helping my knee, but winning the Test helped numb the pain. The painkillers came in useful as well. I took two at the start of play, then two at lunch and two at tea. It helped me get through the day. At the end of each day's play I was also covered in ice, with bags of it strapped to my knees, shoulders, groin and back.

At the end of the tour I had surgery on my knee. It was then they found flakes of bone floating around the joint, which when they became caught would cause my knee to lock up. The reason I was in so much pain was bone had been rubbing against bone because I had worn through my cartilage. This had left a patch of dead bone the size of a 50-cent piece.

England brought in four new players at Trent Bridge for the third Test. I got both the new batsmen, Mark Lathwell and Graeme Thorpe, as I took 5-92 in their total of 321. Boonie made a century as we took a first-innings lead of 52, but England, looking a more determined bunch here, made 422/6 declared. Just before tea on the fourth day, after taking Atherton and Stewart during England's second innings, I felt my groin go. It wasn't a huge surprise, my workload was enormous. Set 371 to win, we were in trouble on the last day at tea on 115/6, but Steve Waugh and Brendon Julian held out in the last session to earn a draw.

There were doubts about whether I would be OK for the fourth Test at Headingley, but Errol and I put in the hours down in London, I even lost some weight, and was passed fit. I met up with the guys in Durham, but sat out the game to stay as fresh as possible.

It was during this game that Steve Waugh found my diet diary in the changing room and proceeded to read it out to the team. I had been employing my own personal dietician for the previous six months and she had asked me to write down everything I ate or drank. Steve found an entry from earlier in the tour when I had visited Planet Hollywood in London following our one-day series win.

On that night I had a bowl of nachos, a dozen chicken wings, a chicken burger, half a chicken burger that someone couldn't finish, a chocolate dessert, 15 pints of lager, a Beetlejuice cocktail and a Terminator cocktail. It took me almost a day to write it all down. OK, I admit that wasn't a healthy day, but I was now being a good boy.

Once again it was great to see us bat first for a long time because I really needed two more days in the shed. We racked up 653/4 declared, with Allan Border making 200, and Boonie and Steve Waugh scoring centuries. The rest had done me good as I took Lathwell, the first of my three wickets, in the first over of England's reply to put them under pressure. It was always going to be difficult for them after spending two days in the field, and they slumped to 200 all out.

As good as Shane Warne's ball was at Old Trafford there was a ball Paul Reiffel bowled to Nasser Hussain here that was its equal. It pitched on leg stump and hit off stump. Paul had taken Craig's place in the side and claimed five wickets in the first innings. He was a bit of an unsung hero on this tour, but none of his team-mates underestimated his efforts. Overall he took 19 wickets at an average of just 20.84.

For the second Test running we bowled for back-to-back innings. It was tough, but I had to keep pushing myself. It was all worth it when we got them all out for 305 to win by an innings and 148 runs. The Ashes had been retained.

When I got Andy Caddick during England's second innings at Headingley, he was the 200th Test wicket of my career. I was very proud to become the seventh member of a club that at that time contained Dennis Lillee, Richie Benaud, Graham McKenzie, Jeff Thomson, Ray Lindwall and Clarrie Grimmett.

If I had finished my career with 199 wickets I don't think I would have gained too much credibility, I would have just been a good bloke lucky enough to play for Australia. As soon as I had taken 200 wickets, people began to think, 'This bloke can really play.' It was a real badge of honour. At the time winning the Test meant more, but looking back I can now see what entering that club did for me.

Though disappointed to lose the Ashes again, the English crowd at Headingley had given us a good reception. Throughout the series, the Pommie fans had got stuck in to me, but fair enough, they had paid their money to come in, and it is not as though the English blokes get offered an armchair in Australia. But, you know what, there is a great affection to the rivalry between the two countries. In pubs, the English fans are great, they want to have a beer and a chat, whereas in somewhere like South Africa they carry on giving you abuse.

I got called 'Sumo' in England because of my bulk, but I loved that. A friend of mine printed up some t-shirts with it written across the chest and flogged them. If you can't take the piss out of yourself, there is something wrong. Early on, Craig McDermott copped a bit of flak too, but it inspired one of the funniest moments of the tour.

In the one-day game at Old Trafford Craig mis-fielded the ball down at fine leg and the crowd got on his back, every time he went near the fence they would shout 'ee-aw, ee-aw' like a donkey. Tim May asked him what that was all about and Craig said he thought it was because he had big ears. No one had realised it before, but we all looked around, and thought, 'Shit, he has got massive ears!'

A few weeks later, between the first and second Tests, we were playing Gloucester at Bristol. Steve Waugh and Tim May had been to a local fun shop and bought ten pairs of these enormous plastic ears. At one stage when Craig was bowling in the game he walked back to his mark and turned around to be faced with all his team-mates wearing these ears beneath our baggy green caps. Craig, the umpires, the batsmen, and all of us fell about laughing for several minutes.

The Ashes might have been safe, but I never considered ducking out of the fifth Test and having a rest. I knew this was my last Ashes tour, and my knee was not going to get the better of me. For a couple of months I had been saying to Paul Reiffel, 'Wait until Birmingham, the pitch will be so green.' But when we got there it was bare! We couldn't believe it.

I knew the Edgbaston curator, Andy Atkinson, as he had been at Essex during my scholarship in 1983. 'Mate, what's going on here?' I asked. He told me that all the Test ground curators had been told to roll out spinners' wickets. 'You're kidding! You guys thought that Tufnell and Such would be better than May and Warne. You were mad!'

This was proved during the Edgbaston Test when Warney and Tim May took 13 of England's 20 wickets as we won again to go 4-0 up in the series. They were an exceptional partnership, one spinning away from the right-hander and one spinning into them. After Gooch's resignation this was Michael Atherton's first Test as captain, but it proved to be the same old story for England.

Exhausted but happy, we made our way to The Oval for the final Test. During the five days there, I can remember Allan Border saying, 'Are you OK? Because you look like rat shit.' I was so tired, but I still took six wickets. It wasn't enough though. While we wanted to go home with a 5-0 series win to surpass the 1989 side's 4-0 effort, it wasn't to be and we lost by 161 runs. A lot of people said it didn't really count for too much, but if you had been in the rooms that night the players were genuinely disappointed. Losing that Test took the shine off it all a little bit.

England brought in Devon Malcolm and Steve Watkin, and we couldn't understand why they hadn't been used earlier as they took 12 wickets between them. Malcolm really made our batsmen dance. 'Look at Devon, how come you can't get the ball over hip high?' Mark Taylor said to me. 'Mate, we've played all summer, this bloke is in his first Test, he wants to win a place in the side, while I want to go home.'

It had been a long, hard tour, but I went home happy with 31 wickets, and the Ashes. But, sadly, I would appear in only two more Tests for Australia. Two weeks after The Oval I had surgery on my right knee back home in Melbourne. I thought I would be fine to play in a few weeks, but the damage was a lot worse when they looked inside and found out I would need more than a routine clean-up. It was as if I had broken my leg because I had to wait for the bone to regenerate. The surgeon said I wouldn't be playing for at least four months. 'What a relief,' was my first wearied reaction.

I missed the whole Australian summer with the series against New Zealand and South Africa. However, I made my comeback on the tour to South Africa in March 1994, but the second Test at Cape Town would prove to be my 53rd and final Test for Australia.

It has been said that my efforts on the 1993 Ashes tour probably brought my Test career to a premature end. I don't agree. I was coming to the end anyway, the truth was my knees, ankles and back were all knackered. It was only a matter of time before I had to make way for the younger blokes, and there was one by the name of Glenn McGrath coming through. At 28, I thought I was going to play forever, but nearing 32, I was physically and mentally spent. Do I regret pushing myself so hard in England? Not for a second. Believe me, it was worth it.

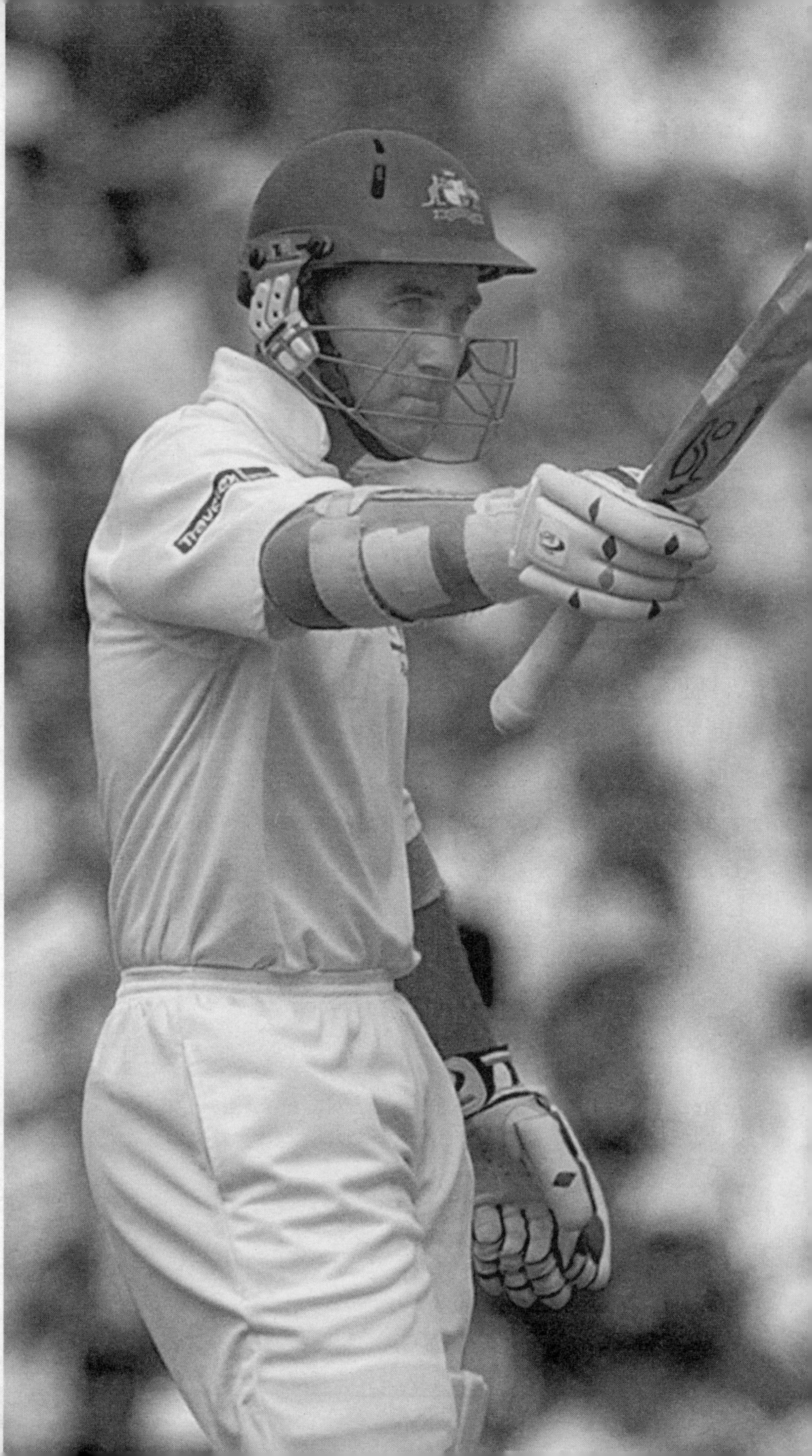

JUSTIN LANGER

Justin Langer – Fourth Test, Melbourne Cricket Ground, 26-30 December 2002

Justin Langer sat seventh in the all-time list of Australia's most successful Test batsmen with 7,696 runs from 105 matches. After making his debut batting at number three in 1993, he played in just eight Tests in six years before becoming an ever-present in the Australian side that won a world record 16 consecutive Tests between 1999 and 2001, and was lauded by his captain Steve Waugh as the best batsman in the world. Dropped again before the 2001 Ashes series, the determined Western Australian left-hander was recalled by the end of the tour and reinvented himself as one of the game's greatest ever opening batsmen alongside Matthew Hayden before retiring after the 2006/07 Ashes series.

Left-handed batsman
Born: 21 November 1970, Perth, Western Australia
Test debut: January 1993 v West Indies
Last Test: January 2007 v England
Test record: 105 matches, 7,696 runs at an average of 45.27

The state of play
Australia had already wrapped up the Ashes by the time Justin Langer posted a big double century to help put them 4-0 up in the series and on their way to a whitewash, though England did save some face with victory in the final Test.

Scoreboard

Australia first innings

J.L. Langer	c Caddick	b Dawson	250
M.L. Hayden	c Crawley	b Caddick	102
R.T. Ponting		b White	21
D.R. Martyn	c Trescothick	b White	17
S.R. Waugh	c Foster	b White	77
M.L. Love		not out	62
A.C. Gilchrist		b Dawson	1
Extras	(lb 11, w 5, nb 5)		21
Total	(6 wickets dec, 146 overs)		551

Bowling	O	M	R	W
A.R. Caddick	36	6	126	1
S.J. Harmison	36	7	108	0
C. White	33	5	133	3
R.K.J. Dawson	28	1	121	2
M.A. Butcher	13	2	52	0

England first innings

M.E. Trescothick	c Gilchrist	b Lee	37
M.P. Vaughan		b McGrath	11
M.A. Butcher	lbw	b Gillespie	25
N. Hussain	c Hayden	b MacGill	24
R.K.J. Dawson	c Love	b MacGill	6
R.W.T. Key	lbw	b Lee	0
J.P. Crawley	c Langer	b Gillespie	17
C. White		not out	85
J.S. Foster	lbw	b Waugh	19
A.R. Caddick		b Gillespie	17
S.J. Harmison	c Gilchrist	b Gillespie	2
Extras	(b 3, lb 10, nb 14)		27
Total	(all out, 89.3 overs)		270

Bowling	O	M	R	W
G.D. McGrath	16	5	41	1
J.N. Gillespie	16.3	7	25	4
S.C.G. MacGill	36	10	108	2
B. Lee	17	4	70	2
S.R. Waugh	4	0	13	1

England second innings (following on)

M.E. Trescothick	lbw	b MacGill	37
M.P. Vaughan	c Love	b MacGill	145
M.A. Butcher	c Love	b Gillespie	6
N. Hussain		c & b McGrath	23
R.W.T. Key	c Ponting	b Gillespie	52
J.P. Crawley		b Lee	33
C. White	c Gilchrist	b MacGill	21
J.S. Foster	c Love	b MacGill	6
R.K.J. Dawson		not out	15
A.R. Caddick	c Waugh	b MacGill	10
S.J. Harmison		b Gillespie	7
Extras	(b 3, lb 21, w 2, nb 6)		32
Total	(all out, 120.4 overs)		387

Bowling	O	M	R	W
G.D. McGrath	19	5	44	1
J.N. Gillespie	24.4	6	71	3
S.C.G. MacGill	48	10	152	5
B. Lee	27	4	87	1
S.R. Waugh	2	0	9	0

Australia second innings (target: 107 runs)

J.L. Langer	lbw	b Caddick	24
M.L. Hayden	c sub (Tudor)	b Caddick	1
R.T. Ponting	c Foster	b Harmison	30
D.R. Martyn	c Foster	b Harmison	0
S.R. Waugh	c Butcher	b Caddick	14
M.L. Love		not out	6
A.C. Gilchrist		not out	10
Extras	(b 8, lb 5, nb 9)		22
Total	(5 wickets, 23.1 overs)		107

Bowling	O	M	R	W
A.R. Caddick	12	1	51	3
S.J. Harmison	11.1	1	43	2

Justin Langer

AS SOON AS I hit the ball I knew it was going for six. While everyone else was in suspense, watching the ball travel through the air in a hushed silence, I just stood there and enjoyed the moment. There were no nerves at all, just a wonderful feeling of stillness and joy. It was like I was in a bubble for that fleeting moment watching the drama unfold in slow motion. For those few seconds in time I felt untouchable.

As the ball landed over the boundary I raised my arms to celebrate reaching a century as the crowd went berserk. This is the reason I play cricket, to experience little moments of magic like that, which you find hard to replicate anywhere else in life. It was simply the most exhilarating moment I have ever had on a cricket field.

I was on 95 on the opening day of the Boxing Day Test against England at the Melbourne Cricket Ground in 2002. The previous ball I had struck for four, so the adrenaline was pumping through me.

A year earlier I had reached a century against South Africa by hitting a six off Claude Henderson at the Adelaide Oval. I had never experienced a moment of such pure happiness on a cricket field before, so I wanted to feel like that again. I also knew this would be even better.

The English spin bowler Richard Dawson ran in to bowl, and I came down the pitch and swung my bat at the ball as hard as I could. I immediately knew where the ball was heading. No one else in the crowd of nearly 65,000 at the MCG realised what was going to happen, but I did because I had felt the power of the shot pulsate through my body.

I had wanted to experience scoring a century in the Boxing Day Test at the MCG since I had seen my heroes Kim Hughes and Dennis Lillee perform here as an 11-year-old watching at home in Perth. It had taken nearly a decade since my Test debut and 58 Tests to achieve it, and looking at the crowd with my arms held aloft I remember thinking, 'It doesn't get any better than this.'

I had been on a long journey to reach that moment, which had tested all of my mental, physical and spiritual strength to the limit. There were times when I didn't think I would make it to the MCG to enjoy that wonderful day. There were times when I was racked with self-doubt, but I continued to believe in myself and kept going. Nothing was going to stop me living out my dreams wearing a baggy green cap.

In January 1993 I received a late call-up to make my debut against the West Indies in the fourth Test in Adelaide. I was a shy but determined 22-year-old about to realise a dream I had harboured for most of my life. The day before the Test I had got the call at home in Perth to say Damien Martyn was injured and I had to get on the next flight to Adelaide. Just hours later I stepped in to the lobby at the Hindley Parkroyal Hotel, and surrounded by players like Allan Border, David Boon and Merv Hughes it felt as though I was on a movie set.

In my room I found a large cardboard box with a gold insignia written on the top, saying 'JUSTIN LANGER – AUSTRALIAN TEST CRICKETER'. I tore it open and rummaged to the bottom to find my baggy green cap. It looked better than I could ever have imagined. I am not ashamed to admit I put it straight on my head and watched myself in the mirror as I jumped about playing hook shots and cover drives.

The next morning unbridled joy was replaced by a terrible bout of nerves as I walked out to face the most feared bowling attack in cricket. Waiting for me with undisguised contempt were Courtney Walsh, Curtly Ambrose, Ian Bishop and Kenny Benjamin. After we had dismissed the Windies for only 252, Mark Taylor was out four balls in to our reply. Now I was in and I felt sick. As I reached the crease the West Indians could smell fear. 'Come on Bishy … this one is scared,' shouted Desmond Haynes to Ian Bishop as he prepared to bowl to me. For the next half an hour until stumps I took a battering. I was hit on the body five times, the doctor had to come on to the field, and I didn't manage to score a single run.

The following morning I made 20 in the first hour before being caught by Junior Murray off the bowling of Kenny Benjamin. In the second innings as we chased 186 to win the Test I managed to stay at the crease for over four hours as I edged my way to 54. At lunch in the second innings, I was already aching and covered in bruises when David Boon said to me, 'Young fella, I just want you to know that Test cricket will never get harder than this, than what you're experiencing right now.'

After watching the top order collapse around me I was ninth man out, and despite a stirring rearguard action from Tim May and Craig McDermott we lost by a single run, the narrowest margin of victory in the history of Test cricket.

Despite making just ten and one in the fifth Test in Perth, I had done enough to convince the selectors I was worth taking to New Zealand. I knew that a good showing against the Kiwis would book me a place on the tour to England later that year. That was what I wanted more than anything. But on tour I was consumed with the fear of failure and again batted to survive rather than to make runs. This mindset contributed to me being out for a pair in the third and final Test at Eden Park.

Two weeks later my Dad broke the news that I would not be going to England. After only five Tests I was dropped. I honestly felt like fainting. I felt physically crushed. I realised now that I had one eye on the Ashes when I should have had both eyes on what was important: making runs against New Zealand. If I had done that I would have gone to England. It was a learning experience: never look too far ahead.

Those first two innings against the West Indies created a perception of me as a player that has been almost impossible to get rid of ever since. Because I was hit on the body several times and slowly accumulated my runs I was seen as a gutsy and gritty kind of player. I didn't want that. I wanted to be seen as a player of natural talent who scored runs with flair.

While Australia toured England I returned to the Commonwealth Bank Cricket Academy in Adelaide. Rod Marsh, who was then head coach, knew immediately what the problem was with my game. 'Batting is about making runs,' he told me. 'You can bat for six hours but if you don't make any runs, you are no good to anyone. It is no good being just gutsy and occupying the crease.'

That was a crucial time as I changed the way I played to become a more aggressive batsman. Often people suggest my game has become more aggressive since I started opening the batting but I am sure this style started to evolve way back in 1993.

It took a long time, however, for the selectors to trust me again. Over the course of the next five years I played in just three more Tests. I was scoring plenty of runs in domestic cricket and banging furiously on the door to be given a proper chance. Allan Border once said I was 'the last picked, and the first dropped' and that was exactly how it felt. The hardest thing to deal with was the horrible feeling of not being wanted.

But that also hardened me up. There is a quote I have pinned to the wall at home that says, 'The pain of discipline is nothing like the pain of disappointment.' I learned that during my years on the fringes of the team. I knew I had to become the best I could be and improve both technically and mentally. I also wanted to become the fittest player in Australia. The concept of concentration fascinates me, so I knew I needed to spiritually change and relax more. I couldn't be so tense and tight, which often happens to young players because they want it so badly. The perception of me was of a very intense young guy. I kept hearing I was one of those players who didn't have much talent, but worked really hard. I was desperate to rid myself of that.

I knew I was making progress because I was called back in to the squad and taken on several tours, including to England in 1997. The only problem was I wasn't being picked for the team. Now the perception of me was of the consummate squad man. I hated that too. I didn't want to be known as good enough to have around the squad, but not good enough to be trusted out in the middle.

During the first Ashes Test at Edgbaston I came on as 12th man while Nasser Hussain was batting. I was chirpy and bubbly and said a few things to him. I didn't hear him at the time, but it has been reported he said, 'Look, I don't mind the others chirping at me, but you're the fucking bus driver of this team. So you get back on the bus and get ready to drive it home this evening.' I reckon Nasser had a point. If the 12th man was like that with me I would have felt the same way. It hurt, but it was true, I was like the bus driver, someone who hangs out with the team but doesn't actually play.

In October 1998 I was given another chance against Pakistan in the first Test in Rawalpindi. This Australian side was so good that you often only got a couple of Test innings to prove your worth. On this occasion I was aware of this as I walked out in the stiflingly hot conditions with us 11/1 in the seventh over. In came Wasim Akram for my first ball and sent down a ball at 150 kilometres an hour that thudded in to my right pad. To my absolute horror the umpire's finger went straight up. I was out for a golden duck. As I shuffled away from the crease those gnawing thoughts of self-doubt came flooding back. Maybe I really wasn't good enough to play for Australia.

Probably because we won by an innings in Rawalpindi I was retained for the Second Test in Peshawar. I knew, however, that I was close to being banished forever. At the Arbab Niaz Stadium I faced one of the game's fastest bowlers, Shoaib Akhtar, for my first ball. It was hot, very hot, and my heart was pounding. 'Watch the ball, watch the ball' I kept repeating to myself, but I didn't see it leave his hand before it struck me in the middle of my right pad. It was plum. I must be out.

The umpire Steve Bucknor was facing me, and he takes an eternity to make a decision. I will never forget staring at him, I have never felt so scared. It felt like someone was holding my head underwater. I knew another golden duck would spell the end. There was no way I could have come back from that.

Bucknor held my career in his hands. He looked to his right and then to his left before stealing one last lingering look at my pads. He looked up and said 'not out'. I was still alive. At that moment I realised only I had control of my destiny. I didn't want to spend the rest of my career playing shield and county cricket. I belonged in the Test arena. I cut Akhtar's next ball for four and didn't look back as I made my way to 116. Nearly six years after my debut I had finally made my maiden Test century.

Despite this century I was denied the headlines. In the same Test Mark Taylor equalled Sir Donald Bradman's highest ever innings for an Australian by scoring 334. This meant I earned the unwanted nickname of Arthur Morris from my team-mates. Morris famously scored 196 in the same Test at The Oval in 1948 in which Sir Donald Bradman was bowled for a duck to miss out on a Test average of 100. For the rest of his life few people remembered Morris had even played in that Test. History was now repeating itself, but I had already lived with the feeling of being the invisible man of Australian cricket for too long, but regardless of that, I knew I had finally taken a huge step forward.

For the next three years no one could accuse me of being invisible as I became a regular in the side. Batting at number three, I played in 33 consecutive Tests, scoring over 2,300 runs, including seven centuries and nine fifties. I made 179 against England in Adelaide, a double century against India at the SCG, and most satisfyingly of all, 127 against the West Indies in Antigua. I knew if I could make a hundred facing Walsh and Ambrose on their home turf I could do it against anyone.

This period of my career also coincided with an era in which we won 16 consecutive Tests to set a new world record. I have no doubt this achievement has been the highlight of my career and while I felt that I had made it to where I always wanted to be, the collective effort was more inspiring than anything I could ever dream of doing personally.

As good a period as this was, a few danger signs started creeping into my game. I remember walking through the arrivals hall at Perth International Airport in September 2000 after arriving home from my third season with Middlesex. I was exhausted after playing seven straight seasons and thought, 'How am I going to get up for another season?' I didn't think I had it in me. In my first game for Western Australia against Queensland Andy Bichel twice got me out for a duck. 'Here we go again,' I thought.

I had decided not to go back to Middlesex the following summer, which meant I knew there was a break in sight. Again I had one eye on the future. We played the West Indies in the summer of 2000/01 and then went to India. I wasn't terrible, but I wasn't great and in eight Tests I only passed fifty twice. I was more interested in that break.

After a four-month rest we set off on the 2001 Ashes tour. I was now pumped about the trip, I couldn't wait to start playing again. After missing out in 1993 and 1997 I was finally going to take England on in their own backyard. On 2 June 2001 I was sitting in my hotel room on the eve of the first Test at Edgbaston when there was a knock at the door. I opened it to see Steve Waugh standing there. My heart sank. I had been dropped. 'Sorry mate, but Marto [Damien Martyn] is in and you are out,' he confirmed.

I wanted to scream, I wanted to shout, I wanted to rant at the injustice of it all, but I said nothing. I had failed to learn my own lessons. I had got sidetracked and given the selectors a reason to drop me. For Steve Waugh to be the messenger of such devastating news made the whole scene incredibly uncomfortable. To me, Tugga is like a brother, he is my great mentor, a man I would want next to me in the trenches. It hurt hearing those words coming out of his mouth.

I was 30 years old and I thought my Test career was over. My overwhelming emotion was anger. I thought, 'I'm going to show these guys', so I trained like a machine to be in the best shape of my life, and technically I was looking good, hitting a million balls in the nets, but something was missing. Mentally, I wasn't in a good place because I was so angry. It taught me about synergy, because at that moment I had none at all. I was fit and doing everything right technically, but I was failing because I was too emotional.

I hit rock bottom when I was out for two against Sussex at Hove. I walked off the ground and shouted at our stand-in captain Adam Gilchrist, 'Look what you guys have done to me!' I really spat the dummy. That night I sat in the bar of the Grand Hotel on the Brighton seafront with Gilly and our coach John Buchanan. I don't normally drink much, but for four hours I knocked back several Budweisers as I spewed out all the emotions that had been simmering away since I was dropped. I told them exactly how I felt and how I was sick of being the easy guy to drop. The most remarkable thing was at the end of the evening John Buchanan gave me a hug!

Two days before the final Test at The Oval the phone rang in my hotel room. It was Steve Waugh telling me that I was back in and would be opening the batting with Matthew Hayden. This came completely out of the blue because I had been playing so badly. It felt like a miracle. My wife Sue, who had flown over in the aftermath of my Hove meltdown, was with me and I told her, 'Whatever happens, I plan to have the time of my life, I am going to have fun, it might be my last Test.' Anger had been stopping me making runs, so I had to change my approach.

That first morning at The Oval felt like Christmas Day. I remember walking out next to Haydos with an enormous smile on my face. When I arrived at the crease, I greeted Andrew Caddick, Darren Gough, Alec Stewart and Nasser Hussain. I smiled and said good morning to them all. They looked a bit shocked. I was so breezy, I had never felt like that before, not even for a charity game. I wanted to have fun. I had plenty of that as I made a century. Like riding a bike my touch all came back to me. I remember hitting my ex-Middlesex team-mate Phil Tufnell over the top a few times and I was pretty emotional when I reached 100 with a square cut off Tuffers. I remember looking up at our balcony with clenched teeth and an expression of 'I told you so' all over my face. It was like I had proven to the guys who had dropped me and to myself that I could still play.

On 102 I got whacked on the side of my helmet by a short ball from Andy Caddick. It was a hell of a blow forcing me to leave the field retired hurt. Everyone was worried, there was blood everywhere, but I didn't have a care in the world. 'I've got a Test hundred,' I kept saying. I was happy to be back in the changing room with Matty Hayden and Tugga thinking, 'I'm back, I'm back.' I was laying on the physio table with blood pouring from my head, but I couldn't stop smiling.

Fifteen months later England came to Australia to contest the 2002/03 Ashes, and they encountered a very different Justin Langer. Since my surprise recall at The Oval I had made the most of my second chance. Driven by the desire that no one would ever take away my baggy green cap again I had batted better than ever, making nearly 1,000 runs, including four hundreds and four fifties.

I had loved doing this with my opening partner Matty Hayden. I cherish my friendship with him, we are great mates and he is the godfather to my daughter Grace. We complement each other as batsmen, and understand each other because our careers have followed such similar paths. Batting with him in each Test is like going to Disneyland, we are like two little kids having the time of our lives.

On their arrival England made familiar noises about regaining the Ashes. We had heard it for 12 years and had yet to see them back up their words. Every time they came to Australia, we heard the same thing about this finally being their year. But not for a moment did we think we could lose this series. People misconstrue that as arrogance, but we don't go in to any series thinking defeat is an option. Steve Waugh drilled it in to us that we should look to win every Test.

We felt invincible because we had such an extraordinary group of players. Most teams might be lucky to have one great player, but we had about seven. We were like the great Chicago Bulls side of the 1990s. I remember speaking to Luc Longley, the Aussie who played for them, and he said a lot of games were won before they even got on the court because of who they were. Teams did not believe they could beat them, and it was the same with the Australian cricket side.

It was an amazing time to walk out on the field with Glenn McGrath, Shane Warne, Adam Gilchrist, Steve Waugh and Ricky Ponting. I always thought to myself, 'We have to do something really stupid to lose.' It didn't matter who the opposition were and what they had planned, we never considered defeat. Before this series Tugga had noticed England were being over complimentary about us in their interviews. He saw it as a sign of weakness, but they were probably just being realistic. They knew how difficult it was going to be to beat us.

Nonetheless, England did have some genuine talent in their side. Andy Caddick is one of the best bowlers I have ever faced, while Steve Harmison and Simon Jones looked young and hungry. They had a lot of experience in their batting with Alec Stewart, Nasser Hussain, Michael Vaughan and Mark Butcher, but maybe they were also too experienced at losing to us. I remember Steve Waugh saying they looked beaten men before the series had even started.

On the opening morning of first Test at the Gabba Nasser won the toss and surprisingly to most put us in to bat. The feeling was that he wasn't showing much faith in his batsmen on what would prove to be a great batting track. We took full advantage and by the end of the first day were 364/2. I made 32 before being caught by Alec Stewart off the bowling of Simon Jones, who not long after was carried off with a sickening knee injury. I was annoyed I had failed to go on to get a big score, especially when I saw how many runs were on offer. But I was delighted to see Haydos make 197 and Punter make 123. The ruthless manner in which we had stacked up those runs and dominated England on the first day set the tone for the whole series.

We eventually finished on 492 all out before England replied with 325. We then had some more fun with the bat, declaring on 296/5. Haydos got another century while I was disappointed to make just 22. We set England a mammoth target of 464. We knew it would be tough for them, but we were still shocked at just how easy it turned out to be. It took just 28 overs and two hours to get them all out for 79.

Often, when we get on a roll we can't be stopped. We had Shane Warne spinning it like a wheel from one end and Glenn McGrath bowling like the wind from other. You are facing the greatest spin bowler and the greatest fast bowler in the history of the game at the same time. Then when one of them takes a break in comes Jason Gillespie. The pitch at the Gabba, which by the fourth day had developed huge cracks, didn't do the English any favours either. The cracks didn't actually play a major role, but psychologically you feel threatened by them and even more under siege.

After the Test we went out as a team and enjoyed ourselves. We actually ended up at the same pub down on the waterfront as the England blokes. We were in one corner celebrating and they were over the other side looking a bit miserable. Sir Richard Branson, who was over in Australia promoting Virgin credit cards, was also there. His PR asked Tugga if he wanted to meet him, so I tagged along too. Did he know who I was? I don't think he knew who anyone was at that stage of the night, but it was still a thrill to have met him.

The first day of the second Test at the Adelaide Oval saw England showing some fighting spirit. An innings of 177 from Michael Vaughan, who we finally dismissed in the final over of the day, helped them finish on 295/4. But I was furious that they had been allowed to get that many. When Vaughan was on 19 I caught him with a low diving catch at cover. It was as clear as anything. Everyone knew I had caught it, he knew it as well as anyone. I walked up to him and said, 'Michael, I promise you I caught the ball.' He gave me no reply. 'Mate, who is going to look like the idiot? It will be me if I am cheating you and I haven't really taken it. I am putting my neck on the line here. I promise you I caught it.' He ignored me.

It went to the third umpire and as happens a lot the cameras couldn't properly see so he was given not out. I really got stuck in to him afterwards, because it was one of the most disappointing moments in my entire career. I believe the players have a responsibility to uphold the integrity of the game and on this occasion, when the opportunity presented itself, this theory was blown out of the water.

To compound it, Michael covered the incident in his book *A Year In The Sun* and was less than complimentary of me. He wrote: 'To say Langer was angry is a huge understatement. He was so red-faced I thought he had turned into something out of a giant packet of matches, this short strand of white with a big red blob on the end of it … For the rest of the morning session, Langer called me every name under the sun and all day kept on giving me plenty … I think if Justin Langer looks back, he may consider he was a little childish.'

He also wrote: 'There were one or two occasions when some of our guys, myself included, had a few words with him on the pitch because we thought he was being a bit of a tit.'

I will say again on my children's lives, and there is nothing bigger you can say, I caught that ball. He questioned my integrity and I was very disappointed about that.

On the second morning England ruined the good work of the previous day by collapsing to 342 all out. In reply Haydos and I put on an opening stand of 101, the foundation for a massive total of 552, thanks mainly to 154 from Punter and 95 from Marto. England folded to 159 all out in their second innings to lose by an innings and 51 run, and put us 2-0 up in the series.

England fared no better in the third Test at Perth where we beat them by an innings and 48 runs to retain the Ashes in the space of just 11 days. This was the third time I had been a part of winning the Ashes and this time was as sweet as ever. We didn't get the urn at the WACA, we had to wait until the final Test in Sydney. But that didn't dampen our celebrations. We play better than anyone and I reckon we celebrate better than anyone as well.

It is my job now to conduct the team song as the toastmaster. It is a tradition passed down from Rod Marsh, David Boon, Ian Healy and Ricky Ponting. We were in the changing room for four or five hours, getting ourselves reasonably drunk, listening to music, talking shit and then singing the team song. It might sound corny, but my greatest memories are not about what happens in the middle, they are when we stand together arm in arm wearing our baggy green caps to sing our team song, 'Under the Southern Cross'. These moments are always special and it would be fair to say I tend to get pretty animated and passionate about our victory celebrations.

The opening day of the Boxing Day Test at the MCG has been my favourite day of the year since I was 11 years old. As a child, I used to spend Christmas Day getting more excited about waking up the next day and spending seven hours in front of the television. The love affair began on 26 December 1981 when I will never forget watching Australia face the legendary West Indies. The day started with my childhood hero Kim Hughes scoring 100 not out against the best attack in the world. He was a brave and talented batsman, who I loved watching at the WACA or on television. The first bat I ever bought with my pocket money was a Kim Hughes Slazenger bat and I used to try and copy him.

I also worshipped Dennis Lillee. He was like a comic book superhero to me. I loved his long hair, moustache and the way he wore his white shirt open to show his gold chain and hairy chest. I thought this was the epitome of cool. At the end of the first day I sat open-mouthed as he ripped through the West Indies top order, removing Desmond Haynes and Colin Croft to reduce them to 6/3. With the very last ball of the day he bowled to the incomparable Viv Richards. My Uncle Rob had played against Richards in World Series Cricket and always fed me stories about his greatness. I will never forget how the whole of the MCG were on their feet, chanting Lillee's name, thrilled to be watching two gladiators going toe-to-toe. Lillee tore in and splattered Richards's stumps, which had me leaping to my feet as the MCG went wild. The West Indies finished the day on 10/4.

From that day it had been my ambition to play in a Boxing Day Test match. I achieved that in December 1996 against the West Indies, but it wasn't enough.

I wanted to do something memorable there, I wanted to score a big hundred and thrive in the same atmosphere that had brought the best out of Kim Hughes and Dennis Lillee all those years ago. By the summer of 2002 I had played at the MCG five times, scoring an 80 and an 85, but that century was proving elusive.

After three low-scoring Tests in this series I was even more desperate for a big score. In between the third and fourth Tests I had some time back in Western Australia when my best mate Ben Beale had a beautiful son who he called Hayden. On the morning of a one-day game against Tasmania I met Hayden for the first time in hospital and said, 'Mate, I'm going to get you a hundred today.' And that is exactly what I did, 114 not out. I was back in the habit of making runs, so I arrived in Melbourne feeling wonderful.

On the opening morning of the Test I walked to the middle alongside Matty Hayden in front of a sell-out crowd of nearly 65,000. I hoped it would prove to be a good omen that the loudspeaker was blaring out U2's 'Beautiful Day'. I drove Andy Caddick for three runs with the very first ball of the innings, but after that things slowed down. At lunch we had only reached 70 without loss. Back in the changing room I went to see our physio Errol Alcott and told him I was worried because I had no energy. I felt really flat. There was something wrong because I couldn't get going.

I don't know what happened, Errol didn't prescribe anything, but in the first 13 overs after lunch we scored 95 runs. The mood among Haydos and I had completely changed. I couldn't believe it as I watched him walk down the wicket and hit Caddick over midwicket. I remember him saying to me when Craig White was bowling, 'If this was a one-dayer I would be belting him ten rows back.'

'Mate, we're on a bit of a roll here, so get it out of your system,' I replied. So I was then treated to the sight of Matthew Hayden twice walking down the wicket and hitting him at least 20 rows back in to the Southern Stand. I helped myself to a pile of runs as well as we both went completely berserk in that second session.

My batting approach on that day was exactly the same as when I made my highest ever first-class score of 342 for Somerset in July 2006. Out in the middle of the MCG I was telling myself to relax my hands just as the bowler gets to the wicket, stand up when he lets the ball go and say 'sharp' to myself so I was completely ready to deal with whatever the bowler had to offer. That is the recipe that works for me. Sometimes you make changes and you mess it up. It is like making a pavlova, if you follow the recipe you will be fine, but if you use one less egg or too much sugar it will be a disaster. Don't mess around with the recipe is the best way to make runs. I followed my own advice and fortunately they came thick and fast.

As we kept the scoreboard ticking over, the England bowlers and fielders increasingly looked like a beaten side even though this was only day one. Whatever Andy Caddick, Steve Harmison, Craig White, Richard Dawson and Mark Butcher sent down I seemed to find an answer. Sure there were some lucky breaks along the way but thankfully I had found a wonderful rhythm to my game and was enjoying using as many strokes as possible, cutting and driving whenever given the chance.

During my innings I shared three century partnerships, with Haydos, Tugga and Martin Love. First Haydos and I put on an opening stand of 195, which saw my great mate make 102. Marto and Punter were out relatively cheaply, which brought Steve Waugh to the crease when we were 265/3. The crowd gave him a great reception, well aware that it could be his final appearance in Melbourne.

Ever since Tugga had been dropped as Australia's one-day captain in February he had been under an almost unbearable amount of pressure to prove that, aged 37 years old, he still had a future as our Test captain as well. After a relatively lean spell with the bat, the feeling was that he really needed runs in Melbourne to prolong his Test career.

After Tugga joined me in the middle of the MCG, Nasser Hussain set a field to allow me singles and put Tugga on strike. He was absolutely furious about being shown such a lack of respect. This seemed to bring the best out of him and he started creaming the ball all over the ground. After every ball he would say to me, 'Why haven't I been doing this all summer? Batting is about backing yourself. Lang, tell me, why haven't I been backing myself? I have waited too long, I should have been batting like this all the time!'

I have never seen him like that. He is usually so calm. By the end of the day he was unbeaten on 62 before being out for 77 the next morning. It was such an important innings for him.

I was 146 not out when we reached 356/3 at stumps on the first day. I can clearly remember the last ball of the day. Andy Caddick had the new ball, which you're always nervous about, but I played the perfect defence, tucked my bat under my arm and headed for the changing room. I have a great photograph on my mantelpiece at home of me raising my bat to the crowd as I walked off the ground. The next day was similar to the first. Although I was physically weary, my concentration felt almost perfect. I was relying on my cues of staying relaxed but sharp and I remained determined to bat for as long as I could.

On reaching 200, the joy was almost as intense as it was on day one when I went to my hundred with a six. The beauty of such milestones is that the crowd at the MCG gives you a reception better than anywhere else in the world. Such receptions make all of the bad days, and trust me there are many of those, all seem worthwhile. It is almost as though you have to live through the bad days to truly appreciate the great ones.

Brian Lara once told me the key to batting is to make the good days into great days. In other words when you get a start, be determined to convert it into a century and when you score a century be even more determined to score a really big century. This advice kept running through my mind throughout day two. 'Cash in, cash in, cash in' was my mantra after the result on Boxing Day and I was focused on making this good day into a great one.

Eventually I was out cutting Richard Dawson and after walking off the ground and into the MCG changing room I sat in my pads for a good 20 minutes reflecting on what had just occurred. Physically I was spent but this was overshadowed by the great sense of achievement and pride that was running through my body. The team was in a fantastic position and I had just realised a dream.

We eventually declared at 551/6 and put England in. By the end of the day we compounded England's misery by reducing them to 97/3. Brett Lee had claimed Marcus Trescothick's wicket, but had to endure a horrific time from the English supporters in the crowd, the Barmy Army. They shouted 'no-ball' at him after every delivery. To be frank, they were having the time of their lives but I took offence to their sledging of one of my good mates.

At the end of play I went to the press conference to talk about my 250, which naturally I was thrilled about, but I made a silly mistake. Asked about the treatment of Brett I said, 'I thought they [the Barmy Army] were a disgrace. These people stand behind a fence drinking beer with most of them 50 kilos overweight making ridiculous comments. It is easy for someone to say that behind a fence, they're within their rights because they've paid their money, but there's still some integrity in life, I think.'

Just like the Barmy Army I am as loyal as a junkyard dog, so I couldn't stay silent and watch my mate getting ripped apart. After my comments the Barmy Army got all sensitive, but I have always thought if you give it you have to be able to take it. I was pleased to get it off my chest. In a lot of ways I am a huge admirer of the Barmy Army in that they are loyal to their team and they provide plenty of atmosphere to cricket grounds around the world. In other ways the Barmy Army say some of the most horrific things. I don't like what they say about Shane Warne and his personal life. People laugh at it, but I don't see much humour in it. There is always a fine line, and sometimes they cross it.

On the third day England were forced to follow on after making 270. While they improved in the second innings, scoring 387, they set us what should have been an easy target of just 107. By the morning of the fifth day England came at us hard and had us 58/3 to give them hopes of pulling off a miracle. At this point Tugga joined me out in the middle. The first thing he said was, 'I'm struggling a bit here ... I'm really feeling dizzy.' He said he had a migraine and it was getting worse.

'Mate, what are you on about? We've got a Test match to win here,' was my reply. Neither of us made it to the end. He fell for 14 to pile the pressure back on, while I made 24 before Andy Caddick got me lbw. Martin Love and Adam Gilchrist guided us over the line to give us a 4-0 lead in the series.

We were now on the brink of becoming the first side to win an Ashes series 5-0 since 1920/21, but the build-up to the fifth Test at the SCG centred on the future of Steve Waugh. Amid blanket coverage the *Daily Telegraph* in Sydney christened this 'The Steve Waugh Test' as the assumption grew that Tugga needed a big score if he didn't want this to be his final Test. There was also a feeling he might decide to retire. Either way, there was a sense that an era in Australian cricket might be drawing to a close unless something dramatic happened in Sydney.

The pressure on Tugga was intense. After the Ashes were retained he became the story. Having been in his shoes, it is a nightmare. Everyone is picking at you, while you torment yourself about how to get out of the rut. I didn't like to see him under so much pressure, but I knew he could deal with it. Never write off a champion, because they always come good.

I had always been in awe of his mental toughness. No cricketer I knew could ever hope to match his strength of mind and character. He would often say to me, 'It is amazing what you can achieve if you put your mind to it.' He had used this approach throughout his brilliant career and I didn't think he was ready to call it a day just yet.

In a press conference before the Test I said I wouldn't be surprised if there was a big knock around the corner for Tugga. It wasn't just bravado, I meant it. I had a gut feeling he was going to be OK. He was in good nick, he had got in the habit after the MCG, but even so I never, ever expected him to do what he did.

After England had made 362, we started our reply in the middle of the second day. I was out for 25 after I had top-edged Andy Caddick to Matthew Hoggard to bring in Steve Waugh at 56/3. He got a huge standing ovation and I was only a quarter of the way off the field and he was already past me on his way to the wicket. He had always said that it was important to get out there quickly and show in your body language that you were relishing taking on the opposition.

Early in his innings I knew he was going to be OK when he hit one of his trademark shots off his legs. I thought this was looking good, especially when he passed 69 to reach 10,000 Test runs. The tension and excitement in our changing room was palpable as he kept going. I was saying, 'He is going to get a hundred, he's going to do it.' A few of the boys rolled their eyes as if to say, 'Oh yeah?' They believed in Tugga, but a hundred at the SCG under this pressure seemed too much of a fairytale.

On the final ball of the day Tugga was on 98. Nasser brought the field in, so I thought he was going to go for a trademark slog-sweep over midwicket. We all held our breath as Richard Dawson bowled to him at a full length and he struck it through the covers to bring up his century. There was total euphoria in our changing room. Around me there were grown men crying. There was a feeling we had just witnessed a miracle and more importantly we all knew our captain had saved himself. He was still alive and looking stronger than ever before.

It was only the end of the second day, but it felt like we had won the Test. We were emotionally spent. When Tugga came back in we all patted him on the back and then he sat down as we all milled around. At the end of the day's play, you normally drift off, it is no big deal, but we all stayed there wanting to savour the moment, wanting to take in this special atmosphere. We knew we had witnessed one of the great moments in Australian sporting history. Tugga's family came in, there were tears and hugs, and the Prime Minister John Howard also popped in to offer his congratulations.

The following morning Tugga was dismissed without adding a run before we were all out for 363. England then proceeded to enjoy themselves in the sunshine. Michael Vaughan got his third big century of the summer with 183 as they made 452 to set us the same target. In a way it didn't surprise me that we failed by a long distance, all out for 226 to lose the Test by 225 runs. By that stage we were both physically and mentally exhausted. We would have loved to win 5-0, but when it came to those crunch moments, we probably didn't have the same ferocity. Still, what's important was we still had our captain, we had won the series 4-1 and were presented with the Ashes to parade around the SCG.

Three and a half years later, when I was playing at Somerset for six weeks during the summer of 2006, I took questions from the floor at a charity dinner. One gentleman asked me what was the best innings I have ever played. Of course, I spoke about making 250 at the MCG.

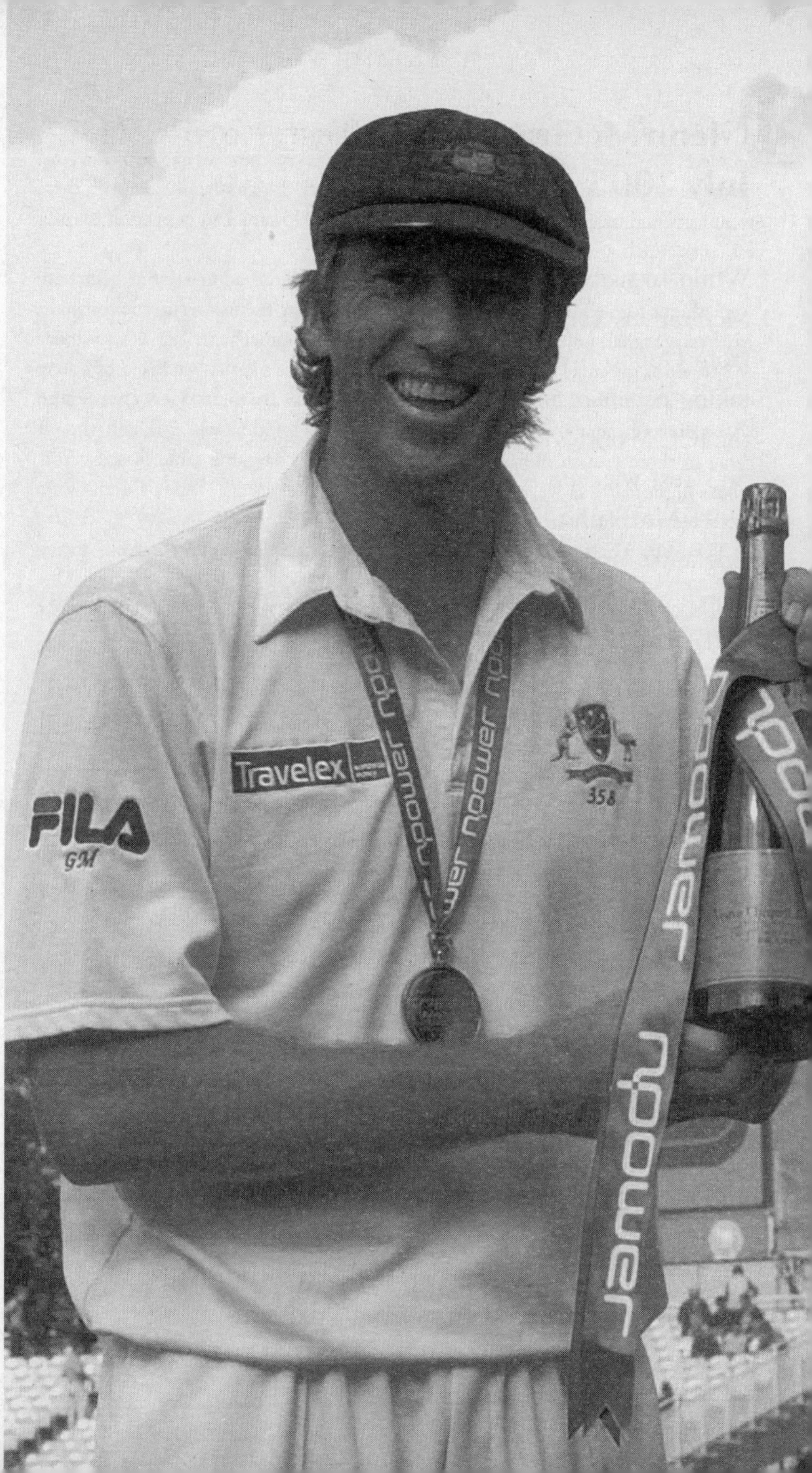

GLENN McGRATH

Glenn McGrath – First Test, Lord's, 21-24 July 2005

While arguably cricket's greatest ever fast bowler, Glenn McGrath is certainly the most successful. In 2005 the man from Dubbo overtook Courtney Walsh as the highest wicket-taking paceman in Test history with his 520th wicket against the ICC World XI at the SCG. He retired with a record haul of 563 Test wickets. After making his Ashes debut in November 1994 McGrath always took his greatest pleasure from being England's arch nemesis, claiming 157 English scalps in 30 matches at an average of just 20.92, and he retired in January 2007 after helping Australia record a 5-0 series whitewash.

Right-arm fast bowler
Born: 9 February 1970, Dubbo, New South Wales
Test debut: November 1993 v New Zealand
Last Test: January 2007 v England
Test record: 124 matches, 563 wickets at an average of 21.64; 641 runs at an average of 7.36

The state of play
Glenn McGrath claimed match figures of 9-82, his 500th wicket and the man of the match award to humble England in the first Test of an extraordinary summer.

Scoreboard

Australia first innings

J.L. Langer	c Harmison	b Flintoff	40
M.L. Hayden		b Hoggard	12
R.T. Ponting	c Strauss	b Harmison	9
D.R. Martyn	c G.O. Jones	b S.P. Jones	2
M.J. Clarke	lbw	b S.P. Jones	11
S.M. Katich	c G.O. Jones	b Harmison	27
A.C. Gilchrist	c G.O. Jones	b Flintoff	26
S.K. Warne		b Harmison	28
B. Lee	c G.O. Jones	b Harmison	3
J.N. Gillespie	lbw	b Harmison	1
G.D. McGrath		not out	10
Extras	(b 5, lb 4, w 1, nb 11)		21
Total	(all out, 40.2 overs)		190

Bowling	O	M	R	W
Harmison	11.2	0	43	5
Hoggard	8	0	40	1
Flintoff	11	2	50	2
S.P. Jones	10	0	48	2

England first innings

M.E. Trescothick	c Langer	b McGrath	4
A.J. Strauss	c Warne	b McGrath	2
M.P. Vaughan		b McGrath	3
I.R. Bell		b McGrath	6
K.P. Pietersen	c Martyn	b Warne	57
A. Flintoff		b McGrath	0
G.O. Jones	c Gilchrist	b Lee	30
A.F. Giles	c Gilchrist	b Lee	11
M.J. Hoggard	c Hayden	b Warne	0
S.J. Harmison	c Martyn	b Lee	11
S.P. Jones		not out	20
Extras	(b 1, lb 5, nb 5)		11
Total	(all out, 48.1 overs)		155

Bowling	O	M	R	W
McGrath	18	5	53	5
Lee	15.1	5	47	3
Gillespie	8	1	30	0
Warne	7	2	19	2

Australia second innings

J.L. Langer		run out	6
M.L. Hayden		b Flintoff	34
R.T. Ponting	c sub (Hildreth)	b Hoggard	42
D.R. Martyn	lbw	b Harmison	65
M.J. Clarke		b Hoggard	91
S.M. Katich	c S.P. Jones	b Harmison	67
A.C. Gilchrist		b Flintoff	10
S.K. Warne	c Giles	b Harmison	2
B. Lee		run out	8
J.N. Gillespie		b S.P. Jones	13
G.D. McGrath		not out	20
Extras	(b 10, lb 8, nb 8)		26
Total	(all out, 100.4 overs)		384

Bowling	O	M	R	W
Harmison	27.4	6	54	3
Hoggard	16	1	56	2
Flintoff	27	4	123	2
S.P. Jones	18	1	69	1
Giles	11	1	56	0
Bell	1	0	8	0

England second innings (target: 420 runs)

M.E. Trescothick	c Hayden	b Warne	44
A.J. Strauss		c & b Lee	37
M.P. Vaughan		b Lee	4
I.R. Bell	lbw	b Warne	8
K.P. Pietersen		not out	64
A. Flintoff	c Gilchrist	b Warne	3
G.O. Jones	c Gillespie	b McGrath	6
A.F. Giles	c Hayden	b McGrath	0
M.J. Hoggard	lbw	b McGrath	0
S.J. Harmison	lbw	b Warne	0
S.P. Jones	c Warne	b McGrath	0
Extras	(b 6, lb 5, nb 3)		14
Total	(all out, 58.1 overs)		180

Bowling	O	M	R	W
McGrath	17.1	2	29	4
Lee	15	3	58	2
Gillespie	6	0	18	0
Warne	20	2	64	4

Glenn McGrath

I HAD WAITED over five years for this moment. Ever since claiming Brian Lara as my 300th Test wicket at the WACA back in December 2000 I had set myself a target far beyond that. I wanted 500. No matter what else I achieved in my career, I knew if I fell short I would never be fulfilled. Something would always be missing. For four months I had been stranded on 499 wickets and now the time had come.

At 4pm on Thursday 21 July 2005, England were 10/0 in reply to our first-innings total of 190 when I took the ball for the first over after tea. As I stood out in the middle I took a brief moment to look around Lord's. To my right I could see my wife Jane in the Mound stand with our children, Holly and James, and also my Mum Bev, and my Dad Kevin, on his first trip outside Australia.

In the previous Test against New Zealand at Eden Park I had never felt completely comfortable. As I approached 500 wickets I was consumed by a strange sense of dread. It crossed my mind, 'Jeez, I'm taking these wickets for fun and Jane's not here to watch me. What if I got to 500 tonight and she missed it?'

I remember dismissing Craig Cumming and the Marshall twins and hearing Ricky Ponting shout to the rest of the team, 'I don't think he wants these wickets boys, he doesn't even look happy.' He was right in a funny way. There was part of me that wanted to wait until Lord's to get to my 500th wicket. I briefly thought I should hold back a bit. How ridiculous does that sound?

Now under the gaze of my family I felt at ease. There was a calmness about me. This was how it was meant to be: playing England in front of a packed house at Lord's. All around me tens of thousands of England fans were celebrating our disappointing first innings total as if they had already won the Ashes. It was time to quieten them down.

I ran in from the Pavilion End and bowled at Marcus Trescothick, watching as the ball reached a good length and kept straight. I knew what would happen. He tried to hit it through square leg, but only succeeded in nicking it into the hands of Justin Langer at third slip. I had finally made it to 500. While I felt immensely proud, my overwhelming emotion was one of relief. That pressure of the previous five and a half years immediately evaporated. The guys made a big fuss of me, crowding around, while I held the ball aloft to applause from all four sides of the ground.

I could not have scripted it any better. I went on to take the next four wickets to reduce England to 21/5. Only once before, seven months earlier when I took 8-24 against Pakistan at the WACA, had I ever felt this powerful, I believed I could take a wicket with every ball. At the end of play I spent some time in the dressing room with my Dad. That was a special moment. We had a beer and reflected on the day with our faces covered in beaming smiles before Jane and the kids joined us. All the time I kept thinking this really was the perfect day.

Twelve months earlier I feared my Test career might soon be over. In July 2004 I was at Marrara Cricket Ground in Darwin making my comeback against Sri Lanka in the Top End series. I had been out of the side for a year after undergoing two operations on my left ankle and now here I was in the Northern Territory fighting to save my place in the Test side.

I had made an unconvincing return to the one-day side on the tour to Zimbabwe six weeks earlier, when it was obvious I was a bit under-done. While we swept the series 3-0, I took just a single wicket. Now the two-match Test series against Sri Lanka was being billed as my last chance to prove I still had a Test career. I was 34 and few fast bowlers keep going at that age. I was told a leading Australian quick had not started a Test after his 35th birthday for more than four decades. Some assumed I had seen my best years and was hanging around vainly hoping to recreate them.

Ahead of this series against Sri Lanka, the chairman of the Australian selectors, Trevor Hohns, was asked if this was make or break for me. 'It could well be,' he said. 'Watching his speed on TV [in Zimbabwe], it wasn't anything to write home about. It's up to him to do the business. It's an important one for him … we need to assess and see whether there is something left for Glenn McGrath.'

The Australian cricket team doesn't carry passengers, so my reputation meant nothing. But I never had any serious doubts about my ability to continue to take wickets, and over the course of those two Tests against Sri Lanka I took ten of them as we won the series 1-0. There was still something left for me.

That year out of the game had been a godsend. Yes, it came with plenty of frustrations, but I never contemplated retiring, it didn't even fleetingly pass through my mind. It was a good break for me, it freshened me up and made me hungry for the game. Shane Warne reflected on his year serving a ban in the same way. It made us both determined to continue our careers for as long as possible. I believed the best was yet to come from me.

Only a few months later I was given a daunting stage to prove this when we toured India. We won there for the first time in 35 years with a 2-1 series victory, and I have honestly never seen some of the boys so pumped and emotional, it meant that much to them. I was happy to play my part by taking 14 wickets over the four Tests, but I wasn't quite back to my best yet.

That moment arrived in the first Test against Pakistan at the WACA in December. At the start of the fourth morning they resumed on 18/1 chasing the massive target of 564. After my first over I wasn't sure how I was going to get through the day, I didn't feel like I had much energy. I found it from somewhere though as by the close of play I had career-best figures of 8-24 and we had won by 491 runs. At one point I had taken the first seven wickets and I thought I might get all ten, but then Kasper [Michael Kasprowicz] ruined it. Still, I couldn't complain, this was the best I had ever bowled. I felt like myself again.

Victories over Pakistan and India are always welcome, but they don't come close to beating the Poms. That will always be the ultimate experience for an Australian cricketer. The desire to go on another Ashes tour had kept me going during those 12 months out of the game. By the start of 2005 I had never experienced losing the Ashes. I had played five series against England and won them all, but there was never any chance of getting bored, it is quite simply the best thing about my job. I just wanted to keep beating the Poms over and over again.

The hype about the 2005 series seemed to start earlier than ever before, mainly because the Poms thought they had a chance of finally beating us. In the previous year they had won a record eight consecutive Tests and a series in South Africa for the first time in 40 years. They seemed to have finally discovered the benefits of a settled side, allowing their guys to perform. We knew retaining the Ashes would be more difficult this time. England had a formidable captain in Michael Vaughan and a team full of players not used to being done over by us. They were young, fresh and ready to step up.

But was I worried? Not in the least. Asked to predict the score of the series I had no hesitation in saying 5-0. This stirred things up over in England, but I wasn't being brash or looking for headlines, I meant it. I thought we could win every Test. If there had been six Tests I would have predicted 6-0. This wasn't arrogance, simply confidence. We were the best team in the world, so there was no point in saying we would win 3-1 because I would have been lying. Our team boasted some of the greatest ever cricketers, so why should we contemplate losing? I thrive on making these big predictions because it makes me work harder and lift my game. It puts an obvious burden on me, but I like that. It is up to the other team to prove me wrong.

Another of my traditions on the eve of a series is to publicly target an opposition batsman. I have done that with some of the biggest names, including Sachin Tendulkar and Brian Lara, and it has worked. I enjoy the challenge of telling a batsman I'm after them. Ahead of this series I chose both Andrew Strauss and Michael Vaughan. It was such a big series I thought I would treat myself to two. Straussy had been a major factor in England's success since his Test debut in 2004. He had made a good start, but hadn't played that much Test match cricket. I hoped it would make him start worrying about me. Cricket is played in the mind as much as on the field. Despite England losing 4-1, Vaughan had scored a lot of runs in the last Ashes series in 2002/03, and now he was captain, I wanted to get at him.

As soon as we had stepped off the plane at Heathrow in the early hours of 5 June we were struck by how Ashes fever was gripping the whole of England. I had not known anything like it. I knew our boys could handle it, but it did occur to me that all the hype might prove too much for the Poms.

Before the Ashes began at Lord's we worked our way through the warm-up schedule of county and one-day games. We got off to a slow start when we were routed by England in the Twenty20 international at Hampshire. Maybe we could laugh that one off as just a bit of fun in the sunshine, but it wasn't as easy when we proceeded to lose to Somerset, Bangladesh and England in the space of four days. Thankfully we quickly improved and tied with England in the NatWest Series final at Lord's and then beat them in the NatWest Challenge.

It hadn't escaped our attention that this was a very different England to the one that had limped home from Australia two and a half years before. They were more aggressive and clearly keen to get in our faces. The one-day final at Lord's showed how they had changed. When they slumped to 33/5 chasing 196 the old England would soon have been defeated, but they kept fighting, stirred by a big partnership between Geraint Jones and Paul Collingwood, and gained an unlikely tie.

What amused me was the enthusiasm with which England and their press leapt on an incident involving Simon Jones and Matthew Hayden in the NatWest series game at Edgbaston as an example of their new aggression. It started when Jones threw the ball straight at Haydos. It was a bad throw right at his chest. Fair enough, if he had played a shot, but he hadn't even left his crease. There was no intention to throw it at the stumps and it wasn't funny how far it was off the mark. Of course, Matthew reacted, he had every right to be unhappy.

Then Jones gives it back, and Strauss and Collingwood race in and start mouthing off too. When you give it to someone there has to be a very good reason for it, but Jones had thrown the ball straight at Matthew. They might have thought they looked tough, but I thought they looked ridiculous. It was all too manufactured for my liking. We wouldn't have pulled a stunt like that, it was un-Australian and against the spirit of cricket.

It wasn't just with their actions, but England were becoming bolder with their words too. In the days before the first Test Matthew Hoggard suggested I might be too old and past my best. My first reaction was to laugh. I genuinely found it funny. I mean, it doesn't really sound like Hoggy to be coming out with the insults like that, does it? To me, it proved he and probably the rest of the England boys were a bit nervous before the start of the series and had decided to start making big statements. I took it as a compliment because it proved I mattered. It was a poor attempt at mind games.

On the morning of 21 July 2005, the Ashes finally began and I had never felt better. Well, I say that, but at breakfast I began to feel my stomach churning. Unusually for me, I had a real attack of the butterflies. I was desperate to finally reach 500 wickets. It had been frustrating to be on 499 for so long because nothing is guaranteed, I could have been hit by a bus and always left one short.

Nerves were replaced by excitement on arrival at Lord's. This is my favourite overseas ground, I absolutely love it. As Steve Waugh once said, it feels like home for an Australian. I even have my own spot in the dressing room right underneath the window where I first sat eight years ago. I love the history and the aura around the place. I remember the first time I played here in 1997 looking at the honour boards in the dressing rooms and seeing all the famous names that had scored a century or taken five or ten wickets. I was desperate to engrave my name up there, and I did with 8-38 in 1997 and 5-54 in 2001. Now on my final ever appearance at Lord's I wanted to get back up there again.

At first it looked like I would be made to wait for that 500th wicket. Ricky won the toss and decided to bat, so naturally I expected to put my feet up for the next couple of days and watch our guys pile up the runs. But it didn't work out like that. From the very first ball you could tell that England were up for it. Steve Harmison tore in with genuine hostility and delivered several really quick balls. With his second one he hit Alfie [Justin Langer] hard on the elbow.

Later he hit Ricky on his helmet with such force that the grille cut his cheek. That is fine, it is part of the game. If a batsman gets hit it is usually his fault for not getting out of the way. But I was disappointed that with blood coming from the cut, all the England guys stood rooted to the spot and refused to enquire how he was. Not even a simple, 'You OK, mate?' I suppose they were making a statement they planned to be aggressive in this series, but I thought it was pathetic.

Harmy was proving he was the real deal. He used his pace, hit the deck hard and was getting good bounce. His radar was on. He made sure we never settled and finished with five wickets. England bowled us all out for 190 in just over 40 overs. It was a bit of a shock, but I remained confident because I knew on that pitch we had scored more than we should have.

At tea, with England 10/0, Ricky took Brett Lee and me aside and said he thought we were bowling too short and asked us to bowl a fuller length. With the first ball after tea I dismissed Trescothick to become only the fourth bowler to take 500 Test wickets. It was a wonderful moment to finally get there. My sponsors Pony had given me a pair of boots with 500 stitched in to the sides in gold. They had wanted me to wear them at the start of the day, so if I got the 500th wicket I would be wearing them, but I didn't like the idea. I thought I would look pretty stupid if I didn't take a wicket all day. So the plan was for Kasper to bring them out at the end of the over in which I took the wicket, but he forgot and came charging out with them under his arm straight after the wicket.

Four balls later, I claimed Straussy, my nominated bunny, with a regulation dismissal. I put the ball on off stump and he nicked it to Warney in the slips. England were 11/2. This was turning into a good day. As a joke Kasper ran back out with my original boots with 501 written in marker pen. I was feeling good, as though I could take a wicket with every ball. Only seven more runs had been added when I uprooted Vaughan's off stump with a quick delivery that kept low.

I enjoyed sending the England captain back to the dressing room. You take out the leader and the rest of the side looks vulnerable. And so it proved minutes later when I got the ball to cut through Ian Bell's bat and pad to clip his off stump.

You only ever dream about playing this well. I had never felt better bowling in an Ashes Test. Underneath their helmets you could tell the English batsmen were worried, they looked uncomfortable facing me. I love bowling at Lord's, coming in from the Pavilion End bowling down the slope. I had simply put the ball in the right place. There really was no magic formula. Sorry, I know people want the finer details and get frustrated with my brief explanations. Batsmen like to think they are the intelligent ones, but I don't see it like that. You bowl in the right areas to them and they are always liable to get bored, do something stupid and nick the ball.

Poor Freddie Flintoff didn't stand a chance. He swiftly followed Bell back to the pavilion for a duck after I had sent down a ball that stayed low to hit his off stump. England were 21/5. I had taken five wickets for two runs in the space of 31 balls. At the end of the day England were 92/7 and we were back on top. By the time I returned to the dressing room our room attendant Peter Lowe had already put up my five-wicket haul on the honours board with some tape and a marker pen. Beating the engravers to it was a tradition we started back in 1997.

The following morning Kevin Pietersen offered some resistance, making 57 to drag England to a total of 155. In the build-up to the series there had been a lot of debate about whether he should replace Graeme Thorpe. The England selectors made the right choice. This was my first look at him in the Test arena and he looked a hell of a player. At one point he hoisted me in to the pavilion for six, which I wasn't too pleased about and soon after I was taken out of the attack. I was furious with Ricky, who said he thought I was never going to talk to him again, but it was nothing personal, I am like that with every captain who doesn't let me get my way.

Pietersen strikes the ball very hard, but it isn't through pure technique, I would say he just murders it, he tries to hit it, you can see the difference. It is not a natural action like Adam Gilchrist, but, hey, he can certainly smoke the ball. He only knows one way to bat, which is both good and bad. Good that he has a lot of confidence and he can score runs quickly, but bad because he gives you opportunities and that means I could always be confident of getting him.

By the end of the third day, we had succeeded in completely turning around the match, making 384 in our second innings before England had stumbled to 156/5 chasing 420 to win. There was a party atmosphere in our dressing room that night, we shared a few beers with the Hollywood actor Hugh Jackman, and all felt that the match was in the bag. They needed a lot of runs with only five wickets left in the shed. The English euphoria of Thursday morning had long gone.

England's only hope was for it to rain for the next two days, so they would have been delighted to draw back their curtains on Sunday morning and see the rain pounding down. There were a few anxious looks in our dressing room when we arrived at Lord's, but I thought the rain would clear to give us the opportunity to finish them off. It arrived late in the day at 3.45pm and we needed less than an hour win the Test.

I soon began to feel as good as I had on the Thursday afternoon. England had only added two runs to their overnight total when I got Geraint Jones playing a poor shot to Jason Gillespie at mid-on and Ashley Giles was caught by Haydos in the gully. I sent Hoggard on his way lbw before wrapping up the Test when Simon Jones edged the ball to Warney in the slips. For a moment I thought he might drop it on purpose because he had four wickets and was desperate to claim a five-for at Lord's for the first time, but of course he held on. I had taken four of the remaining five wickets for only three runs in the space of 23 balls to finish with match figures of 9-82.

As we strolled from the field, the sky was grey and overcast and the stands were half empty, but Lord's had never looked better. I felt more emotional than usual knowing that this was my final appearance at the home of cricket.

The celebrations afterwards with my family made it the perfect moment, something I had imagined for years. It felt quite surreal that here I was now actually experiencing it. Everything had fallen in to place. I had taken my 500th wicket, we had comprehensively won the Test by 239 runs and I was the man of the match.

My only regret is we went across to the England dressing room to continue our celebrations. It was empty by that time, they had all headed home, so we all piled in for Justin Langer to conduct our team song. I suppose it was symbolic; we were taking their territory and saying we owned them. But looking back, I regret that, it wasn't necessary, and if I am honest, I thought it was a bit disrespectful. No one at Lord's or any of the England players complained, but it was still wrong.

That 5-0 prediction was looking pretty good. We hadn't just beaten England, we had really turned them over and I thought it would be hard for them to come back from that. They had shown some early fighting spirit, but the facts are we won in under four days, and it would have been sooner were it not for the weather. England had talked themselves up, but failed to deliver. It promised to be a good tour.

An hour before the start of the second Test at Edgbaston we were warming up on the outfield with a game of touch rugby when Brad Haddin threw a terrible pass way beyond me. I turned to pick up the rugby ball and trod on a cricket ball lined up for the bowling drills. I immediately fell to the ground, and even as I was falling I knew I would miss the Test. I felt helpless, I wanted to rewind time and make it go away. When I hit the deck my ankle was in a lot of pain and I felt nauseous, as if I was on the brink of throwing up. Watching on television, Jane later told me I went as white as a ghost.

I looked up expecting to see my team-mates rushing towards me, but nothing, they weren't even looking at me. The problem is I have a bit of a reputation as a practical joker and they assumed I was just playing around. They only took notice when I shouted, 'Someone needs to get Hooter [our physiotherapist Errol Alcott] now!' They then sprinted over. 'I would be surprised if it wasn't broken,' I told them.

I was helped off the ground and squeezed in to the back of a car and taken to a local hospital where a scan showed I hadn't broken it, but instead ruptured two ligaments in my ankle. I later learned that when it was announced on the loudspeaker there was a change to the original line-ups and due to injury I would now not be playing and replaced by Kasper the news was greeted by an almighty cheer from the crowd. I loved hearing that, absolutely loved it. It meant I mattered. The English crowd feared me. I would hate to be a guy they didn't care about.

I arrived back at Edgbaston after lunch on a pair of crutches and with my leg in an ankle brace to watch England's innings. It wasn't a pretty sight. I am not a good spectator at the best times, but this was dreadful. The England batsmen were hitting our guys all over the ground and by the end of the day had made 407 all out. It had been brutal stuff, they scored at 5.13 an over and managed ten sixes. England's bowling coach Troy Cooley, who now works for us, told me this was the day the whole series turned on its head. He knew the England guys well and could see the transformation in their body language. They were no longer afraid.

This set the tone for the next two days and by the start of the fourth morning we were on the brink of defeat. We needed 107 to win with only two wickets remaining. When we left the hotel I thought we would be back before lunch. While there remains a chance, you never completely give up hope, but this was going to be very difficult. Still, Shane Warne and Brett Lee are fighters and they proved that.

The tension in our dressing room was unbearable as we approached our target of 282. With three runs needed to win I thought we were going to do it, we had come too close to be denied. We were getting ready to celebrate when a ball from Harmy brushed Kasper's glove and was taken by Geraint Jones. Edgbaston erupted around us. We had been on the brink of winning 2-0, and let's be honest we would not have been toppled from that position, but now had to deal with the fact that it was 1-1 and we had lost a live Test to England for the first time for eight years.

The strange thing is that a lot of good actually came from England winning that Test and the Ashes. The game exploded in popularity in both England and Australia. More kids than ever wanted to be cricketers, there were huge waiting lists for coaching clinics, sports shops started selling out of cricket gear and tickets for the next Ashes in Australia were snatched up in hours. The first four days of the SCG Test were sold out in a couple of hours and the first three days at the MCG, 100,000 each day, sold out too.

The 2005 series energised the whole game. In a strange way, it was the best thing to happen to the game in Australia. None of this would have happened if Kasper had hit a boundary instead of getting out with that ball. Now, don't get me wrong, if I could go back in time I would still want those three runs to win the Test and the Ashes, but I have to acknowledge that a lot of good things have happened because we failed.

The jubilant England players soon filed in to our dressing room to share a beer. I was glad they had done that and would continue to throughout the series. A lot of rubbish is talked about socialising with the opposition. Some have said we shouldn't do it because it takes away our mystique and gives the opposition more confidence. The argument is they can see we are just human. I don't agree. Listen, I played cricket as hard as anyone, but afterwards I liked to share a cold beer with the opposition and have a chat. That is the point of cricket and I wouldn't want it any other way. After all, it is only a game.

I had been expected to miss the third Test with it coming just four days after Edgbaston, but Errol worked his magic to allow me to throw away my crutches. I played with some strapping on my ankle to stabilise it, which just goes to prove you don't need that many ligaments. To be honest, I was probably a bit undercooked. I finished with figures of 0-86 in the first innings as England made 444. I wasn't the only one being punished. It was difficult to see my mate Jason Gillespie getting hit all around the ground. He just didn't look himself, and in truth, struggled throughout the tour. England were smart with him, very smart, they went after him with every ball and were unrelenting. I have played a lot of cricket alongside Dizzy and it was uncomfortable. He was dropped after that Test.

England were on top throughout the next three days and by the start of the final day we had been set a target of 423. It was going to be another nervy climax. We knew it was going to be tough surviving the day. From the very first ball our dressing room was quiet and tense. Everyone sat in their lucky seats and only moved for a toilet break.

As our wickets fell throughout the day, one constant remained, our captain Ricky Ponting, who played probably the greatest innings of his career. He was so brave, defended when he had to, but still played his shots. With 25 balls remaining and with Ricky on 156 we began to breathe a bit easier. But at that moment he nicked a chance from Harmy to Geraint Jones and we were plunged back in to despair.

I had little chance to dwell on it as I passed him and walked down the steps to face the last 24 balls. My task was simple: don't get out. I was prepared to take some balls on the body and block them out. Harmy and Freddie were thundering in and doing all they could, but you could tell they were getting frustrated. Was I nervous? Not at all. It was a relief to escape the cloying tension of the dressing room. I was now in control out here. These are the moments you live for as a cricketer, you want to grasp them, not avoid them.

One of the television commentators said I was 'quivering' but I can assure them I wasn't. The only moment was when Freddie hit Brett on the pads and appealed for lbw, I stopped breathing and only began again when I saw Billy Bowden shake his head.

At the start of the final over Stuart MacGill came out to the middle with the instruction to bat two metres out of the crease to take away the chance of being out lbw. I blocked at two balls and then scored from the third. As I passed Brett on my way to the non-striker's end I knew I had played my last part in this Test. It was now up to Brett to survive the final three balls, which he did brilliantly. As he tucked the last one down to the fine leg boundary he and I celebrated and hugged each other. There was a feeling of tremendous relief.

We looked up at the balcony where the rest of the guys were going mad. Celebrating a draw with such fervour was mocked in some quarters, the England guys said it proved we were feeling the pressure. That is plain wrong. We were so happy because we had survived a position we had never been in before, normally we play to win, so batting all day to draw a Test was a new one for us. We were delighted to have met the challenge.

My injury problems returned to haunt me. In the days leading up to the fourth Test at Trent Bridge I began to feel some pain in my right elbow, which saw me fail a fitness test. If watching us lose at Edgbaston was tough, this was a lot worse. I hated every minute on the balcony. England built a commanding lead in the first innings and again we didn't play like ourselves. On the final day, England struggled to make the 129 needed to win, and lost seven wickets before collapsing over the line. We wounded them, but couldn't kill them off. We were now 2-1 down with just one Test left to play.

My fitness for the fifth Test at The Oval was in doubt until the day before. Ricky had said he trusted me to be honest. I would normally try and sneak in the side with a broken leg, but I knew this match was too big. I had to be able to survive the full five days.

Despite England playing so well – they could have been 3-1 up, we still only needed to win the last Test to retain the Ashes. On the first morning I woke up after a good night's sleep fully expecting to win this Test, retain the Ashes and be sitting on the Qantas flight home in six days with a large smile on my face. I was convinced we would salvage our pride. My only slight concern was the weather.

Crucially England won the toss and made 373 in their first innings. It might have been more, but Shane Warne held them back by taking five wickets. The bigger the occasion, the better Warney plays. Alfie and Haydos made a great start to our reply with an opening stand of 185, but, as feared, the weather intervened. We decided to come off for bad light several times because we felt we had time on our side and why jeopardise it by playing in poor conditions when we didn't have to? We felt uneasy at not being out there, but we supported the decision.

By the fourth morning, however, we had no choice. If we stayed in the dressing room we would be handing over the Ashes without a fight. We were forced to play in murky conditions perfect for swing bowling and England took full advantage, reducing us from 281/2 to 367 all out. We had hoped to bat just once in this Test. We knew England would not want to be out there in this light, and at the first opportunity they left the pitch. This was met with a huge roar from the crowd. They knew this meant they were even closer to regaining the Ashes. After the disruption, to have a bit of fun I suggested we re-take the field all wearing sunglasses to convince the umpires how bright it really was. The crowd loved it, but it didn't work and we went off again not long after.

My 5-0 prediction was coming back to haunt me. Whenever I fielded on the boundary the crowd would give me plenty of grief about it. I held up two fingers on each hand to tell them it would end 2-2. Then when the goading got worse I showed them a one and a zero to remind them their soccer team had been embarrassed 1-0 by little Northern Ireland a few days earlier. I was getting desperate!

On the final morning I still believed we would get our hands on the urn by the end of the day, but my earlier supreme confidence had been dented by the weather delays. Still, with the sun now shining and 98 overs to be bowled there was hope. That increased when I got Vaughan and Bell in successive balls early in their innings. I even thought I had a hat-trick when a bouncer to Pietersen nicked something and landed in Ricky's hands, but Billy Bowden turned down our appeals, saying it had hit his shoulder. I have never seen a television replay of it, but I still reckon the ball might have brushed the glove. KP, however, has told me that wasn't the case and that is good enough for me.

We were close to getting KP out before lunch, but both Warney and Haydos dropped him. He was playing horribly, not dealing well with the short stuff, he seemed nervous and not sure of himself. I thought it was only a matter of time before we knocked him over. But after lunch he returned a new man. He decided to trust his game and attack us, and sadly, we had no answers. He was striking almost everything to the boundary. I had never seen anything like it. He was in the zone and we couldn't shift him. The agonising part was that every boundary was leading England to the Ashes and we were powerless to stop him. I eventually got him out for 158, but it was a meaningless wicket, by that time we knew the Ashes were gone. We had expended so much energy in the morning that there was now nothing left in the tank.

Those last few hours at The Oval were torture. I could hear the crowd singing and celebrating the return of the Ashes, champagne corks were popping all over the ground and every trip to the boundary forced me to come face-to-face with an army of gloating England fans. I now know what hell looks like!

Was losing the Ashes as horrible as I had imagined? It was worse. Much worse. I felt sick. I never wanted to be part of an Australian side who lost a series to England, but here I was on the field at The Oval watching Michael Vaughan and his team get their hands on the urn. We were still on the field doing some television interviews when England stepped on to the stage and waited to lift the Ashes. I had the opportunity to escape to the dressing room, but something made me stay and watch the ceremony. It was painful, but I forced myself to watch England lift the Ashes, bounce up and down and spray champagne at each other.

I remember standing on the balcony at Edgbaston in 1997 after England had beaten us in the first Test of that series and watching them celebrate. I hated it, really hated it. I was desperate never to have to witness that ever again. I swore I would do everything I could to avoid it. That was the only motivation I needed to beat England for four consecutive series. They won a few Tests, but they were never live ones, and when we beat them we did it comprehensively. I had managed to keep those painful scenes at bay for eight years, but here they were again.

What made losing the Ashes slightly easier was the firm knowledge that we had lost to the better team. We weren't robbed, we weren't unlucky, let there be no doubt England deserved to win the Ashes. They batted, bowled and fielded better than us. We prepared well and played well, but we were caught out by an England side who took their game to the next level. They set us the kind of stern challenge we had never faced before and the truth is we came up short. We weren't used to teams looking us in the eye and going toe to toe, and we didn't know how to deal with it. It caught us by surprise. We seemed to lack our normal ruthless edge. We created some opportunities, but didn't grasp them.

We weren't complacent, but we just couldn't compete with England's level of preparation, which gave them the edge. They had an extensive support staff of coaches to concentrate on bowling and every small aspect of their game that we couldn't match and you saw the result.

Ahead of the 2005 series, Ricky Ponting said there wasn't an Englishman who would get in to the Australian side. After the series I reckon Freddie might make it as our 12th man! Seriously, Freddie would get in to any side in the world. He was simply awesome, finally fulfilling his enormous potential. He was one of the differences between the sides. His batting was good, but his bowling was amazing. Maybe that was the difference: a few more England players could creep in to our side. Only a few though.

Looking back at the 2005 series I am genuinely proud to have played a part in what is recognised as the greatest series in the history of the game, especially as it included that spell at Lord's and my 500th wicket.

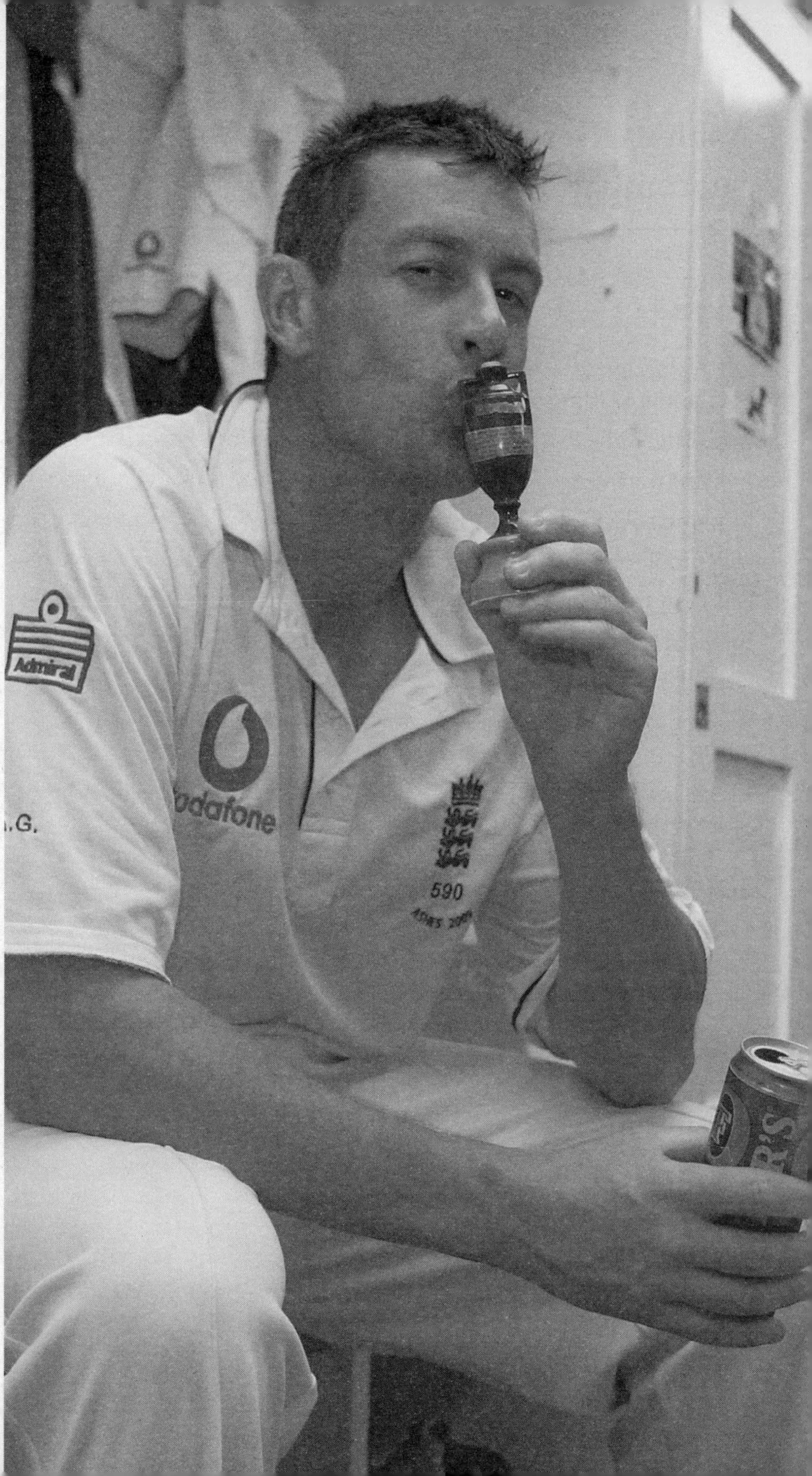

ASHLEY GILES

Ashley Giles – Fifth Test, The Oval, 8-12 September 2005

Ashley Giles began his career as a seam bowler, but after moving from Surrey to Warwickshire in 1992 he was converted into a left-arm spinner. After making his Test debut in 1998, he was England's leading spinner from the tour to Pakistan in 2000 until the Ashes of 2005. The 'King of Spain', a nickname he has enjoyed since a spelling mistake on a souvenir mug, played a major role in England's revival with 31 wickets as they won seven consecutive Tests in the summer of 2004. He is one of only ten Englishmen to take 100 wickets and score 1,000 runs in Test cricket. By far the most important runs were the seven he scored at Trent Bridge and the 59 at The Oval to help England win the Ashes in 2005.

Slow left-arm bowler, right-handed batsman
Born: 9 March 1973, Chertsey, Surrey
Test debut: July 1998 v South Africa
Last Test: December 2006 v Australia
Test record: 52 matches, 140 wickets at an average of 39.60; 1,347 runs at an average of 20.72

The state of play
Kevin Pietersen and Ashley Giles guided England towards their first Ashes triumph for 18 years in a thrilling climax to the greatest Test match series of all time.

Scoreboard

England first innings

M.E. Trescothick	c Hayden	b Warne	43
A.J. Strauss	c Katich	b Warne	129
M.P. Vaughan	c Clarke	b Warne	11
I.R. Bell	lbw	b Warne	0
K.P. Pietersen		b Warne	14
A. Flintoff	c Warne	b McGrath	72
P.D. Collingwood	lbw	b Tait	7
G.O. Jones		b Lee	25
A.F. Giles	lbw	b Warne	32
M.J. Hoggard	c Martyn	b McGrath	2
S.J. Harmison		not out	20
Extras	(b 4, lb 6, w 1, nb 7)		18
Total	(all out, 105.3 overs)		373

Bowling	O	M	R	W
McGrath	27	5	72	2
Lee	23	3	94	1
Tait	15	1	61	1
Warne	37.3	5	122	6
Katich	3	0	14	0

Australia first innings

J.L. Langer		b Harmison	105
M.L. Hayden	lbw	b Flintoff	138
R.T. Ponting	c Strauss	b Flintoff	35
D.R. Martyn	c Collingwood	b Flintoff	10
M.J. Clarke	lbw	b Hoggard	25
S.M. Katich	lbw	b Flintoff	1
A.C. Gilchrist	lbw	b Hoggard	23
S.K. Warne	c Vaughan	b Flintoff	0
B. Lee	c Giles	b Hoggard	6
G.D. McGrath	c Strauss	b Hoggard	0
S.W. Tait		not out	1
Extras	(b 4, lb 8, w 2, nb 9)		23
Total	(all out, 107.1 overs)		367

Bowling	O	M	R	W
Harmison	22	2	87	1
Hoggard	24.1	2	97	4
Flintoff	34	10	78	5
Giles	23	1	76	0
Collingwood	4	0	17	0

England second innings

M.E. Trescothick	lbw	b Warne	33
A.J. Strauss	c Katich	b Warne	1
M.P. Vaughan	c Gilchrist	b McGrath	45
I.R. Bell	c Warne	b McGrath	0
K.P. Pietersen		b McGrath	158
A. Flintoff		c & b Warne	8
P.D. Collingwood	c Ponting	b Warne	10
G.O. Jones		b Tait	1
A.F. Giles		b Warne	59
M.J. Hoggard		not out	4
S.J. Harmison	c Hayden	b Warne	0
Extras	(b 4, w 7, nb 5)		16
Total	(all out, 91.3 overs)		335

Bowling	O	M	R	W
McGrath	26	3	85	3
Lee	20	4	88	0
Warne	38.3	3	124	6
Clarke	2	0	6	0
Tait	5	0	28	1

Australia second innings (target: 342 runs)

J.L. Langer		not out	0
M.L. Hayden		not out	0
Extras	(lb 4)		4
Total	(0 wickets, 0.4 overs)		4

Bowling	O	M	R	W
Harmison	0.4	0	0	0

Ashley Giles

I WANTED TO slow down this moment. I wanted to make it last forever. As I walked off the field with 23,000 people on their feet at The Oval I thought, 'Look at this, I better milk it' but it went by in a flash. It was late on the final day of the series, we were 335/9 and I was out, having made my highest ever Test score, but above all, we had regained the Ashes. It felt like my face was going to explode with happiness.

Not long after, Australia began their second innings. It was a mere formality, they faced four balls before taking the light. But it gave us the chance to come out as a team wearing our caps and all experience this emotionally charged atmosphere. For just a few minutes we could stand in the centre, before the madness really began, and look around as The Oval celebrated the return of the Ashes. We all had silly smiles on our faces and couldn't stop giggling. We had done it. We had really done it. The Ashes were home.

At the start of the summer we seriously believed this could happen. Why not? In the previous two years we had enjoyed almost continuous success under Michael Vaughan and Duncan Fletcher, winning a record eight consecutive Tests in 2004, and a series in South Africa for the first time in 40 years. We hadn't just stumbled on this form; we had brought together the right players, worked hard and executed our plans. We knew the Aussies would be tougher than the West Indies or New Zealand, but there was a feeling we were peaking at just the right time.

Crucially, guys like Kevin Pietersen and Freddie Flintoff had never played Test cricket against the Aussies. I myself had only faced them in two Tests in different series. This meant we weren't weighed down by bad history. In other eras it would have been very difficult for the old guard of Nasser Hussain, Michael Atherton and Alec Stewart to be so positive ahead of an Ashes series because they had been ground down by so many beatings. We didn't have that problem.

We had also met the Aussies in the ICC Champions Trophy semi-final at Edgbaston in September 2004 and didn't have too much trouble beating them by six wickets. That was a huge stepping-stone because it proved we could overcome them. Our confidence grew even more during the one-day series in the month before the Ashes. We beat Australia twice and salvaged a tie in the NatWest Series final at Lord's when I grabbed two runs off the final ball. We also beat them in a Twenty20 game at the Rose Bowl by 100 runs. It was dawning on all of us, 'These guys aren't that big and tough, we can take them on.'

Of course, Glenn McGrath still predicted a 5-0 whitewash, but that didn't bother us. He is a lovely bloke off the field, but he is known for these big statements. We brushed it off as typical Aussie confidence. Did it have us trembling with fear? No chance. It was just banter, and to be honest, I thought we could beat them 5-0 as well.

On the opening morning of the first Test the England team arrived at Lord's on foot. We had been told we couldn't drive to the ground as there was a hospitality tent on our car park, and then we had trouble hailing a taxi, so we walked the mile from the Landmark Hotel in Marylebone, drawing more than a few curious glances as we strode up Park Road.

I have never experienced such an atmosphere at Lord's. When we walked through the Long Room the MCC members were shouting and patting us on the back. They are usually such a reserved bunch. On the field we wanted to hit the Aussies hard from the very first ball. Steve Harmison did that with a spell that saw Justin Langer hit on the elbow and Ricky Ponting on the helmet with such force that it cut his cheek. I don't know if it was a conscious decision, but none of us went to see if he was OK. Normally we're good lads, but maybe this was a show of strength. 'Just get on with it' was our attitude. I asked how he was afterwards, but at the time it was tense and we didn't want to break that. He was on his feet and looked all right. If he had gone down we would have all been around him.

That first day was the most draining I have ever had on a cricket field and I didn't even bowl a single ball. For the first three hours, the Aussie wickets kept tumbling until we had them all out for 190. We were on a real high and they were going crazy in the Long Room again. Then McGrath went and spoiled the party. He took our first five wickets with only 21 runs on the board. From delirious joy to despair in ten overs. I was the last of the 17 wickets to fall that day as we finished on a pitiful 92/7. We would never recover.

By the Saturday morning the Australians were batting well in their second innings and setting us a daunting target that would eventually reach 420. Michael Vaughan later told us he could see us physically shrinking and becoming intimidated again. He wasn't wrong. We were still drained from the first day and the thought running through my head was, 'Fucking hell, what have we done? We've thrown away this game already.'

That was confirmed on a drizzly Sunday afternoon as we slumped to 180 all out to lose by 239 runs. I lasted just two balls before McGrath got me. Some of the Aussies, certainly not all of them, were quite disrespectful, chirping away as we headed to a heavy defeat. When they knew they were going to win, there was no need to rub our faces in it. I hadn't forgotten that at The Oval, which made victory even sweeter.

But back then a horrible silence descended on the dressing room. It was dreadful to lose so easily after all the hype. Maybe that got to us, but either way, we were all shocked. We didn't join the Aussies for a drink at the end of play because we were too embarrassed. We had been compared to them and yet they had thrashed us easily.

Then the criticism from the papers and former players began to rain down. Suddenly we were all rubbish. They said we weren't good enough to beat Australia and could even lose 5-0. In one Test we had gone from heroes to zeroes, the success of the last year forgotten. Myself, Geraint Jones and Ian Bell were pushed to the end of the plank as the chosen scapegoats. I was disappointed with my performance, I hadn't taken a wicket, but I wasn't on my own, and with the exception of Harmy and KP we had all failed.

Two days after Lord's I was sitting at home flicking through *The Times* when I came across a piece entitled 'Why playing Giles is akin to taking the field with only ten men'. It quoted the former Zimbabwe Test player and current director of cricket at Derbyshire, Dave Houghton, saying, 'What use is [Ashley Giles] in the side? He's not going to get wickets against the Aussie batsmen and he's not going to make any runs against their bowlers. With him, England are effectively playing ten against 11. They should either include another specialist batsman or pick a spinner who can bat.' Already painfully raw, this really hurt me. I had enjoyed a good couple of years, but one bad Test and I was set upon. All I wanted was some respect, but it felt like I was pissing against the wind.

The next day I played for Warwickshire in a one-day game against Kent at Canterbury. The crowd were dreadful to me, which was upsetting as they were English supporters. I also received a letter from a fan, which I thought might say 'keep your head up, Gilo' but instead it said, 'Stop your fucking whingeing, you're not good enough.'

At Edgbaston, Chris Foy from the *Daily Mail* asked for a few words. In my state of mind, I should have said no, because I was still upset and angry. Instead, I had a bite back at my critics. 'Unfortunately, it feels like a lot of ex-players don't want us to win the Ashes, either because they didn't or because they were the last people to do it,' I told him. 'That might sound bitter, but that's the way it feels.'

I really got nailed after that. The abuse got worse because I had the temerity to answer back. The attitude was who is he to have a go at us, what does he know? I felt like the world was on top of me. It just went on and on. People who had never met me started having a go. It really descended into personal abuse. I was called 'dead wood', 'a namby pamby', and 'precious'.

My head was full of rubbish when I arrived at Edgbaston for the second Test. I walked in to the dressing room and the first person I saw was Michael Vaughan. 'Alright Gilo, had a good week?' 'To be honest, it hasn't been the best one of my life,' I laughed. 'Why, what's wrong?' He didn't have a clue; he had been away with his family and ignored the press. Vaughany was right when he told me I looked haggard.

It had been one of the hardest weeks of my life. I kept thinking, 'Why does everyone think I'm shit? Maybe it is because they're right.'

I felt my head was going to explode. On the Wednesday night I started to clear my mind and focus on the game with the help of our team psychologist Steve Bull. He said, 'I'm not letting you out of my sight until I am convinced you have got the rubbish out of your head and are focusing on this Test.' I felt better when I left him.

I was still incredibly nervous on the first morning, but I knew my home crowd at Edgbaston would support me. They are always a raucous and fiercely patriotic bunch, so it is a great place to come when you're down. I knew they would look after me, and I wanted to give them something to shout about.

We got off to a flyer on the first day with KP, Tres and Freddie sending the ball to all points of the ground as we finished on 407 all out. In the Australian reply on the second day Ricky Ponting had effortlessly made his way to 61 off 76 balls and seemed destined for another hundred when I tempted him to sweep and he top-edged the ball to Vaughan at short fine leg. That wicket meant a lot. It offered a tremendous release, which you could see in my reaction. I loved the fact that the rest of the guys swarmed around, rubbing my head. I then got Michael Clarke and Shane Warne as we knocked them over for 308. The troubles of the previous week began to float away.

Though we only made 182 in our second innings, by the end of the Saturday Australia were 175/8 chasing a target of 282. They needed 107 more runs with only Warney, Brett Lee and Michael Kasprowicz left, so there was a superb mood among the guys. We thought we had won. It had taken three days and we were back in the series. We went out for dinner that night excited about being on the brink of squaring it at 1-1.

That last day was ridiculous. You don't take anything for granted against the Aussies, but we only needed two good balls to win. When we stepped on the field it felt as though the crowd were already celebrating. But as Warney and Brett whittled down the target we all grew quiet. We were beginning to feel uncomfortable until Warney trod on his stumps 62 runs short. I thought it was then curtains for the Aussies. Freddie was charging in and reversing the ball, so he would surely quickly get that final wicket. But it didn't happen and their target kept getting smaller; 50, 40, 30.

When they needed 20 I started to feel sick. Brett and Kasprowicz were batting well and their edges and mis-hits were falling safely. Standing at gully, I glanced over at Andrew Strauss, who said, 'This is getting tricky.' The rest of the boys were looking at each other in disbelief. We thought it would be 1-1, but we were about to go 2-0 down. Vaughany remembers us all going missing. That wasn't because we had given up, but we were away in our own thoughts like, 'How the fuck have we thrown this game away? How are we going to get off the field because we will be murdered if we throw this away?'

I had another more immediate problem. I couldn't see a bloody thing. It was very bright, the crowd was packed in right at my level, and if anyone cut Freddie, the ball was coming straight out of the crowd. I was thinking, 'How the fuck am I going to see this ball?' I have to catch it, anything else was unthinkable.

When they needed 15 Simon Jones dropped a chance at third man from Kasprowicz. 'That's it, that was our one chance and we've blown it,' I cursed to myself. For what would prove to be the last over I was down at fine leg, I remember Brett driving Harmy through the covers and I thought that was it, it had gone for four and we had lost, but I hadn't seen we had a man at deep point, so it was just a single.

Finally, with Australia needing just three to win, in came Harmy and forced Kasprowicz to glove one to Jonah [Geraint Jones]. At first I wasn't sure if he was out, but when the boys went up I knew we had done it. I remember running around in circles on my own for about a minute lost in my own little world. Realising I looked a complete idiot, I thought I should join my team-mates. What a fine line between defeat and victory, and we were just the right side of it. We couldn't have come back from 2-0 down against this side, no chance.

That afternoon we went out on Broad Street in Birmingham, and everywhere we went we were applauded. But if the Aussies had got three more runs we wouldn't have been able to show our faces. Sitting with our beers we were all still in a state of shock, we kept puffing out our cheeks and saying, 'That was close.'

Four days later we took the momentum of Edgbaston in to the third Test at Old Trafford. After winning the toss we were treated to a wonderful innings of 166 from Michael Vaughan. He shocked me, because he had been struggling for form and had ten other guys to worry about, but managed to play a brilliant knock. When he does it, he does it big. He was aggressive and his timing was superb, but his running was ordinary, so you can't have everything. This set the foundation for a first-innings total of 444.

The Australians didn't look so confident now. They clearly weren't used to dealing with this pressure. In their reply I removed both openers. I got Langer when he edged the ball for Belly to claim with a lightning reaction catch at short leg and then Hayden lbw. The most satisfying wicket was Damien Martyn with a ball that pitched outside leg stump, but clipped the outside of his off stump.

Rain ruined much of Saturday, so we finally got the Aussies out for 302 on the Sunday before we scored quickly to declare on 280/6. It meant Australia needed 423 runs to win, or more pertinently they had 108 overs to survive. Hayden and Langer kept us at bay on the Sunday night to set up an extraordinary final day.

On the Monday morning 20,000 people were turned away from the gates of Old Trafford. I got there early, full of nerves because I wanted to get on with it, and couldn't believe the mass of people. Those that did make it in saw Australia offer plenty of resistance, chiefly through their captain Ricky Ponting, but we were taking wickets regularly enough to feel confident we would win. When we got rid of the normally obdurate Jason Gillespie for a duck it left Australia at 264/7 at 4.20pm.

More than two hours later we were getting desperate. We had finally seen off Ponting for 156, and now needed the wicket of Lee or McGrath in the final 24 balls. I stood in an England field of seven slips, a short leg and a silly mid-off, hoping Freddie, who continued to amaze me, or Harmy could get a nick. It never came.

There was some consolation, but not much, from the sight of the whole Australian squad jumping around on their balcony celebrating a draw. But, above all, this was a lost opportunity. I had let the team and myself down. We needed one wicket, but I couldn't deliver it. I didn't even get one in the entire second innings. That night driving home to Birmingham I felt terribly low, and the sense of disappointment stayed with me for a couple of days. A few sessions on the piss and playing golf with my mates helped get it out of my system. And I had learned my lesson. I didn't pick up a paper.

At the start of the fourth Test in Nottingham we were more convinced than ever we could win the series. The Australians were on the run. After winning the toss Straussy and Tres put on 105 for the first wicket, but the Aussies came back to have us 241/5 early on the second day. The key to winning the whole series was the 177-run partnership between Freddie and Jonah, which began at this point and helped us finish on 477.

Freddie's innings of 102 saw him come of age. If you play like he did against the best team in the world you have earned the right to greatness. On television they might look daunting, but in the flesh they weren't. As soon as he shared a field with the Aussies he quickly realised, 'These guys aren't that great.'

After Australia had finished the second day wobbling on 99/5 Adam Gilchrist was hoping to guide them away from trouble the next morning when he nicked a ball towards Straussy at second slip. I was at gully and thought he had no chance, but he hung in the air to grab the ball before holding on to it when he hit the floor. I thought, 'It is all going our way.' They never recovered and were all out for 218, allowing us to ask them to bat again for the first time since 1988. None of them had ever had to follow on before; they didn't know what was happening.

Further evidence they were rattled came when Ponting was run out by our substitute fielder Gary Pratt in their second innings. He was not at all happy. While waiting for the third umpire's decision he started shouting at us. He also had a go at Fletch on his way back to the dressing room, though I don't think Fletch helped by coming out on the balcony. Ponting felt we were using too many substitute fielders, but on this occasion Simon Jones was having a scan in hospital, so we didn't have a choice. And we're not exactly going to have the worst fielder in the world patrolling cover. For Ponting to react like that was ridiculous and showed they were under the cosh. All the way through that game they had whinged about decisions. We were clearly getting under their skin.

On the fourth morning Australia resumed on 222/4, and while we didn't take a wicket for a while, there was no panicking, we continued to bowl with discipline, so they couldn't come at us. Eventually Warney cut loose and gave me a bit of a clout, but I got him stumped by Jonah for 45. They were all out for 387 and we now needed just 129 to go 2-1 up.

'Come on, lads, finish it for us,' was how the rest of us felt towards the openers. We wanted a nice easy finish. We made a good start, cheering every run, but then Warney got Vaughan and Tres and suddenly we were 36/2. The nerves began to get worse. Somehow I knew I was going to have to play a part in this game. Waiting to do that, I have never known nerves like it. I was literally shaking.

I couldn't sit still, so I went in to the coaches' office to be with Duncan and Troy Cooley, our bowling coach. 'I am absolutely shitting myself … I'm not sure how I am going to cope,' I told Fletch. He looked me in the eye. 'At least you can do something about it if you're called upon.' 'Yeah, but I don't want to, I want the other guys to do it.' It didn't look like I was going to get my way as Strauss and Bell were both out in the space of three balls to leave us 57/4.

The coming together of Freddie and KP brought some relief as they made their way past 100. We got all boisterous in the dressing room, but it soon fell flat when Lee removed KP. When that happened I left the coaches' office to sit in the main dressing room with my pads on.

Fifteen balls later Lee got Freddie too and I was in. It was 111/6. I got up and remember everyone looked at me without any confidence because of my famously miserable record against Warne.

Heading down the stairs with my helmet and gloves on, my nerves evaporated. I put my cricket head on to get ready for Warne. 'Right, keep your leg out the way, and if he bowls in line look out for the quicker ones,' I told myself. 'Brett Lee is bowling quickly, it is reversing and keeping low, so keep your head up and don't fall over. Get over the bounce.'

I had been in the middle for just eight balls when Jonah played a shot to break the game, but only succeeded in putting it down Kasprowicz's throat at long off. We were 116/7. In marched Hoggy, he is a gutsy bugger who knows how to hold a bat. He had a stupid grin on his face. 'Come on, me and you will get it done,' he said. 'I should warn you Brett Lee is bowling 95 mph in-duckers, good luck!' The Aussies were chirping a bit, but it wasn't personal, they were just trying to keep a tight handle on the game. I shut everything else out, there were only the four of us, me, Hoggy, Brett and Warney, out there.

We needed 13 runs. Warney had already got me out four times in the series, so I was naturally wary of him. I thought he would bowl a lot of sliders and try to line me up for an lbw and he should have thrown in a lot more of his big leg breaks too. I was making a conscious effort to keep my front foot on leg stump so if he sent down something straight and quick I could play it. 'Come on, you twat, concentrate,' I kept saying to myself. 'Keep your head up, keep your leg out the way, watch the ball, watch the ball.'

Hoggy relieved the tension with a wonderful drive through extra cover for four, and after I had taken two from a shot to long leg we needed just two more runs. Warney then bowled me one on the leg stump, I clipped it, frankly I timed the shit out of it, but it hit Simon Katich at short leg. I had decided when the target got down to two, anything up there I was going to try and hit hard and if it missed a fielder it was all over. But I got the next delivery wrong, it was a slider, so I went for a big drive only for it to go through the gap of my bat and pad. I thought he had bowled me, but it missed off stump.

Then Warney tossed another one up at me, which I just tried to lean on. It wasn't the best timed shot, but there was no one there apart from mid-on, so we ran two. We had won. Oh, that felt good. That meant everything. I clenched my fist, lifted my bat to the sky and hugged Hoggy. We were in front with one to go. God, it felt good.

Back in the dressing room everyone was slapping me on the head, there were loads of cuddles, everyone was going mad, Freddie looked particularly demented. Before I knew it, I had a big Geordie on top of me; Harmy dived on me and wrestled me to the floor. The whole team naturally had a big night out in Nottingham before Hoggy and me got up early to speak to the press. We both had terrible hangovers and looked a bit shabby in front of the cameras, but I didn't mind, I could get quite used to this hero thing.

In the aftermath of Trent Bridge, we all mentioned the fact that if we had got that wicket at Old Trafford we would have won the Ashes by now and could have gone on the piss for the week before The Oval. Instead we had to face up to the hardest week of our lives. The country had gone cricket-mad. You couldn't turn anywhere without being recognised, which is unusual for cricketers. I tried to stay away from anything to do with the Ashes, which was tough as it was being hyped as the biggest sporting event in England since the 1966 World Cup Final and plastered all over the newspapers, radio and television. Even the weather reports came live from The Oval.

My wife Stine had something of a premonition in the week of the fifth Test. She woke up one morning and said, 'I've just had the strangest dream, you were all on a bus and everyone was waving at you.' I had heard brief mention about an open-top bus tour if we won, but I had never mentioned it to her. Weird. She can be funny like that.

At the back of my mind I feared there could be a cruel twist with the Aussies snatching it at the end. I was looking up at the sky, hoping a monsoon would descend on London for the next week. But on the first day the sun shone and Warney spun his magic to take five wickets. Even so we were reasonably pleased to finish on 319/7 with Straussy getting a century.

On the second morning I resumed on five and progressed to 32 as we finished on 373 all out. It was crucial to drag it out for a little bit longer. While I had only got seven at Trent Bridge, it was a huge step to overcome the Warney factor, and in the build-up to The Oval I had enjoyed a prolonged session with Merlyn, the bowling machine which attempts to simulate his bowling action. I was patient and played myself in to a bit of form, which would prove more than useful for the second innings.

We never expected the Aussies to make it easy and Langer and Hayden then scored 112 without loss as we failed to take a wicket in an uninterrupted session for the first time in the series. After tea, before a ball had been bowled, Australia returned to the field, but then took the surprising decision to leave due to poor light. Walking off, we kept our heads down, so they couldn't see the glee on our faces. It wasn't our problem. The longer they stayed off the field the more chance we had of winning.

On the Saturday Langer and Hayden both reached centuries, but rain and poor light came to our aid again, washing out 53 overs. By the Sunday morning the Aussies had no choice but to bat in the gloom. It was great for bowling, but awful for fielding. At one point I was at fourth slip when Freddie was bowling and I couldn't see a thing. If it came my way the ball was going to clean me up.

Australia started the day on 277/2, but an amazing spell from Freddie and Hoggy got them all out for 367. They lost their last seven wickets in just 90 balls. Freddie was awesome; we couldn't get the ball out of his hand. His attitude was this was the final Test and there was no point in leaving anything behind. It was all or nothing now. Their innings came to a close when I caught Lee's slog deep on the long-on boundary.

On the Sunday night six of us went to a Pizza Express near the hotel with our wives. Around the table we were all distant, thinking about the following day. At various times we all weren't there. You had to shout to get us out of our trance. You couldn't avoid thinking we were on the brink of the biggest day of our lives.

I got to my hotel door on Monday morning and didn't want to leave. I did, but I didn't. I was almost overpowered by nerves, it was like going to the gallows. I know Fletch had a wobble too. Everything I did, taking the lift, walking through the lobby, I thought the next time I do it the Ashes will have been decided and our lives might have changed forever.

At The Oval Fletch took the chat and he was visibly shaken. You don't normally get that from him, but you could hear the tension in his voice. Looking around all the guys had a mask of anxiety, and were clearing their throats and fidgeting a lot. It promised to be both the worst and the best day. We needed to bat for around 60 of the 98 overs to make sure of a draw. If I was shaking and nervous at Nottingham, I was far worse now, I was a physical wreck at the start of our innings.

After resuming on 34/1, the sight of McGrath removing Vaughan and Bell in successive balls to leave us 67/3 made me worse. The Ashes were slipping away.

Hoggy and I went in to the dining room at The Oval to hide from the action. We started playing rummy, something we had never done before. Then someone put their head around the door to tell us Tres was out. This can't be happening, we don't deserve this.

By lunch we had lost Freddie too and were 126/5. At the start of the afternoon session I went and sat in the coaches' office with my pads on. I was gently shaking and felt sick. The fitness coach Nigel Stockill came in and said, 'Are you alright?' and got me a glass of water. 'Can you just sit down and talk to me for a while, not about cricket, just about anything,' I asked him. We had some general chit-chat before Geraint Jones got tumbled by Shaun Tait. I was in.

It was 199/7 and we were in serious danger of throwing away the Ashes. My mouth was dry and I was breathing quickly as I walked down the steps to join Kevin Pietersen, but as I stepped over the rope it all became clearer again. I was focused and cricket thoughts flooded my head: Tait is reversing it, get your legs out of the way, watch the ball, get your face straight.

I had to stay with Kev, that was my job. We just tried to relax each other, he kept saying 'keep going, George' to make me laugh. It has been said a few times I look like the actor George Clooney, something I am not going to argue with. Together we would count our way through every ball in an over, five, four, three, two, one, and then again. We then counted down 12 balls over two overs and kept upping it as our confidence grew.

At tea we had made it to 221. Everyone was really chuffed, but I knew we weren't there yet. I went and sat in the coaches' room again and kept telling myself to focus. I wanted no part in the premature celebrations. You never know when you're safe with the Aussies. Even if it got down to them needing ten an over for 25 overs they could still do it.

After tea we began to gradually pull away. The Ashes were getting closer every time Kev struck the ball to the boundary as he made his way to 158. It was a joy to watch such raw power and supreme confidence up close. Kevin was very relaxed, he is just incredibly confident all the time. Some of the shots he played were ridiculous, he took on Warney, hitting him for a succession of sixes and fours.

Brett Lee was bowling at 95 mph, but I didn't feel any fear. I thought, 'You are going to have to kill me to get me out because I'm not going anywhere.' I would do whatever it took to stay in. I wanted the Ashes that much. During the same spell Kev nonchalantly hit Brett over the longest boundary in to the crowd in front of square. How on earth did he do that?

Incredibly, Kev had been under some pressure before this Test as he hadn't scored a century so far in the series. He is always going to fall in to that trap because of his confidence, but I love that about him. We need to create more Kevin Pietersens. When he first joined the side I remember thinking if this bloke thinks he can be bolshie in this dressing room he has got another thing coming, but he fitted in straight away and gave us a new lease of life. He is full of the odd bit of bullshit, but it doesn't harm anyone, it is good fun. Beyond the bravado, he is a very professional man and a brilliant cricketer.

When we reached 300 I began to feel pretty good. There wasn't a specific moment I thought we had done it, just a gradual easing of the tension. But I know I was there on the field when we won the Ashes. You can't buy that. It will stay with me forever.

My role was to be Kev's chaperone, but I also managed my highest Test score of 59. I was proud as I gave everything against the best bowlers in the world in a pressurised situation. That told the real story of Ashley Giles, and whatever the doubters had said earlier in the series they couldn't take that knock away from me. I had proved what I could do for the team.

After I was ninth man out we didn't add any more runs to finish 335 all out. Australia then faced those four balls in their second innings before taking the offer of bad light. Back in the dressing room there was a bit of confusion about what was happening until the umpires Rudi Koertzen and Billy Bowden popped their heads around the door, and said, 'We want you to keep it quiet, but we're going to call the game off, congratulations.' We all jumped up and down and went mad. Job done. There is a bond between the 12 players that will remain forever because we feel like we have been through a couple of world wars together.

Of course, we had a big night out. I remember being drunk, but the adrenaline was still running through me so I didn't feel so bad. Arriving back at the hotel in the early hours, I woke up my two kids and whispered, 'We won the Ashes, we won the Ashes.' After three hours' sleep, I jumped straight out of bed with no hangover. I was so excited. 'Let's get breakfast, let's get the kids ready,' I told Stine. 'It is only 6am, go back to sleep,' she said. But I couldn't wait to continue the celebrations. I put the telly on and the first thing I saw was a live shot of a reporter in our hotel reception saying Andrew Flintoff was still in the bar. What sort of state would he be in?

Later on we all stumbled on to an open-top bus, slightly concerned there would only be a few people on the streets. But our fears were allayed when we turned the first corner and saw people five deep along the route, and others hanging out of windows and standing on roofs. Straussy and I looked at each other like kids, we couldn't believe it. We got off at Trafalgar Square to greet the 20,000 who had gathered under Nelson's Column. It was a moment I wished could last forever.

Afterwards we made our way down Whitehall to meet the Prime Minister at Downing Street. It was basically a photo opportunity for Tony Blair. We were exhausted and disappointed to discover they didn't have any alcohol, but they soon managed to find some. KP chatted to Cherie Blair like they were best mates, but when she moved on, he asked, 'Who was she?'

Then it was on to Lord's for a few presentations, by which time we were rocking again and had found our second wind. Back at the hotel I had a choice between falling in to bed and sleeping for 16 hours or jumping in to the shower and getting ready for another night out. You only win the Ashes for the first time once, so I jumped in the shower and headed down to the hotel bar.

On the Wednesday lunchtime I drove home to Birmingham, which finally gave me a few hours to myself. Listening to the James Blunt CD I had played all summer, I had the opportunity to think back to everything we had been through over the last seven weeks. That really was a lovely moment, just letting it all sink in. We had won the Ashes.

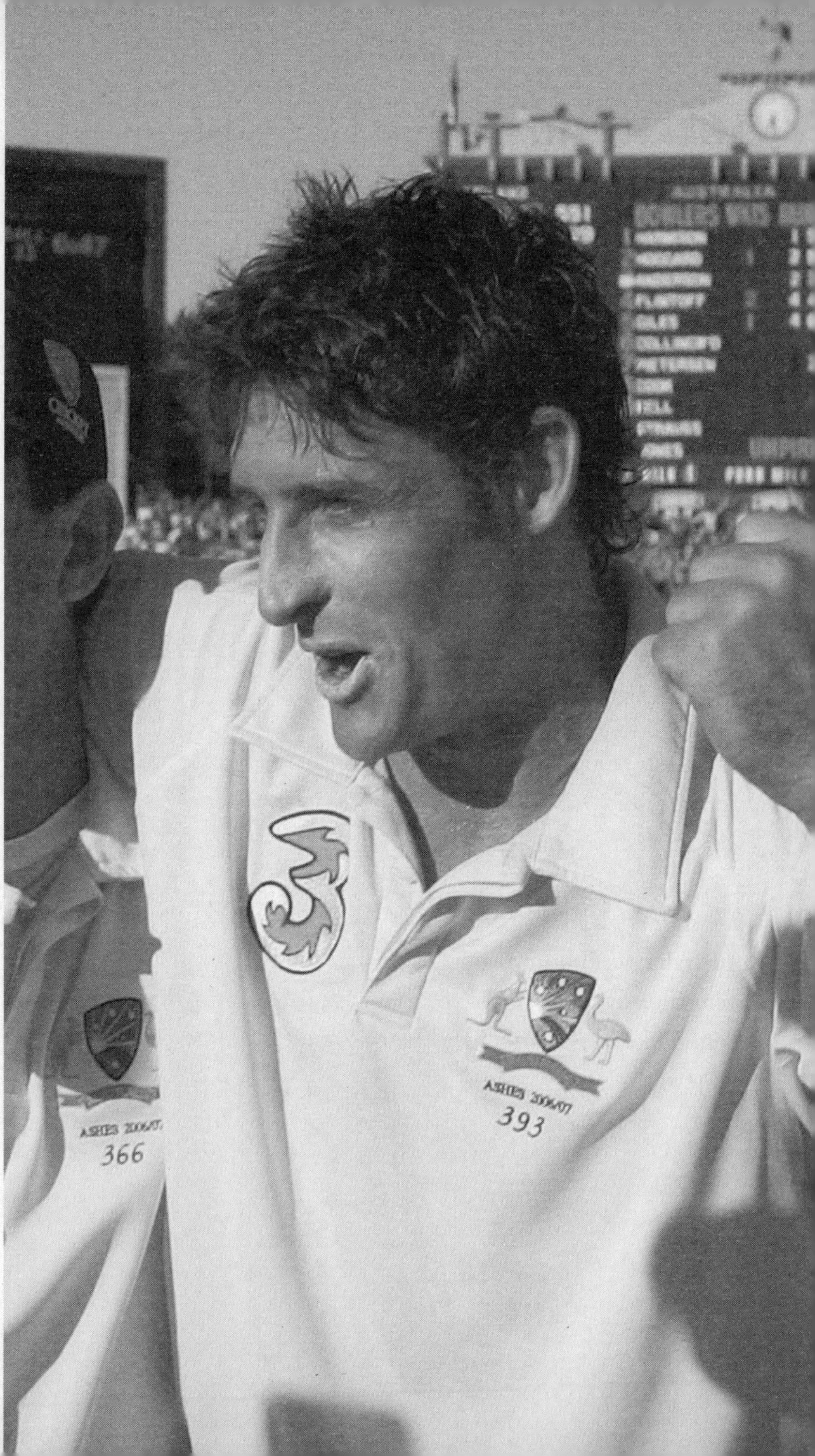

MIKE HUSSEY

Mike Hussey – Second Test, Adelaide, 1-5 December 2006

Mike Hussey had to score 15,313 first-class runs, more than anyone else in the history of the game, before he earned his Test debut in November 2005. He was certainly more than ready, and in his first two years accumulated an incredible average of 86.18. A hugely popular figure in the dressing room and affectionately known as 'Mr Cricket', he played 79 consecutive Tests before retiring in January 2013 as Australia's 12th highest run-scorer of all time.

Left-handed batsman
Born: 27 May 1975, Mt Lawley, Perth
Test debut: November 2005 v West Indies
Last Test: January 2013 v Sri Lanka
Test record: 79 matches, 6,235 runs at an average of 51.52; seven wickets at an average of 43.71

The state of play
Australia, seeking to regain the Ashes after losing them in 2005, were already one up in the series and two important knocks from Mike Hussey doubled their advantage on the way to a 5-0 whitewash.

Scoreboard

England first innings

A.J. Strauss	c Martyn	b Clark	14
A.N. Cook	c Gilchrist	b Clark	27
I.R. Bell		c & b Lee	60
P.D. Collingwood	c Gilchrist	b Clark	206
K.P. Pietersen		run out	158
A. Flintoff		not out	38
G.O. Jones	c Martyn	b Warne	1
A.F. Giles		not out	27
Extras	(lb 10, w 2, nb 8)		20
Total	(6 wickets dec, 168 overs)		551

Bowling	O	M	R	W
B. Lee	34	1	139	1
G.D. McGrath	30	5	107	0
S.R. Clark	34	6	75	3
S.K. Warne	53	9	167	1
M.J. Clarke	17	2	53	0

Australia first innings

J.L. Langer	c Pietersen	b Flintoff	4
M.L. Hayden	c Jones	b Hoggard	12
R.T. Ponting	c Jones	b Hoggard	142
D.R. Martyn	c Bell	b Hoggard	11
M.E.K. Hussey		b Hoggard	91
M.J. Clarke	c Giles	b Hoggard	124
A.C. Gilchrist	c Bell	b Giles	64
S.K. Warne	lbw	b Hoggard	43
B. Lee		not out	7
S.R. Clark		b Hoggard	0
G.D. McGrath	c Jones	b Anderson	1
Extras	(b 4, lb 2, w 1, nb 7)		14
Total	(all out, 165.3 overs)		513

Bowling	O	M	R	W
M.J. Hoggard	42	6	109	7
A. Flintoff	26	5	82	1
S.J. Harmison	25	5	96	0
J.M. Anderson	21.3	3	85	1
A.F. Giles	42	7	103	1
K.P. Pietersen	9	0	32	0

England second innings

A.J. Strauss	c Hussey	b Warne	34
A.N. Cook	c Gilchrist	b Clark	9
I.R. Bell		run out	26
P.D. Collingwood		not out	22
K.P. Pietersen		b Warne	2
A. Flintoff	c Gilchrist	b Lee	2
G.O. Jones	c Hayden	b Lee	10
A.F. Giles	c Hayden	b Warne	0
M.J. Hoggard		b Warne	4
S.J. Harmison	lbw	b McGrath	8
J.M. Anderson	lbw	b McGrath	1
Extras	(b 3, lb 5, w 1, nb 2)		11
Total	(all out, 73 overs)		129

Bowling	O	M	R	W
B. Lee	18	3	35	2
G.D. McGrath	10	6	15	2
S.K. Warne	32	12	49	4
S.R. Clark	13	4	22	1

Australia second innings

J.L. Langer	c Bell	b Hoggard	7
M.L. Hayden	c Collingwood	b Flintoff	18
R.T. Ponting	c Strauss	b Giles	49
M.E.K. Hussey		not out	61
D.R. Martyn	c Strauss	b Flintoff	5
M.J. Clarke		not out	21
Extras	(b 2, lb 2, w 1, nb 2)		7
Total	(4 wickets, 32.5 overs)		168

Bowling	O	M	R	W
M.J. Hoggard	4	0	29	1
A. Flintoff	9	0	44	2
A.F. Giles	10	0	46	1
S.J. Harmison	4	0	15	0
J.M. Anderson	3.5	0	23	0
K.P. Pietersen	2	0	7	0

Mike Hussey

'ONE MORE, JUST one more run, that's all we need,' I kept whispering to myself, but it was becoming increasingly hard to stay calm.

My heart was racing, pounding in my chest, while my throat was tight, and I began to feel a bit nauseous as I battled to keep my nerves and the tension inside the ground from overwhelming me.

Over the first two days of the Test England had made 551/6 declared, and no side in the history of the game batting first had made so many runs and declared and gone on to lose, so at that stage none of us harboured any thoughts of winning. We thought saving it was still possible, but actually winning it? Not a chance. But now here we were in the final overs of the last day and just a run away from completing an unprecedented comeback.

Amid the heat, the noise, and the unrelenting tension at the Adelaide Oval, it was me, little old Mike Hussey, out in the middle with the task of guiding Australia to this incredible win.

We had been set 168 runs to win from 36 overs, and after hitting each boundary, as we edged closer, I couldn't help punching the air. I understand I was winding up the England captain Andrew Flintoff, but that was never my intention, it was simply the adrenaline coursing through my body, I couldn't stop myself.

With one run to win, I remember looking at Jimmy Anderson beginning his run-up and getting impatient. 'Hurry up, hurry up and bowl,' I thought, as I just wanted to get some bat on the ball. It didn't matter where he bowled, this wasn't the time to be technical, I just wanted to hit the ball and scamper down the other end.

As he gained speed and approached the wicket, I was thinking, 'Watch the ball, watch the ball and hit it! Hit it anywhere!'

As soon as I hit the ball through the covers I instinctively knew it was the winning run, and at that moment I was consumed with this incredible sensation, a surge of emotion, it was like nothing I had ever felt before as I let out a scream, ran down the wicket and jumped in to the air.

Hitting that run is the one memory I will take to my grave. It was the best feeling an Australian could ever have on a cricket field while playing against England; it felt like a miracle, a bit like a dream, I couldn't believe we had done it, and I thought as I looked around a delirious Adelaide Oval, 'It will never get any better than this.'

It was only two years before I had come to accept I would never experience moments like this. I thought my moment had gone; I would never play Test cricket for Australia, and no matter what I did and how many runs I scored in state cricket I was never going to wear a baggy green or be invited in to the inner sanctum of the Australian dressing room.

It was when I was dropped by Western Australia at the end of the 2002/03 season that I thought my chance of playing Test cricket had gone for good. I was now so far removed from being in consideration for the Test side I had no choice but to make my peace with it and accept it.

It was a deeply frustrating time. I thought I was good enough, but it was my misfortune to be playing at a time when vacancies in the Australian Test side almost never came up.

I think in the five years of Steve Waugh's captaincy between 1999 and 2004 only seven players made their Test debuts for Australia, and some of them were only for a few Tests if someone was injured and then they would be ushered back out of the side again.

In any other era I would have got in the side, but I had to wait and wait. I was desperate for a baggy green, I did everything I could, and probably went over the top in my training to make them notice me, but this was a once-in-a-lifetime set of players, arguably the greatest side ever, so there was never an opening for me.

But I wasn't distraught by this. I thought if I never played for Australia in a Test match I could still be fulfilled by my career, having scored over 15,000 first-class runs, played for Australia A and played county cricket in England. I was very proud of that.

I was always a very intense character, forever heaping pressure on myself, but when I realised I wasn't going to play Test cricket a burden was immediately lifted from my shoulders. I would just have to go back to enjoying my cricket and not put too much pressure on myself, and from that moment I started playing better than ever and my opportunity finally came.

I had been a part of the one-day side on the 2005 tour of England, but when the Test series started it was difficult to leave the boys and go back to playing county cricket with Durham.

Later that summer when Australia were struggling there was speculation I might replace Matthew Hayden at the top of the order, but I thought, 'Holy cow, I don't want to make my debut under so much pressure.' I didn't think I would be the great white hope for Australia. I didn't want that. I didn't think I could have an impact.

But later that year at the age of 30 I was finally handed that baggy green for my first Test against the West Indies at the Gabba as Australia rebuilt after narrowly losing the Ashes to England.

My long apprenticeship proved to be the making of me, because when I finally got my chance I was ready. I had done the hard yards in state cricket and knew my game, I felt like I had a better chance to stay in the side, I had a mountain of runs in the bank, and knew what to do. I accumulated a healthy Test average of over 75 as we won ten of my first 11 Tests.

After so long on the outside this was cricketing utopia for me, but it was about to get even better during the Ashes series of 2006/07.

When I was growing up all I wanted to do was to play for Australia against England in the Ashes. When I was a kid I used to sit up late at night with my Mum and Dad with my bag of peanuts and a soft drink watching the Test matches over in England.

For some reason, when the Ashes were played in Australia it didn't give me the same buzz as watching it late at night on television or listening on the radio from England. I remember Michael Slater scoring a hundred at Lord's in 1993, and the goose bumps on my arms when he punched the air. You just think how good that must feel.

The Ashes has always had this magical feel about it. What I love about the Poms is they truly love their cricket, and they love all the traditions, and still turn out in big numbers for the Test matches. They really know their stuff compared to the other countries.

The 2005 Ashes series was an historic one, which galvanised the whole of cricket. Its importance to Test cricket was huge, and I have even heard Australians say they wouldn't change the fact we lost because what it did for Test cricket was more important.

So the build-up to the return series in Australia at the end of 2006 was incredible; I have never known those levels of interest or excitement. All the newspapers were full of cricket, it was hard to get tickets to the Tests, and the hype seemed to be out of control.

It had come as a shock to the psyche of Australian cricket not to be the holders of the Ashes after winning eight straight series between 1989 and 2003. We had got used to it being ours, so to suddenly see an England captain lift up the urn was very difficult for us.

We really felt the weight of expectation from the Australian public; this was more than just another Test series, even more than just another Ashes. After the excoriating pain of so narrowly losing the 2005 Ashes in England this was a series we simply had to win.

But trust me, if the Australian public were desperate to regain the Ashes, it was nothing compared to the determination of the players.

Inside the dressing room, champion players like Shane Warne, Ricky Ponting and Glenn McGrath were completely consumed with winning back the Ashes. Nothing else mattered to them.

I have never been a part of any Australian team so focused and intense; the thought of regaining the Ashes was everything to these guys despite what they had already achieved in their long careers so far, this was what they really wanted above all else. They might have played in excess of 100 Test matches, but these five in the summer of 2006 were the most important.

You could see it in their eyes, this was more than just sport, they were still hurt from 2005; this was about their reputations. They didn't want revenge; they wanted redemption.

I know that losing in 2005 prolonged Shane Warne's Test career by another 15 months; he put off his retirement just so he could play in this series and win back the Ashes.

About three months before the start of the series we were taken away for five nights to a boot camp in Queensland with the aim of toughening us up and fostering our team spirit.

Let there be no misunderstanding, there was absolutely no sense of luxury or even comfort to the camp. It was organised by a security company run by a former member of the SAS and staffed by ex-military guys, and isolated out in the Bush we were tested both mentally and physically to our limits. It was tough, really tough.

At the start of the camp we had to line up wearing just our jocks, and almost like in the movies when you see people enter prison, we were handed only the bare minimum; two pairs of underpants to last five days, two trousers, two shirts, two socks, a water bottle and a sleeping bag.

We had to hand over all our phones and iPods, you were allowed no electronic gear or anything personal whatsoever, although Shane Warne managed to smuggle in a couple of packs of cigarettes.

Everyone got on board with it, no one whinged or complained. The truth is we were too scared to speak out after the guy running the camp, a Sergeant Major figure, lined us all up and yelled and screamed at us. No one was brave enough to stand up to him.

One of our first tasks was we had to drag 20-litre jerry cans filled with water up a mountain, and stop every ten metres to do push-ups. If you didn't do them properly there were penalties of more push-ups, and if your team didn't stand in a straight line there were more penalties, and if you didn't help your mate there were even more penalties, so by the time we had suffered through all of that and hauled ourselves up to the top of this mountain the guys were a complete mess. I remember seeing some of them dry-retching in absolute agony.

That night we were only given soup and bread to eat, and afterwards we were exhausted so we collapsed in to our sleeping bags, but after only a couple of hours of sleep we were woken up by explosions going off all around us. Our guide screamed, 'Get up and get out now, it's not safe here!'

It was pitch black, there were bombs exploding around us, and we had to pack up our supplies and get out of what was a dangerous area. The sleep deprivation really kicked in as we trekked through the night for about an hour to find a new base, but the idea was to see how we reacted when we were tired and under pressure.

After five days of relentless team building exercises, which included pushing cars and abseiling down rock faces, very little sleep and living out in the bush, I was spent. I had nothing more to give and couldn't wait for a hot bath, which I laid in for about an hour.

Inside the camp we developed a real bond and also an excitement about what was coming up. We now had a shared experience, a reference point, so when things got hard we knew we could keep going because it couldn't have been as hard as that trek on the first day or being woken up in the middle of the night.

Ahead of the series there was talk this Australian side was too old, that too many of us were over 30. The name 'Dad's Army' was mentioned, but this only spurred us all on to prove people wrong.

Despite how the series would unfold there was never any sense this England side would be anything but very, very difficult to beat.

When England arrived in Australia we saw them as a very talented side who were a real threat, and could beat us. We had a deep respect for them; only the year before they had gone toe-to-toe with a truly awesome Australian side and beaten them.

Ricky told us he wanted us to be more aggressive than normal to England. Of course we should be civil and polite, but he didn't want us to be over-friendly. He wanted us to send the message that they were here for a battle, not to make friends. 'You can catch up after games, that's fine, but during games we are here for business,' he told us. He didn't want us to be too matey, we should use their proper names, not nicknames, so Kevin Pietersen was 'Kevin' and not 'KP' and Andrew Flintoff was 'Andrew' and not 'Freddie'.

We didn't think this England team were there for the taking or vulnerable in any way, and we certainly didn't see the appointment of Andrew Flintoff as captain as a weakness. It was quite the opposite, we thought such a big character leading with confidence and bravado would galvanise all the other English players.

On the sunlit morning of 23 November 2006 the most anticipated Ashes series ever finally began with the first Test at the Gabba.

None of us will forget that first ball. I was out on the balcony as Steve Harmison stormed in against a wall of noise and bowled straight to second slip. I was stunned as the crowd roared its delight. However, I never felt it set the tone for the series.

There were some nerves around, a new ball can be slippery, so I didn't read too much in to it. In the 2010/11 series Andrew Strauss got out in the first over for a duck in the first Test and it didn't set the tone for that series as England beat us 3-1, so it is ridiculous to think it had any impact. A lot of cricket still had to be played.

We were 79/1 when Ricky Ponting made his way out to the middle. He had waited 15 months for this moment and was determined to make the most of it as he hit the ball all around the ground.

I joined him at 198/3 and together we put on a partnership of 209, with Ricky helping himself to a mammoth 196. I was in awe of him, he was so positive and aggressive, and gave the rest of the batting order the confidence to play with freedom.

I would make 86 myself, and I remember looking around and thinking, 'How good is this? Life doesn't get any better than playing in an Ashes series.' But it was brought to an end when Flintoff bowled me; he came around the wicket, I played a solid defensive shot, but he snook the ball through.

I departed on 407/4 before we pushed on to 602/9 declared, a hugely intimidating first-innings score which acted as a statement of intent, but it was a great batting pitch so now it was over to our bowlers, particularly Glenn McGrath, who used all their pent-up hurt from 2005 to skittle out England for just 157. You might have expected Ricky to enforce the follow-on, but instead we had another bat. His thinking was there were cracks appearing on the pitch, which were only going to get worse, and to also give our bowlers some time to freshen up. We would make England suffer more, making 202/1 to set them an impossible 648 to win.

Even though we would comfortably triumph by 277 runs, England put up a fight in their second innings. Kevin Pietersen and Paul Collingwood both got in to the 90s so they had shown they could still be a threat in this series.

And so it proved over the first two days of the second Test in Adelaide as England dominated us before eventually declaring on 551/6 in their first innings. It was their biggest total in Australia for two decades.

It was a long, hard slog out in the middle as we watched their batsmen take advantage of a very good Adelaide batting pitch. The talk in the field amongst the boys was the real England had finally turned up, the one we had expected all along.

Once again Pietersen and Collingwood batted brilliantly, putting on a partnership of 310 for the fourth wicket. We simply didn't look like we were ever going to get them out. The only way was with a run-out, which is what happened to Pietersen on 158.

Paul Collingwood went on to make 206 as he feasted on our bowlers. Shane Warne went for 1-167, apparently his worst ever figures in Test cricket, and it was a strange sight to see him treated like that. Shane was talking to Collingwood all the time, making fun of him being awarded an MBE for winning the Ashes the previous year when he played in just one Test, but it wasn't working here.

Walking from the field after England had declared on 551/6, I remember thinking it was a good thing they had taken two days to make the runs as we might just be able to save the Test. The talk amongst the guys was 'OK, we can save this' but there was no talk about winning, which seemed to be beyond us now.

But even saving the Test appeared to be in jeopardy when we slumped to 65/3 after the dismissals of Justin Langer, Matty Hayden and Damien Martyn. Then Ricky played another captain's innings to haul us back from the brink and went on to make 142, taking advantage of being dropped by Ashley Giles at deep square leg when he was on only 35.

Just like at the Gabba, Ricky and I batted well together, putting on a partnership of 192, but it was far from easy, we had to work hard for every run all day; the England bowlers really kept on at me.

It took me 212 balls to reach 91, a good knock, but again I was disappointed not to reach a century, because I felt I had worked hard before I chopped a delivery from Matthew Hoggard on to my stumps after the second new ball had been taken. It was 286/5 when I trooped back to the dressing room still concerned as we remained so far behind. It was beginning to look desperate.

But a century from Michael Clarke and good knocks from Adam Gilchrist and Shane Warne pushed us on to 513 all out and only 38 runs behind England, and so at the close of play on the fourth day with England now 59/1 in their reply, we thought we had saved the Test. I went home that night convinced we would be back in the morning to see the game peter out into a draw.

But the next morning when we regrouped Ricky was bouncing around, full of energy. He was convinced we could still win this, while Shane Warne kept muttering 'we can do this, we can do this' but I could see some of the guys, including myself, looking around with sceptical looks, thinking, 'Are you really sure?'

In the team meeting John Buchanan stood up and said, 'We can win this Test, but the only way it will happen is if we all believe it.'

'What is the best way to win this Test?' Buchanan asked us. 'Is it to go all-out attack, set attacking fields and try to go for wickets all the time even though they will score runs more quickly? Or do we go for a more patient approach, and try to give them no runs at all, give them no chances and stop them scoring, so the pressure slowly builds, and if we can grab a wicket then we can go on a roll?'

The belief of Ricky, Shane and John Buchanan was infectious, and together as a team we decided to pursue the latter approach, giving them no runs to build up the pressure. They had sold us a dream and we bought in to it. I thought, 'OK, let's go for it.'

Walking out on to the field at the start of day five, I noticed there wasn't much of a crowd in; clearly they didn't expect anything but a draw. And this is what the England batsmen Andrew Strauss and Ian Bell were playing for, being safe, but it was also our bowlers and a deteriorating pitch that didn't let them score.

In the first ten overs of the day England only managed to add ten runs to their overnight total, so it began to appear as though our plan was working and the pressure was slowly suffocating them.

After 45 minutes with England 69/1 we made our first breakthrough when Strauss appeared to get something on a delivery from Shane Warne and I held on to it at short leg. I saw the ball flick the pad, and Shane went up, so I went up with him even though I wasn't sure, but Steve Bucknor lifted his finger. It was a soft one, and if the review system was being used it wouldn't have stood. When you saw the replay there was a gap between his bat and the ball.

England had only added another run when a panicking Ian Bell was run out, and suddenly you could feel the balance of the game shift. We now had the momentum. Dread and real discomfort was beginning to engulf England's batsmen at the wicket, and I thought, 'Jeez, we might actually have a chance here.'

Kevin Pietersen strode to the wicket, a few boundaries from him and England would again be reassured, but he lasted only five balls with Shane Warne brilliantly bowling him around his legs. England were now 73/4, and sinking in to trouble.

Next in was Flintoff, and he looked as though he wanted to be positive, he wanted to take the game back, and if he could get a quick 50 then the game would be back in his favour. But Brett Lee quickly got him for two with his reverse swing and England were 77/5.

We could all sense something special was happening. We were looking around at each other, all thinking the same thing, Ricky and John's plan and bold words were coming true right in front of us.

No one was working harder than Shane Warne, who would bowl unchanged for two sessions, and take 4-29 from 27 overs. It was a superhuman effort from him, shrugging off the stupor of his first innings. He was utterly possessed, he wanted this so, so badly, and summoned up all his immense talent to help secure victory.

Warne kept up the pressure and took the wickets of Ashley Giles and Matthew Hoggard as England failed to rid themselves of their increasing panic and slumped to 129 all out, having lost their last nine wickets on this day for 60 runs in 42 overs.

The win was now on. We needed 168 from 36 overs, but we had to do it on a deteriorating pitch on the last day. As we got ready there was an excitement in all of us, but it was tempered by a sense of anxiety and nervousness as well because we had come so far, and were well aware it would be dreadful not to finish the job now.

I was extremely nervous, hoping the openers would get us off to a good start, and maybe I wouldn't even be needed, but at 33/2 I found myself walking to the middle batting at number four.

I had been promoted over Damien Martyn because the idea was to have a left-hander out there as it was going to be difficult for the right-handers to score quickly with Ashley Giles bowling over the wicket in to the rough. We needed to keep the scoreboard ticking over, and so needed a left-hander to mix up Giles's line and length.

I entered the game with us still a long way off from our target, still needing 135 runs to win, and thought, 'Let's get another partnership going with Ricky.' I knew I had to score quickly, work the ball around, I wanted to stay calm and steady the innings.

It immediately felt like a one-day game. There was a lot of cat and mouse going on, while they were trying to preserve the runs, and trying to pick up wickets. If they got us to six down they could still win it, and if we chased too hard, we could certainly lose it.

If I was going to do anything I first had to combat my nerves as I could feel my heart racing in my chest. I had never known anything like this before. Here I was out in the middle with the task of bringing Australia home in an Ashes Test. It was down to me, a whole nation was expecting me to do it.

The nerves never left me, I just learned to deal with them, and the adrenaline actually brought the best out of me. I was finding the gaps in the field pretty well, and running hard between the wickets, turning comfortable singles in to twos.

Throughout the afternoon the crowd built up quite quickly, at tea time it seemed half full, but then word spread around the city we were getting close and they opened the gates, so at the end of the day it was packed with about 20,000. The crowd was making a huge amount of noise, counting down every run, while the electronic scoreboard told us exactly how many more we needed.

With just over 13 overs remaining we still needed another 47 runs after Ricky had fallen for 49, and Damien Martyn lasted just four balls to leave us 121/4 and bring Michael Clarke out to the middle.

As we got closer it was getting hard to stay calm, the crowd was getting louder, the emotion of the day was getting the better of us, we were so excited like little kids. Michael is a pretty nervous sort of guy too, so we were counting down the runs.

There was one moment when we needed 25 runs to win when Kevin Pietersen threw a ball in to the keeper Geraint Jones and it hit the rough just short of him and ran away for five over throws. 'Hang on a second, this looks like it is going our way.' And maybe when we needed about five runs, with six wickets remaining, I thought we were going to get there, but this all-consuming tension was always there.

At around 6.45pm when Jimmy Anderson came in to bowl and I hit him through the covers for the winning run, all the nerves and tension immediately evaporated to be replaced by sheer joy and relief.

I looked up to the dressing room where on the balcony the boys were punching the air and hugging each other, and while I was caught in a flurry of shaking hands with England players and the umpires, they had run on the pitch to share the moment. The guys were patting me on the back and shouting, 'You bloody beauty!'

I was stuck on the field for the next half an hour as we went over to the scoreboard end and thanked the fans for their support. It was hectic for me, speaking to the media, and all the while trying to properly take in what we had just accomplished.

Back in the dressing room, I cracked open a few beers, and slumped down on a chair, looking around at the scenes of celebrations, still finding it hard to believe we had won.

Shane Warne was particularly animated, it meant so much to him, and he had played such a huge part. He was very, very excited. He had taken some criticism from the England coach Duncan Fletcher before the Test, so he was desperate to show he could still do it. There was a real emotional out pouring from Warnie.

We performed a boisterous rendition of our team song, 'Under the Southern Cross', three times and then the England players began to filter in. Flintoff was the first through the door, and though he and his team were clearly shattered, it was a show of character to come in and share a beer, because if that was me, and I had suffered a defeat like this, I would have been sulking for a few hours. I am not sure I would have had the courage to come in and say 'well done'.

The rest of the night was a blur, after all the effort and emotion of the day I had sculled three beers quickly so I was light-headed.

We woke up the next day with heavy heads, and went straight to the airport to fly to Perth for the next Test, but it soon became clear Damien Martyn wasn't there with us. At first we just thought he had a few too many beers the previous night and had overslept his alarm, but then the boys started hearing whispers he had retired.

It came as a real shock, it wasn't something we were expecting, it wasn't something he had even let on about. Damien and I got on well, we played a lot of state cricket together, but we were never especially close. I sent him a text, but he disappeared, he snook off to Sydney for a few days to get away from the spotlight.

At 2-0 up in the series we knew we now needed to win just one more Test from the next three to regain the Ashes, and we wanted to get it done as soon as possible.

Despite the crushing nature of their defeat at Adelaide, we never thought it would be easy. We didn't believe England were vanquished, we thought they would still come at us hard, which is what happened in the first innings at the WACA. I scored 74, but we were bowled all out for 244 on the first day.

But the England batsmen couldn't continue the good work of their bowlers and made just 215 in their first innings to give us a narrow lead. We weren't going to slump again and make the same mistakes, so we came out again with a better attitude.

In our second innings I made 103, which in front of my home crowd, including my family, in an Ashes Test was the realisation of a dream. The one shot that stands out was the one to bring up my century. I didn't put it where I wanted, a pull shot off Steve Harmison that went straight down the ground, but I didn't care.

When I was given out we were 357/4, and doing well, but then Adam Gilchrist strolled to the wicket, and did what he always did best; transformed the game and took it away from the opposition.

It was stifling hot, and earlier in the day I had done all that hard work in getting to my century in 156 balls, then Gilly comes out and smashes a century in 57 balls, the second fastest in the history of the game.

It was great to watch, but because it was so hot, I have had so many people tell me they had to leave the WACA at tea so they missed Gilly's century, which helped push up on to a total of 527/5 declared to set England 556 to win.

But England would crumble in their second innings, and we won by 206 runs to regain the Ashes when Shane Warne got one through against Monty Panesar. It was a surreal moment, my first Ashes win, and it just felt incredible to be a part of this team. We made the most of it but Ricky wanted us to always be humble too.

It meant so much to the guys who had been through the pain of 2005. There were a few tears shed between Matty Hayden, Justin Langer and Ricky Ponting. They had regained more than just the Ashes; for them, they had now also had their redemption.

Shane Warne sat in the corner looking around at the celebrations and said to us, 'You know, there are certain things I'm really going to miss about the game, and this is one of them, being a part of a winning team and celebrating with your mates.'

All our ears perked up at that and we started to think he was going to retire soon, and three days later he made it official when he announced he would walk away from the Test side after the series.

More than ever, he was the star attraction at the fourth Test in Melbourne. They really support their local players there, and on the first morning the crowd started chanting for Warnie, telling Ricky to get him on, so as soon as he started to warm up the whole ground of about 90,000 people erupted.

Shane was fond of saying he had a great script writer throughout his career, and he didn't let him down again as it wasn't long before he spun one through the gate of Andrew Strauss to celebrate his 700th Test wicket. It was the moment everyone had come to see.

The Test was all about Shane, who took seven wickets, as we triumphed by an innings and 99 runs over just three days, and it ended with him being carried on the guys' shoulders around the MCG. He is the best player I have ever seen. I was lucky to field at short leg for several Tests, so had the best seat in the house to watch him at work, and how he would try to work batsmen out, the way he spoke to them and to umpires. He had a great knowledge of the game, and he knew exactly how to use his talent.

I didn't know him that well before I came in to the Test side, but I'll never forget how welcoming and gracious he was towards me. I was pretty nervous, you don't know what these guys think about you, do they even think you deserve to be there? But I'll always remember before my first Test against the West Indies at the Gabba, Warnie standing in the dressing room toilets in his underpants puffing on a cigarette. He turned to me and said, 'Huss, I know you're nervous, but you don't have anything to prove to us, you deserve to be here mate. Just play your way and you'll enjoy success at this level.' For Shane Warne to say that to me meant everything. I felt I belonged and it relaxed me straight away.

Following on from Shane's retirement, two more champions, Glenn McGrath and Justin Langer, announced they too would be retiring after the fifth and final Test at the Sydney Cricket Ground.

It had been mentioned we had a poor record in dead rubbers, and in recent years Australia had missed the chance to inflict a whitewash on England, either winning 4-0 or 4-1, and in fact no side had won every Test in an Ashes since 1920/21 so we wanted to achieve that, and send off Shane, Glenn and Justin on a high.

We granted them their wish and won by ten wickets with Matty Hayden hitting the winning runs to complete a 5-0 series whitewash.

We had done well not to let the emotion of the occasion overwhelm us, but afterwards I know it got to a few players. I had never seen Ricky so emotional, he was crying in the dressing room, because he had shared so much with the three guys retiring. I know Adam Gilchrist wore sunglasses on to the field to hide his own tears.

There was a great family atmosphere and all the players had their wives and kids on the ground with them. The crowd stayed for a long time afterwards as we did a lap of honour of the ground to show our respects to both our own fans and the Barmy Army.

This is the reason you play the game, to experience these moments. But while I remember feeling happy, I was also thinking, 'Things are going to get a lot tougher now, because guys like Shane, Glenn and Justin are simply irreplaceable.'

But after a few beers back in the dressing room the tears were replaced with laughter, and despite their acute disappointment the England team joined us. I remember having a good chat with Alastair Cook and you could see the glint in his eye, this was going to make him a harder and better player in the future.

And in the next two series this is exactly what happened when Cook played a leading role in England winning the Ashes in both 2009 and 2010/11, so that series in 2006/07 would be the only Ashes I won in my career, making the memories even more special.

After celebrating long in to the night at the ground we were invited on to a 32-metre yacht owned by the Australian businessman James Packer, and it was there bobbing about on Sydney harbour that we sang our team song.

I wanted to enjoy that night as much as possible, because I knew things were about to get a lot harder. Surrounded by my team-mates as we drifted past the Heads with the Sydney skyline twinkling in the background I wanted that night to last forever.

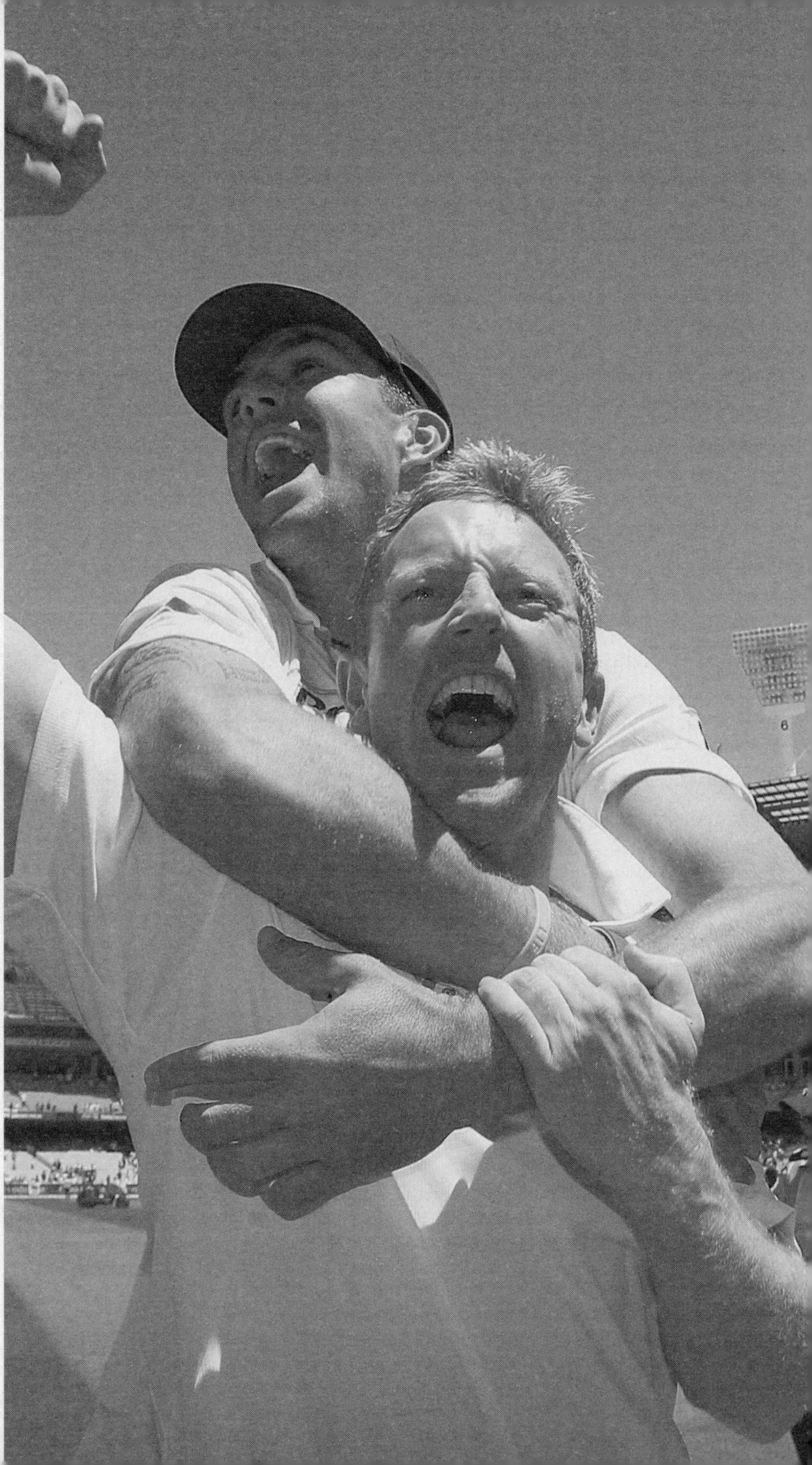

Paul Collingwood – Fifth Test, Sydney Cricket Ground, 3-7 January 2011

'I know I was a limited player,' admits Paul Collingwood in this book, but that didn't stop him enjoying a long and successful career with England in all formats of the game. The ultimate team man; Collingwood was always a dogged presence at the crease and one of the world's best fielders, who won the Ashes three times, while also captaining England to the Twenty20 World Cup in 2010.

Right-handed batsman, right-arm medium-pace bowler
Born: 26 May 1976, Shotley Bridge, County Durham
Test debut: December 2003 v Sri Lanka
Last Test: January 2011 v Australia
Test record: 68 matches, 4,259 runs at an average of 40.56; 17 wickets at an average of 59.88

The state of play
The Ashes were already heading back to England with the tourists 2-1 up but Australia could still tie the series by winning in what became Paul Collingwood's final Test. England had the last laugh however, winning by an innings for the third time in the series.

Scoreboard
Australia first innings

S.R. Watson	c Strauss	b Bresnan	45
P.J. Hughes	c Collingwood	b Tremlett	31
U.T. Khawaja	c Trott	b Swann	37
M.J. Clarke	c Anderson	b Bresnan	4
M.E.K. Hussey		b Collingwood	33
B.J. Haddin	c Prior	b Anderson	6
S.P.D. Smith	c Collingwood	b Anderson	18
M.G. Johnson		b Bresnan	53
P.M. Siddle	c Strauss	b Anderson	2
B.W. Hilfenhaus	c Prior	b Anderson	34
M.A. Beer		not out	2
Extras	(b 5, lb 7, w 1, nb 2)		15
Total	(all out, 106.1 overs)		280

Bowling	O	M	R	W
J.M. Anderson	30.1	7	66	4
C.T. Tremlett	26	9	71	1
T.T. Bresnan	30	5	89	3
G.P. Swann	16	4	37	1
P.D. Collingwood	4	2	5	1

England first innings

A.J. Strauss		b Hilfenhaus	60
A.N. Cook	c Hussey	b Watson	189
I.J.L. Trott		b Johnson	0
K.P. Pietersen	c Beer	b Johnson	36
J.M. Anderson		b Siddle	7
P.D. Collingwood	c Hilfenhaus	b Beer	13
I.R. Bell	c Clarke	b Johnson	115
M.J. Prior	c Haddin	b Hilfenhaus	118
T.T. Bresnan	c Clarke	b Johnson	35
G.P. Swann		not out	36
C.T. Tremlett	c Haddin	b Hilfenhaus	12
Extras	(b 3, lb 11, w 5, nb 4)		23
Total	(all out, 177.5 overs)		644

Bowling	O	M	R	W
B.W. Hilfenhaus	38.5	7	121	3
M.G. Johnson	36	5	168	4
P.M. Siddle	31	5	111	1
S.R. Watson	20	7	49	1
M.A. Beer	38	3	112	1
S.P.D. Smith	13	0	67	0
M.E.K. Hussey	1	0	2	0

Australia second innings

S.R. Watson		run out	38
P.J. Hughes	c Prior	b Bresnan	13
U.T. Khawaja	c Prior	b Anderson	21
M.J. Clarke	c Prior	b Anderson	41
M.E.K. Hussey	c Pietersen	b Bresnan	12
B.J. Haddin	c Prior	b Tremlett	30
S.P.D. Smith		not out	54
M.G. Johnson		b Tremlett	0
P.M. Siddle	c Anderson	b Swann	43
B.W. Hilfenhaus	c Prior	b Anderson	7
M.A. Beer		b Tremlett	2
Extras	(b 11, lb 4, w 3, nb 2)		20
Total	(all out, 84.4 overs)		281

Bowling	O	M	R	W
J.M. Anderson	18	5	61	3
C.T. Tremlett	20.4	4	79	3
G.P. Swann	28	8	75	1
T.T. Bresnan	18	6	51	2

Paul Collingwood

IT WAS THE perfect end to the perfect tour. Sitting on the outfield of the Sydney Cricket Ground next to the square surrounded by my team-mates as we swapped stories having just won the Ashes in Australia for the first time in a generation I could not have been more content, and I knew, however hard it had been, I had also made the right decision to retire from Test cricket.

On that final day of the fifth Test we had taken the six remaining wickets we needed to retain the Ashes and win the series 3-1.

At around five o'clock after we had sprayed each other with champagne, knocked back several beers, and posed for countless photographs it was our coach Andy Flower who suggested we left our dressing room and took a stroll out to the middle of the field.

The England fans had long gone, drifting away to celebrate in the bars of Sydney, the media had filed their reports and gone home, and it was just us in this vast stadium, which was now completely empty.

Still wearing our whites and blue caps, some nursing a beer, and some sucking on large cigars, we sat down on the grass. All of us instinctively knew this was a special moment, something different, which we would always remember.

Where so recently there had been such noise and colour, there was now a wonderfully still silence. I had never heard birds tweeting in a cricket ground before, and never felt so calm and peaceful.

There was nothing more to worry about, no more Tests, no more training sessions or team meetings to remember, we were finally free to reflect upon what we had achieved together.

It was our bowling coach David Saker who first spoke about his most cherished memories from the previous two months, and then spontaneously we all went around the circle and took our turn, one by one to give our own thoughts and memories. Some told a joke, and as most of us were half-cut there was a lot of laughter, while others offered a deeper and more meaningful contribution, telling us how much the tour had meant to them and how in a small way it had also changed them.

This showed how comfortable we were with each other, and how a bond had developed among us as we had triumphed in Australia.

Only two days earlier I had been devastated to score only 13 in my final Test innings. I wanted 100, and I wanted that fairytale.

But as I looked around at this scene, surrounded by the happy and laughing faces of my team-mates I now realised I could never have imagined a better way to bow out of Test cricket.

Four years earlier I had been stood on the same outfield of the Sydney Cricket Ground consumed with a very different emotion.

We had just been whitewashed 5-0 by the Australians, and as I watched them bounce up and down on a stage holding aloft the Ashes I can honestly say I had never felt worse on a cricket field.

It was the toughest tour I had ever been on, seven weeks of relentless humiliation and defeat, and by the end of it I was utterly demoralised; bitter, beaten, and exhausted. You almost felt lifeless, like all the blood had been drained from your body.

Australia were ruthless, and though we didn't know it at the time, three of their greatest ever players, Shane Warne, Glenn McGrath and Justin Langer, were all determined to go out on a high.

They gave us nothing, no easy runs or easy wickets. They got us on the ground and never stopped stamping on our throats.

In the second Test at Adelaide I scored 206 in our first innings, and became the first Englishman in 70 years to score a double hundred in Australia. I am rather fond of that knock as I did it against an attack of Shane Warne, Glenn McGrath, Brett Lee and Stuart Clark.

It is a good tale to tell, the day I scored a double ton against that lot, but it has a dreadful ending, and two days later it meant little as we collapsed in the second innings to hand Australia victory and leave me with my head between my knees fighting back the tears.

It was torture. We just kept on losing, and as the tour progressed we played some terrible cricket because we had lost all confidence in ourselves, and each other. It really was horrific.

There seemed no escape. Even away from the grounds the Australian public and media hounded us. We got abused in restaurants, and it wasn't nice for our families when they joined us.

I can remember getting back to my hotel after one really bad day in the field, putting on the television and slumping on to the bed. A story came on the news about a local woman who was celebrating her 100th birthday. When they interviewed her, she said, 'Well, I've enjoyed a better innings than those bloody Poms!'

I famously got some personal ridicule from Shane Warne out in the middle during one Test. He was determined to sledge me about getting an MBE for playing one Test in the 2005 series. By that point I had had enough, but it didn't make it worse, truth is I found it funny. Obviously he had a problem with it, but I didn't.

I can remember sitting in an ice bath with Monty Panesar after we had lost the series 3-0 at the WACA, both feeling devastated. I said, 'Monty, we have to make sure we're never in this position ever again. I can't take this feeling again, it's absolutely horrible.'

By the end of the fifth Test at Sydney we had lost twice more, so it only got worse. I forced myself to watch Australia lift the urn. All players should, you're showing respect to your opposition, and it also fuels your determination for the next time you face them.

We were so monumentally pissed off we had allowed this to happen. There was no way I was going to put myself through this again, so the only thing to do was to win here. I resolved to come back in four years' time and win the Ashes.

In between the two tours of Australia, there was of course the 2009 series in England, which we won 2-1. I enjoyed regaining the Ashes, and playing in all five Tests this time, instead of just the one of 2005, but it didn't completely make up for what we had endured in Australia. Not by a long way. We still had unfinished business.

By the summer of 2010 under the leadership of Andrew Strauss and Andy Flower we had developed into a well-organised side, and with series wins over Bangladesh, home and away, and Pakistan at home we were heading towards our ultimate aims: winning in Australia and becoming the number one Test side in the world.

We had been too sloppy in 2006/07, undercooked and badly prepared. We were determined not to make the same mistakes again, so around four weeks before we set off for Australia we found ourselves summoned to meet at Gatwick Airport at 4am.

All we had been told was to bring our passports and meet there. None of the players knew anything more. Even the most organised man in the world, our manager Phil Neale, knew nothing.

It was the morning after the Professional Cricketers' Association dinner at the Hurlingham Club in London, which is normally a big piss-up, so some players came straight from there still drunk, while others had an early night and arrived wearing a back-pack.

We were ushered on to a flight to Munich and when we landed we were met by two ex-Australian policemen who stuck us on a coach and drove in to the Bavarian forest. We had to swap all our personal items; watches, mobile phones, iPads and laptops for a back-pack of basic clothes, cooking utensils and a torch.

Then we simply walked in to the forest for the next four days. It was tough, they really pushed us and took us out of our comfort zones, so we never knew the time and had to sleep in tents in the forest.

Some of the lads said it felt like a form of torture, it was that bad. On the first day we trekked through the forest in all weathers for about 25 miles. If we didn't keep to their strict rules we were given a punishment and had to drop and give them 50 press-ups.

We were also handed two bricks each and had to keep hold of them, they were never allowed to drop, while we were running up and down hills. It was agony. It took us to the brink of breaking down. We were cold, tired, wet, hungry and thirsty, and they kept pushing us. I know there were some who came close to giving up.

No matter how hard things were, they would ask you to do another drill, and you would think 'you are kidding me' but you always found the strength from somewhere. What we learned from those four days was when you think you have nothing left you can still do it.

Those bricks were signed by the camp leaders and came around Australia with us. We put them on the benches in each dressing room as a constant reminder. All you would have to do is come in from a hard session in the field and look at those bricks to realise it wasn't that bad, and you could still win this game of cricket.

On 29 October 2010 we left for Australia absolutely determined to retain the Ashes. I had been waiting four years for this moment. Here lay the route to redemption, to finally rid ourselves of the horrible memories of that dreadful 2006/07 tour.

The press like to trot out the cliché of players having mental scars about playing in Australia, and it is true. I had been scarred by that experience in 2006/07, and was maybe a little too cautious and anxious about playing there, but I was pleased to be surrounded by a squad of such determined characters, including some new young players who didn't know or care about what was to come.

I can remember being in team meetings, and saying to the guys who hadn't toured Australia, 'Listen, this is really hard work.' The younger players would sort of shrug, their innocence was a good thing. They hadn't experienced what it was like to play in Australia, so they would say, 'It doesn't have to be like that. If we play well we will win.' It was a good point.

A strange thing happened when we landed in Australia: the Aussies were nice to us. It was completely different from four years earlier because they were so welcoming. It was very disconcerting.

On the day we arrived in Perth we went and had a coffee in the suburb of Subiaco, and people were coming up to us and saying, 'Good luck, we hope you win.' We couldn't work out what was going on, it was like they were sick of their own team, and they wanted us to win. I think they really enjoyed the brand of cricket we were playing, how ruthless we were. Or maybe they just knew they were about to get beat.

This was my fourth Ashes series, so you would have thought on the first morning of the first Test at the Gabba I would be nice and relaxed, but no, I was absolutely riddled with nerves.

It is so hard to explain the nerves and the sense of trepidation going in to an Ashes series. The build-up, the days before, the training sessions, everything about it is different, the sense of expectation is heightened. The butterflies are constantly there in your stomach. It isn't just another cricket match.

There are a lot of nerves because you simply don't know what is going to happen. It is like going in to the unknown. It is like you start all over as a cricketer. Doubts begin appearing in the back of your mind that you never knew you had. It is very weird. It is the most intense pressure you can experience as a cricketer.

When Andrew Strauss was out third ball for a duck I couldn't help thinking 'oh no, not again' and we didn't ever recover from that moment, making just 260. My contribution was just four before I was caught by Marcus North off the bowling of Peter Siddle.

Then we found ourselves trailing by 221 runs after the Aussies made 481 in their first innings. In previous years there would have been no coming back from that and we would have lost.

But this was a different side. We are great scrappers, the deeper the hole, the better we play, and by the end of the Test we had secured a draw that felt more like a win after our batsmen had made 517/1 in our second innings. Look at that again – 517/1!

You could not have had a more one-sided draw and we now knew the Aussies were there for the taking. Everyone was now questioning their bowling attack, whereas before the series they had been saying how good the Australian seamers were and how much pace they had, and what they could do with the ball.

Now they had no answers and were panicking, 'How are we going to get these guys out?' Alastair Cook, Jonathan Trott and Andrew Strauss had all made centuries.

I was sat there watching it, the next after Kevin Pietersen to go in, but I never thought I would be batting. I didn't get pad rash, as I didn't put them on. I just didn't think they would ever get out.

Once Alastair Cook gets a rhythm going and a system with his batting, you know exactly what he is going to try and not try. His shot selection, what he hits and what he leaves is incredible. He knows his game so well it is very difficult to get him out.

There is this serene calmness about him when he bats that I wish I could replicate. He doesn't get flustered, he doesn't even sweat, and seems to enjoy pressure.

Everyone loves Alastair. I would think it would be very, very hard, nigh-on impossible, to fall out with him. He doesn't do arguments, he is very calm, very level-headed. He has a lovely manner.

Aside from all these runs there was an incident at the Gabba when Australia were batting that demonstrated this was a very different England side. Brad Haddin was giving one of our young bowlers Steve Finn some fearful abuse, trying to goad him by saying, 'You're shit, you shouldn't be here.'

This was something we had talked about. If someone gets abuse we stick together. If someone has a go at us, we go back at them hard, so as a team we started getting at Haddin and he was soon out. This time we had prepared for everything. Andy Flower had organised a response for every possible scenario. What happens if we're

2-0 up? Or what happens when we're 2-0 down? Everything that could happen on the pitch he had a plan for it. Everything had been spoken about and dissected before it actually happened.

The second Test took me back to Adelaide, scene of my double hundred and that horrible collapse four years before, but walking back in here brought back only good memories. I love playing there, it feels like an English ground with a lovely playing surface.

My smile got even wider when we took three Australian wickets for only two runs in the first two overs, and we bowled them all out for 245. We all knew something special was happening. This was our time.

We racked up 620/5 declared as I made what would be my highest score of the series by far of 42. For a time I batted with Kevin Pietersen as he went on to make an incredible 227.

I loved batting with KP, we had some great partnerships. Yes, he's a bit different, but I always got on with him, and enjoyed his company. KP has always been good to me, we've never fallen out.

Yes, he comes with some real nonsense, some very silly things have come out of his mouth, but most of the time he doesn't mean them, and he never minds when you put him back in his place.

Australia were put back in again and were wobbling at 238/4 by the end of the fourth day. On the final day the only thing standing in our way was the weather as a huge downpour was predicted, but fortunately we took the six wickets we needed before lunch and bowled Australia all out for 304 before the rain came to win by an innings and 71 runs and go 1-0 up in the series.

As we had wrapped up the Test so early we stayed drinking in our dressing room for six hours and got hammered.

Sitting in there watching the rain pound down on the covers I suddenly got the urge to do a swan dive across them. For years I had jealously watched as drunken fans had skidded across them, so I fancied doing it myself and went for it.

I didn't want it to come across as a piss-take towards the Aussies, it was just a spur of the moment thing. The lads were egging me on, so dressed in just the little skins boxer shorts I wear under my whites I rushed down to the centre of the field for my big moment, the only problem was in my haste I didn't notice a piece of string surrounding the covers so I tripped over it and fell flat on my face.

The whole team would then fall flat on their face in the third Test at the WACA. After Australia had made 268 in their first innings, we started well in our reply before collapsing from 78/0 to 187 all out.

After Australia made 309 we were set 391 to win, but did even worse than our first innings and were all out for 123. Mitchell Johnson took nine wickets in the Test, and once he got the ball swinging back in to the right-handers he caused a lot of problems.

Despite losing our lead in the series we never got too despondent or thought 'here we go again'. We had been beaten by a side who were better than us on this occasion on a fast and bouncy track, but we knew we could come back. In the past you could think we had no chance against them, but this was different.

Amid the temporary gloom there was one special moment for me when I caught Ricky Ponting off the bowling of James Anderson in the Aussies' first innings, when Ponting had scored 12. It was probably the best catch I ever took in Test cricket!

I have since heard Andrew Strauss say it was his one abiding memory of the whole tour because of the way we took down their captain in such a dramatic manner. It sends a message, because when he hit that ball he would never have expected to be out, but there he was trooping back to the dressing room.

I saw it come off the bat, and I thought 'I'm not going to get this' and a split second later I felt the ball stick in my hand. It was an amazing feeling. For that split second when you're still in the air and you know you've got the ball safe it is incredible. It was pure instinct, my body and hands just reacted to the ball.

I can remember being on the floor and Straussy coming up to me and shouting, 'You've still got it, Colly, you've still got it!' He was trying to help me through what was becoming a hard time for me, and it was good to know I had guys trying to buff up my ego.

On the opening day of the fourth Test at the mammoth Melbourne Cricket Ground we experienced a dream day, a day where everything went right, and when we knew we were going to do it.

We bowled Australia out for just 98 and then at the close of play were 157/0 in reply. The lads were all shaking their heads in disbelief and saying, 'If Carlsberg did Boxing Days …' It was the perfect day. Everything went right, and we knew we had hurt them. This felt like revenge for everything the Australians had put us through.

It was a day that was meant to happen.

There were around 85,000 fans at the MCG. It should have been a cauldron of noise, but you have never heard such a large crowd go so quiet. I think they were struggling to understand what had happened, and I don't think we could grasp it either. It was just too good to be true.

Unsurprisingly Australia never recovered from that first day, as we built up a huge first-innings lead of 415 after making 513 all out, but unfortunately I contributed only eight runs to that total.

Australia made just 258 in their second innings to lose by an innings and 157 runs, and although we obviously knew it was coming when Tim Bresnan took Ben Hilfenhaus's wicket to confirm we had retained the Ashes I felt this huge surge of emotion.

The feeling was pure euphoria. We had conquered Australia in Australia, something if I am honest I thought I might never do.

Andrew Strauss had brilliantly captained us in Australia. He was always very well prepared. He knew how he wanted the team to operate, and created a great atmosphere in the dressing room. I know he came from a posh background and posh school, but that didn't matter, he got on with everyone.

The iconic image of that Test win and indeed the whole series was of the team doing the sprinkler dance in front of the Barmy Army as we celebrated at the MCG.

At the time I can remember Andrew Strauss being worried it might look too triumphant, and I shared that view. You have to be careful. You have to respect your opposition, but at the same time the sprinkler had become so special to us, it was like our team motto, our team war dance if you like. It was something we were doing among ourselves for our fans, it wasn't to take the mickey out of our opponents. We had such a laugh doing it with Graeme Swann leading us, and me just tucked in behind him.

I am proud to say the sprinkler was my idea. Two months earlier Graeme Swann and I had been chatting in the dressing room at the Adelaide Oval during a rain delay in our tour game against South Australia when we started talking about silly dance moves like the robot and the moonwalk. I showed them how to do the sprinkler. I honestly can't remember where I first saw it, but the lads loved it and before long they were all doing it.

Amid all those celebrations at the MCG I had also come to realise my time as a part of this team was coming to an end.

After five innings I had scored just 70 runs, and while I had experienced patches of bad form before this time it felt different, because I knew I had no fight left in me.

The idea of retirement first drifted through my mind during the third Test in Perth. I was batting on a fast pitch, and every ball felt quicker than usual. I was getting some bouncers and seriously worried that if they got one straight I was going to be knocked out.

My family were over for this game, and I could see my family watching from a box, my two little girls, Shannon and Keira, smiling and waving their '4' cards. It just made me think, 'What are you doing this for? Why are you putting your life in danger?' When you start thinking like that you know you're pretty much finished.

I first mentioned these thoughts to my wife Vicky in Melbourne, and then broached the subject with Andy Flower. I told him I would have to change my technique to carry on. I was asking him for his opinion, but by his reaction I knew it was time to go! While I was happy to be a part of a team who were winning in Australia, something I had never experienced before, I carried the pressure of my lack of form with me throughout. It was agony, I couldn't score a run, and just couldn't find any answers.

I was hurting inside and knew I was close to being dropped, there was talk of replacing me with Eoin Morgan for the final Test, so it was increasingly obvious. But

I wanted to go on my terms, not be pushed, and just held on to my place for the fifth Test in Sydney.

Though we had already retained the Ashes, we knew we had to win in Sydney as well. Coming home with a 2-2 draw just wouldn't have been the same as a 2-1, or hopefully 3-1 win.

We wanted to go that extra yard and inflict the same pain on the Australians that they had on us for so many years.

You could see we had broken Australia down, stripped them of any confidence when they failed with the bat again, making just 280 in their first innings. I even got a wicket, bowling Mike Hussey, and after all the pressure I had been under it was one of the best moments of my career. I have that ball at home as a souvenir.

At the end of the second day with us at 167/3 I went for dinner with my former captain Michael Vaughan. I asked him about my predicament and he gave me some great advice: 'You can never go too early, but you can go too late.' I knew what he was saying.

On the third day I walked out for what I knew would probably be my final Test innings. I was desperate to get a good score, desperate to contribute to the team, and so was devastated to be walking back to the dressing room having made just 13. I was in such poor form, it was no surprise, I wanted to take the bowlers on, but got out to Michael Beer coming down the wicket.

Back in the dressing room, Graeme Swann offered me no sympathy. 'Colly, I have to say you are the ugliest batsman in world cricket except for Paul Harris. Your pull shot isn't bad, but the rest is absolutely dreadful to look at.' I wanted to tell him I would no longer be inflicting that on him, but bit my tongue. Later that night I told the England managing director Hugh Morris I intended to retire from Test cricket at the end of the series.

My plan was to announce it after the Test, but I bumped in to our security guy Reg Dickason, who changed my mind. 'Colly, you should do it on the fourth day.' 'Nah, I don't want a swansong. It's not about me.' 'But there are a lot of people who might want to celebrate your Test career.' I had never really thought about it like that, I just wanted to slide away, but Reg talked some sense.

At 9.45am on the fourth day I gathered the boys together in a circle on the field and told them this would be my final Test.

I couldn't look any of them in the eye for fear of crying, so I bowed my head, and said, 'It's my time to go, I have loved playing with you, and playing for England is an amazing experience, never take it for granted, cherish it and moments like this, winning in Australia. I have always given it my best shot.'

After that I was filled with relief and could enjoy my last days in Test cricket. I tried to take it all in, and made sure I wore sunglasses most of the time to hide any tears as I stood in the slips and looked at the England flag fluttering on top of the SCG pavilion.